THE
TAILHOOK
REPORT

THE
TAILHOOK
REPORT

[The Official Inquiry into the
Events of Tailhook '91]

OFFICE OF THE
INSPECTOR GENERAL
(Department of Defense)

St. Martin's Press | New York

DESIGN BY JAYE ZIMET

ISBN 0-312-10392-8

First Edition: June 1993
10 9 8 7 6 5 4 3 2 1

CONTENTS

CONTENTS

PUBLISHER'S NOTE

For the past 18 months, the molestations and acts of indecency that occurred at the 35th Annual Tailhook Symposium in Las Vegas in September 1991 and the official responses to those acts have been the subject of extensive press coverage, Congressional scrutiny, and public outrage. Arguably this has resulted in the recent sweeping changes seen in the U.S. Navy's policies regarding sexual harassment, the role of women in the service in general, and the expanded combat opportunities for women in specific. It has certainly ended or derailed the careers of several of the most senior Navy officials, while over 100 additional officers, junior and senior, still face the prospect of courts-martial or disciplinary action stemming from the events of Tailhook '91.

The Tailhook Association, a private, nonprofit social/professional organization of naval aviators, contractors, and others involved in naval aviation, has hosted an annual professional conference at the Las Vegas Hilton for decades. (In 1991, over 4,000 naval officers attended the weekend conference.) The U.S. Navy has consistently provided significant support and cooperation to the conference and to the Association. While the quality and usefulness of the conference has been unchallenged, the social or "party" aspects of the conference had been growing increasingly out of control in the years before 1991. As the following report documents, this progression had been noted with concern by the Tailhook Association and some senior Navy officers in the years prior to the 1991 conference and yet no effective course of action was adopted to curb or control that behavior. In the view of the authors of this report, Tailhook '91 was one of the "tamer" of the recent conventions and still they were able to identify 90 victims of indecent assault by naval officers as well as numerous other acts of indecency over the weekend of the conference.

Unlike the previous Tailhook Symposiums, however, the events of Tailhook '91 caught the attention of the press and Congress. Over a month after the conference, in the face of an impending article in the *San Diego Union* and the official complaint of assault at Tailhook '91 lodged by Lt. Paula Coughlin, then–Secretary of the Navy H. Lawrence Garrett III took the first official action. He directed the Navy to end all support for the Tailhook Association (support that included providing the Association with free office space and transporting Navy officers to the annual conference at an estimated cost of $400,000 in 1991) and to aid an investigation into the events of Tailhook '91. A week later, Chief of Naval Operations Admiral Frank B. Kelso removed Rear Admiral John W. Snyder, Jr., from his prestigious post as commander of the Patuxent River Naval Air Test Center for "his apparent failure to take timely and appropriate action" when his aide, Lt. Paula Coughlin, reported to him her abuse at Tailhook '91. In the press reports of the time, Rear Admiral Snyder's transfer to a lesser post was described by an unnamed Navy source as "the kind of thing where they leave a pistol on the table and everybody leaves the room."

The full investigation promised by then–Secretary of the Navy Garrett failed to materialize. The report issued by the Navy Inspector General and the Naval Investigative Service in April 1992 did establish that many senior officers in attendance at Tailhook '91 were aware of the assaults and acts of indecency that took place and failed to take appropriate action. However, the report identified few of the officers who took part in the assaults, and it cited the large-scale lack of cooperation on the part of the officers and their Commanding Officers as the reason. Significantly, it was discovered that the NIS had failed to include in its final report 55 pages of interviews, one of which placed Navy Secretary Garrett at the scene of many of the indecent assaults that occurred at Tailhook '91. When, in early June of 1992, this omission became public knowledge and criticism mounted for the meager results of the investigation (including some accusing the Navy of a "whitewash"), Secretary Garrett turned the Tailhook inquiry over to the independent Office of the Inspector General.

Lt. Paula Coughlin, in apparent frustration over the Navy's lack of action and in response to a rumored whispering campaign against her, publicly identified herself and described her attack at Tailhook '91 in press interviews in late June of 1992. In response to the articles and news stories about Lt. Coughlin, and reportedly angry over the Navy's handling of the entire affair, the White House requested and received Secretary Garrett's resignation.

On July 1, 1992, Vice Admiral Richard M. Dunleavy (Assistant Chief of Naval Operations at the time of Tailhook '91) retired from the Navy at a reduced rank. During both the initial investigation by the NIS and the subsequent inquiry by the Office of the Inspector General it was established that Dunleavy had witnessed the famous "Gauntlet" at Tailhook '91 and had taken no action. The two admirals in charge of the initial ineffective investigation were reportedly forced to resign as well.

Published in February of 1993 and released to the public in late April of 1993, the following report by the Inspector General is a devastating indictment of the behavior of the officers at Tailhook '91 and of the senior officers' failure of leadership in the matter. An exhaustive account of the much-disputed events of Tailhook '91, it is likely to be the most complete report of what has come to be regarded as the most wide-ranging scandal in the history of the U.S. Navy. In the press conference following the release of this report, Admiral Kelso, Chief of Naval Operations, said, "Tailhook brought to light the fact that we had an institutional problem with women . . . it was a watershed event that has brought about cultural change." With the establishment of far stricter rules regarding sexual harassment and the accountability of the commanding officers regarding charges of harassment brought to their attention, the implementation of an extensive training program on that issue, and the expansion of women's role in the U.S. Navy, that cultural change in already in progress.

The investigative files on 140 individuals were referred back to the Navy by the Inspector General for investigation and possible courts-martial or disciplinary action. The Navy and Marine Corps have set up military panels—headed by Major General Charles Krulak for the Marine Corps and Vice Admiral Joseph Reason for the Navy—to determine what action or punishments, if any, are appropriate. With the statute of limitations on many of the charges due to run out in September of 1993 (two years after the events of Tailhook '91), any such decisions must be made soon. As of this writing no actions regarding these 140 individuals have been publicly announced.

FOREWORD

February 1993

In this report, we have attempted to describe the events that occurred at the 35th Annual Symposium of the Tailhook Association (Tailhook '91) in as complete a manner as possible. We determined that at least 90 indecent assaults took place and a considerable amount of improper and indecent conduct occurred. Although our purpose is not to shock or offend readers or to sensationalize the accounts of the various incidents, there are sections of the report that contain graphic language. After considerable reflection regarding how best to present our findings, we determined that general descriptions and euphemisms failed to convey a full impression of the prevailing atmosphere in which the assaults took place.

We have used a few pictures* from the more than 800 obtained during the investigation where we believe a picture would significantly enhance the readers' understanding of the general situation or particular event. Some of the pictures are offensive and not in good taste, but they add to any description of what took place. We chose not to use many of the pictures, particularly those depicting indecent exposure, because they did not convey any better understanding than the descriptions used in the report.

It is important to understand that the events at Tailhook '91 did not occur in a historical vacuum. Similar behavior had occurred at previous conventions. The emerging pattern of some of the activities, such as the gauntlet, began to assume the aura of "tradition." There is even some evidence to suggest that Tailhook '91 was "tame" in comparison to earlier conventions. Although there were some attempts made in past years to curb improper behavior, such attempts were ineffective. In fact, many of the younger officers who

*Publisher's Note: The 14 photographs included in the Government Printing Office version of The Tailhook Report have been omitted.

[*xi*]

attended Tailhook '91 felt the excesses that occurred there were condoned by the Navy. This belief is understandable given that the Navy continued to support the Tailhook Association and the annual convention notwithstanding the knowledge on the part of many senior Navy leaders of significant misconduct that had taken place at prior conventions. More disturbingly, the evidence indicates that at least one former high-ranking civilian Navy official engaged in lewd behavior at a prior Tailhook convention in front of junior officers. There is no excuse for the misconduct and unbecoming behavior that occurred at Tailhook '91. However, to be fair to those engaged in nonassaultive activities, such as indecent exposure and drunkenness, the reader must keep in mind that an atmosphere was permitted to develop over a period of years which encouraged officers to act in inappropriate ways.

Finally, we recognize that the effects of Tailhook '91 have had a negative impact on the morale of many members of the Navy. We believe that neither the entire Navy nor the aviation community generally should be judged on the basis of the misconduct of some officers at Tailhook, and we commend the many loyal and dedicated Navy and Marine Corps aviators who continually perform their duties in an exemplary fashion.

INSPECTOR GENERAL
DEPARTMENT OF DEFENSE
400 ARMY NAVY DRIVE
ARLINGTON, VIRGINIA 22202–2884

April 12, 1993

MEMORANDUM FOR SECRETARY OF DEFENSE
SUBJECT: Report of Investigation: Tailhook '91—Part 2, Events of
the 35th Annual Tailhook Symposium

We have completed the second of two reports regarding Tailhook
'91. The enclosed report describes what transpired at the Las Vegas
Hilton Hotel between September 8 and 12, 1991. The report, which
was completed in mid-February, provides information on the status
of our investigation as of January 31, 1993.

Misconduct at the 1991 Tailhook Symposium was more widespread than previously reported by the Navy. We identified 90 victims of indecent assault. In addition, we documented a significant
number of incidents of indecent exposure, and other types of sexual
misconduct, as well as other improprieties by Navy and Marine
Corps officers. We established that more than 50 officers made false
statements to us during the investigation.

Investigative files on at least 140 officers are being referred to the
Acting Secretary of the Navy for consideration of appropriate action.
All individual files and records developed during the investigation
will be made available to the convening authorities for review. Administrative or disciplinary action may be warranted against other
officers whose actions and conduct are described in these records.

In addition, investigative files regarding the 30 Navy flag officers,
2 Marine Corps general officers, and 3 Navy Reserve flag officers
who attended Tailhook '91 will be forwarded to the Acting Secretary
of the Navy after you have had an opportunity to review them. I
believe the files pertaining to the flag officers should be evaluated
outside of the convening authorities to determine whether action is
warranted with respect to the responsibility of each flag officer for
the overall leadership failure that culminated in the events of Tailhook '91.

I would appreciate being advised of the actions taken by you or the Navy with respect to the report. I will, of course, make myself and the OIG staff available to discuss the matter further with the new Secretary of the Navy, the Chief of Naval Operations, the Commandant of the Marine Corps, the convening authorities and their legal staffs.

Derek J. Vander Schaaf
Deputy Inspector General

THE
TAILHOOK
REPORT

SECTION I
EXECUTIVE SUMMARY

This report covers Part 2 of our inquiry into events relating to the 35th Annual Symposium of the Tailhook Association (Tailhook '91) held at the Las Vegas Hilton Hotel from Thursday, September 5 to Sunday, September 8, 1991. The inquiry was initiated in response to a request from the Secretary of the Navy on June 18, 1992.

This report is primarily focused on the events at Tailhook '91; Part 1, issued on September 21, 1992, detailed our review of the Navy investigations of Tailhook '91 and related matters. Part 1 of the report concluded that the scope of the Navy's earlier investigations should have been expanded beyond the indecent assaults to encompass other violations of law and regulation as they became apparent and should have addressed individual accountability for the leadership failure that created an atmosphere in which the assaults and other misconduct took place. In that regard, the first part of our report examined the actions and inactions of Navy leadership responsible for the Navy's investigations of Tailhook '91.

In conducting the second part of our inquiry, we interviewed over 2,900 people who attended Tailhook '91 and obtained documents and other evidence relating to crimes and misconduct by naval aviators at Tailhook '91.

The symposium aspects of Tailhook '91 were found to be reasonably educational and professionally presented. We noted, however, that the Navy knowingly supported and encouraged the attendance of as many as 4,000 naval officers despite the fact that at most only 2,100 people—including contractor personnel and other non-Navy people—actually registered for the professional aspects of the conference, and even fewer actually attended the professional events. Navy support also included the use of naval aircraft and other vehicles, as well as the use of various administrative personnel to facilitate attendance by naval officers. By virtually all accounts, large numbers of officers attended for the sole purpose of participating in the "social" aspects of Tailhook '91.

Many attendees viewed the annual conference as a type of "free-fire zone'' wherein they could act indiscriminately and without fear of censure or retribution in matters of sexual conduct and drunkenness. Some of the Navy's most senior officers were knowledgeable as to the excesses practiced at Tailhook '91 and, by their inaction, those officers served to condone and even encourage the type of behavior that occurred there.

Our investigation disclosed that 83 women and 7 men were assaulted during the three days of the convention. Virtually all the assaults took place in the third-floor area (including the adjoining patio which continued to be open to the public during the convention) of the Las Vegas Hilton Hotel where the squadron hospitality suites were located.

Through the use of detailed interviews and other investigative techniques, 23 officers were determined to warrant referral to the Navy for having participated in indecent assaults, and an additional 23 in indecent exposure. In total, 117 officers were implicated in one or more incidents of indecent assault, indecent exposure, conduct unbecoming an officer or failure to act in a proper leadership capacity while at Tailhook '91.* Further, 51 individuals were found to have made false statements to us during our investigation. Evidence concerning all such matters has been referred to the Navy and/or the Department of Justice for appropriate action. In this regard, it is noted that we anticipate further referrals with respect to officers implicated as a result of our continuing investigation into the indecent assaults. It should also be noted that the number of individuals involved in all types of misconduct or other inappropriate behavior was more widespread than these figures would suggest. Furthermore, several hundred other officers were aware of the misconduct and chose to ignore it.

In this regard, the Navy is being given access to our entire investigative files so as to allow Navy authorities to determine whether additional violations of laws or regulations are supported by evidence obtained during our investigation.

Information, to include transcripts of interviews, concerning all flag officers who attended Tailhook '91 has been provided to the

---

*All statistical information contained in this report is based on data completed through January 31, 1993. Inasmuch as our investigation is continuing with respect to certain indecent assaults, it is expected that additional individuals will be interviewed and that further referrals may be made to naval authorities.

Office of the Secretary of the Navy for consideration as to any required remedial action.

Our inquiry was greatly aided by the cooperation of the Secretary of the Navy, the Chief of Naval Operations and the Commandant of the Marine Corps.

SECTION II
SCOPE AND INVESTIGATIVE
METHODOLOGY

A. SCOPE

The scope of our investigation encompassed the following areas:

1. Indecent assaults*

2. Indecent exposure

3. Conduct unbecoming an officer

4. Dereliction of duty, as well as failure to act in a proper leadership capacity†

5. False statements and false swearing during the course of our investigation

*Indecent assault is a crime under Article 134 of the Uniform Code of Military Justice (UCMJ). The elements of the offense are: "(1) That the accused assaulted a certain person not the spouse of the accused in a certain manner; (2) That the acts were done with the intent to gratify the lust or sexual desires of the accused; and (3) That, under the circumstances, the conduct of the accused was to the prejudice of good order and discipline in the Armed Forces or was of a nature to bring discredit upon the Armed Forces." Lesser included offenses of indecent assault include assault and assault consummated by a battery (Article 128, UCMJ), indecent acts (Article 134), and attempts (Article 80).

†Failure to act is punishable as a dereliction of duty under Article 92 of the UCMJ. The elements of that offense are: "(a) That the accused had certain duties; (b) That the accused knew or reasonably should have known of the duties; and (c) That the accused was (willfully) (through neglect or culpable inefficiency) derelict in the performance of those duties." A duty may be imposed by statute, regulation or custom of the Service, and actual knowledge need not be shown if the individual should have reasonably known of the duties.

[5]

We found it necessary to conduct a comprehensive investigation because the earlier Naval Investigative Service (NIS) investigation focused almost exclusively on indecent assaults. That investigation found that a total of 26 women, 14 of them naval officers, had been assaulted at Tailhook '91. Although an NIS interim report dated February 1992 listed 18 naval officers who were considered to be suspects or subjects, the NIS final report of investigation, issued in mid-April 1992, identified only three indecent assault suspects—one naval officer, one Marine Corps officer and one foreign military exchange officer.* In late April 1992, the Commander, NIS, referred 11 specific "case summaries" to cognizant Navy and Marine Corps flag officers ". . . for such disposition as [they] deem appropriate." However, in his memorandum to the Commander in Chief of the U.S. Pacific Fleet, the Commander, NIS, stated that the allegations regarding two Navy captains included in the 11 "referrals" were in one case "unsubstantiated" and, in the other, "uncorroborated."

The Naval Inspector General (IG), after reviewing the NIS investigative report, but without conducting a comprehensive investigation of his own, forwarded for further review the names of 32 officers and one civilian for consideration of administrative sanctions. Six of these individuals were referred for questionable personal conduct, 6 were referred for standards of conduct issues involving contractor hospitality suites, 4 were referred for failure to act, and 17 were referred because they were commanding officers of squadrons which hosted or contributed to the funding of hospitality suites that featured lewd entertainment or behavior.

We also received a memorandum from the Navy Judge Advocate General (JAG) dated July 2, 1992, in which he listed 80 individuals referred ". . . to the chain of command for appropriate disciplinary or administrative action." The list of 80 names included some of the 11 and 33 names specifically referred to the chain of command by the NIS and the Naval IG, respectively. The list of 80 also included 56 names which had not previously been mentioned as referrals. In total, the NIS and the Naval IG identified 95 names which were considered for referral.†

---

*The NIS report also contained information regarding a Marine Corps lieutenant colonel with respect to his possible obstruction of the NIS investigation. In pursuing this matter, we found insufficient evidence to warrant such a referral.

†The Navy JAG informed us that the additional names contained in its list of 80

The Naval IG also commented in his report with respect to the Navy's use of military aircraft to support attendance at Tailhook '91. Further, the Naval IG noted that various forms of impropriety such as instances of indecent exposure and excessive alcohol consumption were apparent. Neither the NIS nor the Naval IG, however, conducted comprehensive inquiries into those latter areas nor did they pursue the matter of leadership accountability.

B. METHODOLOGY

Due to the large number of witnesses and their geographic dispersion, we approached our review on a geographic rather than on a "lead-by-lead" basis as would normally be done in investigating crimes such as indecent assault. Our investigation into the events at Tailhook '91 began 10 months after the actual convention. Witnesses were scattered literally around the world at Navy and Marine Corps bases, as well as aboard naval ships. We assembled a task force of investigators which, after reviewing available information received from the Navy, developed a detailed plan for use in conducting interviews of attendees and other witnesses.

The task force, consisting of over 40 investigators, conducted interviews at Naval air stations throughout the United States as well as on four aircraft carriers, including the USS *Saratoga* while it was deployed in the Mediterranean Sea, the USS *Ranger* while deployed

included names provided by NIS as potential suspects in various misconduct. The Commander, NIS, had prepared referral letters dated June 23, 1992 to 5 flag officers for all of the names on the list of 80. In his letter, the Commander, NIS, stated, "I have been directed to refer [these individuals] to the chain of command for appropriate action." The NIS advised that the reason the letters were never sent was because the Department of Defense (DoD) IG had requested that all criminal or administrative disciplinary actions be held in abeyance pending the completion of the DoD IG investigation. Our review of the NIS and the Naval IG referrals led us to conclude that many of the actions or inactions cited did not rise to the level of impropriety necessary to warrant a referral when viewed in the overall context of Tailhook. For example, the list of 80 included the names of many field grade officers who were referred simply because they had attested to the fact that they had witnessed the gauntlet and described what they had seen. They were referred presumably for their failure to take action. Of the 117 referrals we are providing to the Navy for misconduct at Tailhook '91, only 30 are also included in the Navy and Naval IG referrals.

in the Persian Gulf, the USS *Nimitz* deployed off the western coast of the United States, and the USS *Independence* while deployed in Japan. Interviews were also conducted in Canada, Japan, Europe, the Middle East and various other locations at which witnesses were found to be stationed. A total of 26 investigative and 4 administrative support work years were expended in the effort as of January 1, 1993.

Inasmuch as neither the Navy nor the Tailhook Association maintained comprehensive records that reflected the identity of all attendees, we sought to identify witnesses through various other means. That process included:

1. Analysis of Navy and Marine Corps flight records.

2. Review of Hilton Hotel guest registers pertaining to rooms reserved by the Tailhook Association.

3. List of approximately 1,680 named registrants furnished to us by the Tailhook Association.*

4. Questionnaires completed by officers and civlian employees at the request of the Navy, Marine Corps and the Air Force.

5. Information garnered through interviews of other witnesses.

6. Information received through the Department of Defense Hotline or in anonymous letters sent directly to our Tailhook task force.

*Tailhook Association records reflect the names of approximately 1,680 registrants. The Association contends that an additional 500 people registered while at Tailhook '91 but the Association failed to record the names of those individuals. Of the 1,680 named registrants, approximately 900 were active duty or Reserve officers. The remaining attendees consisted of contractor personnel, Government civilian employees, retired officers and members of the general public.

7. Information developed through the NIS and the
Naval IG investigation.

Although the Tailhook Association reserved approximately 1,000 rooms at the Hilton, that number did not come close to accommodating the estimated 4,000 officers that attended Tailhook '91. Thus, our attempts to identify all attendees were hampered by the fact that there were no records for hundreds of officers who slept on the floor of squadron hospitality suites or in rooms occupied by other officers. Further, our investigation disclosed that attendees stayed at hotels throughout the Las Vegas area, while others stayed at the homes of local friends or relatives. Still others stayed in motor homes or simply slept in vehicles driven by officers from such locations as San Diego and El Toro, California. Due to the proximity between Naval Air Stations in California and Las Vegas, hundreds of officers drove their personal vehicles to Tailhook '91.

During the course of our investigation we interviewed* a total of 2,911 people. Tables 1 and 2 depict the demographics of those interviewed.

In addition to the above cited interviews, we conducted 314 reinterviews involving critical witnesses.

We also note that, as of January 31, 1993, more than 1,500 ad-

TABLE 1

All Interviewees by Affiliation

United States Navy (Male)	2,021
Civilian (Female)	305
United States Marine Corps	298
Civilian (Male)	123
United States Navy (Female)	84
United States Air Force (Male)	63
United States Air Force (Female)	9
Other Male	8
Total Interviewees:	*2,911*

*Of the 2,911 people interviewed, 108 were interviewed telephonically rather than in person.

TABLE 2

Navy and Marine Corps Officer Interviewees by Rank

Ensign (Navy)/2nd Lieutenant (Marine Corp)	71
Lieutenant, Jr. Grade (Navy)/	
1st Lieutenant (Marine Corp)	1,232
Lieutenant (Navy)/Captain (Marine Corp)	352
Lt. Commander (Navy)/Major (Marine Corp)	239
Captain (Navy)/Colonel (Marine Corp)	92
Admiral (Navy)/General (Marine Corp)	37
Admiral (Navy)/General (Marine Corp) Ret.	43

*Note Marine Corp and Navy ranks are grouped by equivalent ranks for each service.

ditional individuals are either known or believed to have attended Tailhook '91. Those individuals were not interviewed either because (1) they refused to discuss details of Tailhook '91 with us,* (2) we were unsuccessful in contacting them during the investigation, or (3) their names came up only on an incidental basis and no information was developed that indicated an interview was warranted.

Throughout the interview process, we continued to identify new victims, witnesses and suspects. The need to fully address these emerging leads contributed to the time needed to complete the investigation.

Finally, we note our belief that a substantial number of other, unidentified individuals attended Tailhook '91. Neither the Tailhook Association nor the Las Vegas Hilton Hotel attempted in any way to limit access to the third floor area. Thus, for example, several witnesses cited the presence of female attendees who could not be specifically identified or otherwise located. Similarly, many retired and Reserve officers are believed to have attended who were not identified during our investigation. In an effort to identify possible witnesses, we requested that local newspapers and other media publicize the task force presence in their area, noting our local and headquarters telephone numbers and the fact that we welcomed contact

*The category includes certain nonmilitary attendees, as well as military attendees who invoked their rights against self-incrimination.

with any attendees or anyone else having information concerning Tailhook '91. The articles resulted in several telephone calls to the task force, thereby identifying additional witnesses.

In addition to conducting witness, victim and suspect interviews, the task force used a full range of other investigative techniques, some of which are described below.

1. *Photographs of Officer Interviewees.* As part of our interview process, we photographed military officers and later used those photographs to develop groups of pictures needed to assist victims and witnesses in identifying specific individuals knowledgeable of the events at Tailhook '91.

2. *Polygraphs.* This technique was used on 34 occasions, in accordance with DoD Directives regulating the use of polygraphs.* Officers taking the polygraph examination executed signed waivers indicating they consented to the examination and had been fully apprised of their legal rights prior to the test. Findings disclosed that 14 of the tests indicated the officer was nondeceptive, 12 indicated deception, and 8 were inconclusive or no opinion was rendered by the polygraph examiner.† Twelve of the officers made admissions to the issues under investigation as a result of the polygraph examination.

3. *Subpoenas.* A total of 19 DoD IG subpoenas were issued in support of our investigation. Twelve of those subpoenas related to photographic evidence believed to be in the possession of the subpoenaed party. The remainder of the subpoenas related to business records and other documentary evidence relevant to the investigation.

4. *Undercover Operations.* This technique was used in an effort to further corroborate information concerning a specific

*DoD Directive 5210.48 and DoD Regulation 5210.48R.

†"Inconclusive" indicates that a polygraph examination was conducted, however, the examiner could not reach a conclusive opinion. "No opinion" indicates that the examination was terminated, either by the examiner or examinee, before completion.

indecent assault. The operation was successful in obtaining additional corroboration.

5. *Consensual Monitoring*. Four conversations were recorded with the consent of one of the parties, in accordance with DoD Directive.* The conversations related to knowledge of indecent assault activity in the gauntlet and other criminal activities.

6. *Immunity*. Throughout the investigation, we considered whether individuals suspected of involvement in criminal behavior at Tailhook '91 should be offered immunity in exchange for other information of specific concern to the task force. In each instance, a "proffer"† was required. A total of 15 suspects or their attorneys engaged in immunity discussions with us and 3 submitted proffers. We requested and received two grants of immunity from naval authorities in regard to the matter.

7. Computer Analysis. Due to the enormous volume of information collected, the use of computer data bases played a significant role in recording and cataloging witness statements and other evidence.

8. *"Candid" Photographs*. We obtained more than 800 photographs during the investigative process. The photographs range from simple scenes depicting people conversing on the pool patio to pictures of indecent exposure and various other activities that could be characterized as conduct unbecoming an officer. In virtually every instance in which activity relevant to the investigation was shown, we were able to identify those individuals represented in the photographs. In every case of male indecent exposure, the individuals involved were found to be Navy or Marine Corps

---

*DoD Direction 5200.24.

†In the context of a grant of immunity, a proffer is a written offer from the suspect or the suspect's attorney, to the Government, of what the individual would say if that individual were to be granted immunity from prosecution. The proffer cannot be used as evidence in any subsequent prosecution.

officers. In every case of indecent exposure depicting women, the individuals were found to be civilians.

9. *Other*. In addition to the above techniques, the task force used various other accepted law enforcement tools such as surveillance, confidential sources of information and consent searches.

SECTION III
THE TAILHOOK ASSOCIATION

A. BACKGROUND

As described in our September 1992 report, the Tailhook Association is a private organization composed of active duty, Reserve and retired Navy and Marine Corps aviators, Defense contractors and others. The annual Tailhook Symposium began as a reunion of naval aviators in 1956. In 1963, the annual reunion moved from San Diego to Las Vegas, where it was expanded to include a number of seminar sessions relating to naval aviation, as well as other professional development activities.

We questioned attendees about the scheduled symposium events and reviewed material, including videotapes, taken throughout the symposium. A copy of the agenda for Tailhook '91 is in Appendix A. From all reports and appearances, the symposium events were professionally presented and of educational value to people involved in naval aviation. No instances of impropriety were found to have occurred at official symposium functions or in the exhibit area.

In addition to the educational forums, the Association, in conjunction with various Defense contractors, hosted formal dinners, lunches and various sporting events (a golf outing and a 5-kilometer run) during the convention. One of the dinners centered around the Association's annual presentation of awards to aviators who had distinguished themselves in various aspects of naval aviation. On Friday and Saturday nights, the dinners featured speakers of interest to the Association's members. The Chief of Naval Operations and the Secretary of the Navy were the respective speakers at the two dinners at Tailhook '91. As with the educational events, we found no instances of impropriety at any of the scheduled functions.

B. PROFESSIONAL
ASPECTS OF TAILHOOK '91

In order to provide the Tailhook Association and the Navy the opportunity to present their views of the professional aspects of Tailhook '91, we invited them to provide formal comment for use in this
report. Both organizations availed themselves of that opportunity
and submitted brief discussion papers (Appendices B and C, respectively).

The single, most talked about topic with regard to the Tailhook
'91 formal agenda was the Flag Panel. That event attracted more
attendees than any other symposium function and did not require
registration as a symposium attendee. Contrary to some media accounts, we found that the Flag Panel was conducted in a responsible
and professional fashion. The Flag Panel was comprised of eight
Navy admirals and one Marine Corps general. Officers attending the
event addressed a variety of questions to members of the Flag Panel
who responded in a generally straightforward manner.

Questions relating to the possibility of women flying combat aircraft elicited strong reactions from attendees. A female officer asked
the panel whether women would be allowed to fly aircraft in combat.
Her question drew a slight reaction from some members of the audience in recognition that this was a sensitive issue. Vice Admiral
(VADM) Richard M. Dunleavy, who fielded the question and first
displayed some unease in addressing the issue, responded by saying
that the Navy would do as Congress directed, indicating that women
could be flying aircraft in combat within a year thereafter.

Witnesses told us that VADM Dunleavy's response was not ac-
ceptable to either side in the argument. Those who supported the
concept of women in combat felt that VADM Dunleavy had not
shown sufficient support for their position, whereas those attendees
who rejected the proposed role of women in combat believed that
VADM Dunleavy, as Assistant Chief of Naval Operations (Air Warfare), had not properly defended the interests of male aviators. One
male officer in the audience stood up and forcibly stated his personal
objections to women in combat. In response to the officer's statement, the audience erupted into loud cheers and applause.

Although some witnesses opined that the "mood" of the attendees changed for the worse as a result of those exchanges, we found
insufficient evidence to support the theory that male officers later

turned their frustrations over this policy matter into violent acts against women on the third floor.*

Perhaps most important in this discussion is that, although the Flag Panel drew the largest crowd of any symposium function, the crowd was estimated to have been no more than 1,500 to 1,600 people, including contractor and civilian personnel. That is especially telling when compared with the fact that, even by conservative estimates, overall attendance at Tailhook '91 was placed at more than 4,000 people. Our investigation disclosed the vast majority of attendees did not register for the conference and did not attend symposium functions. Rather, many officers merely attended the social aspects of Tailhook. Parties were held on the third floor, where virtually all the assaults and most other improprieties occurred. It is especially pertinent to note that of the 117 officers found to be involved in misconduct,† only 26 appeared as named registrants on the Tailhook Association list of symposium attendees.

C. RELATIONSHIP BETWEEN THE NAVY AND THE TAILHOOK ASSOCIATION

The Tailhook Association has depended on substantial support from the Navy and from contractors doing business with the Navy. Senior aviation leaders told us they viewed the Association as an integral part of naval aviation. Thus, they felt justified in lending Navy support required by the Association, especially with regard to the annual symposium.

The relationship between the Navy and the Tailhook Association dates back to the first Tailhook reunion. Historically, Tailhook Association membership has been comprised of naval aviators and those with interests in or otherwise associated with naval aviation. Active and retired naval aviators serve on the Association's Board of Directors and a senior naval aviator, usually stationed at Naval Air

*However, one female aviator reported that, immediately following the Flag Panel, she was verbally harassed by male aviators who expressed to her their belief that women should not be employed in naval aviation. They also accused her of having sexual relations with senior officers while deployed on carrier assignment.

†Includes indecent assault, indecent exposure, conduct unbecoming an officer and failure to act in a proper leadership capacity.

Station (NAS) Miramar, is normally appointed as the Association's President. Other Association leadership positions such as Vice President, Secretary and Treasurer are generally held by active duty, Reserve, or retired aviators. The Tailhook Association advised us that, as of August 1992, there were 15,479 individual and 10 corporate members.*

The Navy support of the Tailhook Association is apparent in the Association's former occupancy of Government-owned office space located at NAS Miramar. The Association headquarters occupied 2,500 square feet of office space at NAS Miramar on a rent-free basis from July 1984 to December 1987 and again from May 1990 until December 1991. The rent-free arrangement was severed when the Secretary of the Navy withdrew Navy support for the Association in October 1991. The decision resulted from public disclosures of misconduct by naval officers at Tailhook '91. The Association is currently located in private office space in the San Diego area. Plans to construct a Tailhook Association headquarters building funded by the Association at NAS Miramar are currently being held in abeyance.

The Navy authorized and supplied transportation by military aircraft in support of Tailhook '91. According to the Naval Air Logistics Office (NALO), the aircraft, primarily C-9s, transported approximately 1,730 attendees to and from Las Vegas. The NALO advised us that 37 aircraft missions were flown, including 17 missions solely dedicated to Tailhook and 20 missions that had been combined with other, non-Tailhook requirements. Those flights originated at various military air bases throughout the United States. The NALO reported that the missions required approximately 325 flight hours. We determined this resulted in a cost of nearly $400,000 for fuel and contract maintenance.† Other transport aircraft, as well as small training planes and fighter jets, were used by some officers as transportation to Las Vegas. In at least one instance, officers rented a private plane and charged the cost to the Navy under the guise of a "training" flight.

The Naval IG investigation concluded that subordinate commands

---

*Corporate membership numbered 52 just prior to Tailhook '91 but declined dramatically over the ensuing year as a result of adverse publicity arising from Tailhook '91.

†The costs cited do not include pay and allowances for flight crews and local maintenance expenses.

believed that Navy guidelines, as well as current and historical instructions from the NALO regarding Tailhook technically permitted the use of aircraft in all cases where an officer was traveling on travel orders, whether those orders were funded or unfunded.* Nonetheless, the Naval IG properly criticized the Navy for allowing such widespread use and the apparent and perceived abuses that accompanied that use. Our investigation also disclosed many instances in which attendees were transported to Tailhook '91 by C-9 aircraft despite the fact that they had been issued no orders whatsoever.

Since 1974, the Navy has transported officers and even civilian staff, spouses and friends to Tailhook conventions using Navy aircraft. An exception occurred in 1975, after a Government Accounting Office inquiry criticized the Navy for failing to adequately control and oversee the use of such flights.† The Secretary of the Navy denied attendees the use of military aircraft for Tailhook purposes. Attendance at that year's convention was greatly diminished and use of military aircraft in support of Tailhook resumed in 1976.

Our investigation disclosed that, in addition to military aircraft, other official vehicles such as buses and vans were used to transport attendees to Las Vegas and that enlisted personnel were occasionally the drivers of those vehicles.

To our knowledge, fewer than 10 of the Navy or Marine Corps officers who attended Tailhook '91 were required to take annual leave for that purpose. Additionally, countless duty hours were spent by suite administrators and Association committee members during the months prior to the convention in preparation for the 3-day event.

The Association assumed most of the costs relating to transportation, accommodations and, in some instances, per diem for approximately 63 committee members, 50 of whom were active duty or Reserve officers. To the best of our knowledge, the Navy did not require active duty officers to take annual leave for the day or two prior to the symposium opening to attend meetings in preparation for the convention.

The symposium portion of the convention was supported in large

---

*The topic of aircraft use was addressed by the Naval IG in his report on Tailhook dated April 29, 1992. Directives used by the Naval IG in determining the propriety of operational support airlift use in support of Tailhook included DoD Directives 4500.43 and 4515.13-R and OPNAVINST 4630.25B and 4631.2B.

†Comptroller General Report titled *Alleged Use of Military Aircraft for Other Than Official Purposes-DoD*, Report Number B-156819 dated September 1975.

part by the Navy. Although various Defense contractors also participated as presenters in some of the educational seminars, the Navy was the primary source of seminar speakers and played an integral role in determining the agenda for each year's symposium. The Navy provided funded orders for seminar speakers and military personnel who were given awards at the symposium. We found no evidence of any effort by the Navy to require actual registration for the symposium in order to attend the social functions at Tailhook.

SECTION IV
WITNESS AND NAVY
COOPERATION

We found the Secretary of the Navy, the Chief of Naval Operations and the Commandant of the Marine Corps were fully supportive of our efforts and went to all necessary lengths to ensure that our logistical and scheduling needs were met. The Navy also assisted in identifying Tailhook attendees and adjusting flight and training schedules where necessary to make officers available for interview. Perhaps most important was the Navy's designation of "points of contact" (POCs) to work with us in scheduling interviews and to act as facilitators in solving any and all logictical problems. The POCs, generally officers of the rank of commander or captain, accomplished all required tasks, including arranging the transportation of our agents onto various aircraft carriers, helping to identify and locate retired officers and, in general, helping to facilitate our interviews.

In contrast to the organizational cooperation described above, we found a wide variance in the level of cooperation shown by aviation officers. Most of the officers interviewed responded in a serious and cooperative fashion. Other officers were far less cooperative and attempted to limit their responses so as to reveal only minimal information. Many officers refused to offer information pertinent to the investigation unless asked very specific questions. For example, a common tactic taken by many officers in response to general questioning was to answer that they simply had no knowledge of the subject. However, we experienced a number of situations in which facts disclosed later in the investigation suggested that many of the same individuals did indeed have pertinent knowledge or information. A typical response to questions posed in followup interviews was that the investigator had not asked the "right" question. It is our belief that several hundred of the 2,384 naval officers we interviewed responded in that fashion.

The evidence revealed that other officers deliberately provided false information to us. Some squadron members appeared to maintain unified responses that were often contradicted by the testimony of witnesses not assigned to those squadrons. Similarly, individual officers specifically lied to us about their activities unless directly confronted with conflicting evidence. In one instance, a Navy lieutenant repeatedly denied that he indecently exposed himself. After he was shown a photograph clearly depicting him publicly exposing himself at Tailhook '91, the officer told us he had lied because he did not know that we had a picture and his career was worth the risk of being caught in a lie.

A second officer, a Marine lieutenant colonel, lied to us about his own improper activities, as well as those of his squadron mates. The same officer had previously alleged to us that he had seen Lieutenant (LT) Paula Coughlin seeking souvenirs in the Rhino suite on the morning after her assault. The officer later retracted the allegation after he was found to have supplied other false information to our investigators.

In many instances, we were able to overcome attempts to mislead our investigators. In many others, however, we were not. Collective "stonewalling" significantly increased the difficulty of the investigation and adversely affected our ability to identify many of those officers who had committed assaults. In the absence of specific conflicting testimony or physical evidence, an individual officer's statement that he or she neither saw nor heard of anything improper occurring at Tailhook '91 had to be accepted at face value.

Our investigators encountered repeated and deliberate attempts to obstruct their efforts. For instance, some witnesses who had been identified as having taken photographs at Tailhook '91 told us that they had misplaced or destroyed all such photographs. However, when these individuals were presented with a DoD IG subpoena, in most cases these "lost" photographs were produced. One Marine Corps aviator's commanding officer (CO) informed us that, after the aviator was interviewed, he overheard the officer telephone other aviators and tell them what they should and should not say to investigators relating to improper activity engaged in at Tailhook '91. A few officers reported the existence of a "Lieutenants' Protective Association (LPA)" and a "Junior Officers' Protective Association (JOPA)." The LPA and JOPA were described as being an allegiance among officers. One officer told us that, according to LPA and JOPA "rules," a junior officer will not "give up" another junior officer just because he has done "something stupid."

Naval aviators are typically known by their nicknames or "call signs." In one instance, aviators in a squadron denied they were known by call signs. However, we later learned that they did, in fact, use call signs. We strongly suspect that the initial denial by these officers was intended to conceal their involvement with a woman who was indecently assaulted in the gauntlet and that these aviators were aware that the woman knew them only by their respective call signs. In fact, they had earlier given her a poster autographed with their call signs.

In situations in which the interviewee was considered to be a suspect or subject of criminal or other improper activity, we advised them of their rights under Article 31, UCMJ, and we respected their right to seek legal counsel and afforded them the opportunity to consult with an attorney. In every location where we conducted interviews, defense counsel was immediately available to interviewees through the Naval Legal Services Office (NLSO).

SECTION V
SQUADRON HOSPITALITY
SUITES

A. BACKGROUND

The primary venue for social activity at Tailhook '91 was the squadron hospitality suites. The majority of the Navy and Marine Corps officers who attended Tailhook '91 told us they did so for two primary reasons: to take advantage of the professional symposium and to socialize with other aviators. The socialization centered around the third floor squadron hospitality suites.

In the early years of Tailhook the conventions revolved around social gatherings and parties held in various hospitality suites that were funded and operated by Defense contractors. Those suites offered free food and beverages to all Tailhook attendees. The growth in the number of contractor suites in the early 1970s is attributed to efforts of the Tailhook Association to increase the number of contractor or corporate sponsors.

Hospitality suites continued to be sponsored by contractors until the Association notified its corporate members in the late 1970s that, as a result of existing rules and DoD regulations* governing the relationship between contractors and DoD employees (both civilian and military), this practice would no longer be sanctioned by the Association. Those rules and regulations placed strict limits on the receipt by DoD employees of gratuities, including liquor and entertainment. They were intended to deter military and civilian employees from providing favorable treatment to contractors in return for gratuities. Tailhook Association officers told us that the Directive was the primary reason for the shift from contractor-sponsored hospitality suites to squadron sponsorship of the suites. As one Association employee opined, contractors sponsored the suites to facilitate

---

*DoD Directive 5500.7, dated May 6, 1987, superseding the previous DoD Directive dated January 19, 1977.

meeting key military personnel in the naval aviation community. Contractors felt such meetings were important and would encourage those personnel to "like the contractors when it came time to buy stuff." He went on to say that the practice ended only when "Congress outlawed it." We were further told by Captain (CAPT) Frederic G. Ludwig, Jr., President of the Tailhook Association during Tailhook '91, that the Association began to host what has become known as the "President's Dinner" as a legitimate means of allowing the senior naval leadership to socialize with the contractors.*

According to the Executive Director of the Association, the U.S. Navy Air Test and Evaluation Squadron (VX-4)† was the first squadron to host a hospitality suite after issuance of the new DoD rules and regulations. In the ensuing years, other naval squadrons and commands also sponsored suites by collecting funds from squadron members to defray the operating costs of such suites. Witnesses opined that with the increase in squadron hospitality suites, competitiveness emerged among the squadrons to outdo one another with respect to having the most popular suite. One naval officer told us it was that mentality that led to excessive consumption of alcohol and an increase in rowdy, boisterous behavior at the conventions. Over the years, the officer witnessed drunkenness, strippers, public nudity and consensual public sex acts that he attributed to competition among officers in various squadrons.

By many accounts, the increase in rowdy and improper behavior culminated at Tailhook '85. As a result of such behavior, the Association received a number of complaints and subsequently held a special Board of Directors meeting on September 26, 1985, to address those complaints. One complaint from a Tailhook board member and squadron CO to the Tailhook Association read:

> As a member of the board and as a professional aviator I feel that several issues should be reviewed and

---

*The President's Dinner, at which the Chief of Naval Operations was the featured speaker, was held on Friday, September 6, 1991. Attendees included 250 industry and military dignitaries.

†Naval aviation squadrons are commonly referred to by their alphanumeric designations. The letters designate the type of squadron. For instance, "V" indicates fixed-wing aircraft and "H" indicates helicopter. The numbers represent a particular squadron. The glossary at Appendix D defines the alphanumeric squadron designations and Naval command acronyms referenced in this report.

corrected by the Association prior to Hook '86. I viewed with disdain the conduct, or better put, the misconduct of several officers and a lack of command attention which resulted in damage and imprudent action.

The encouragement of drinking contests, the concept of having to drink 15 drinks to win a headband and other related activities produced walking zombies that were viewed by the general public and detracted from the Association/USN integrity.

Damage to the Hilton should not be tolerated and restitution should be made by the command in charge of the suite.

Dancing girls performing lurid sexual acts on Naval aviators in public would make prime conversation for the media.

The minutes of the special board meeting identified the most pervasive problems in the suites to be excessive drinking and lewd behavior and reported possible solutions for those suite-related problems. Those solutions included limiting the number of suites, black-listing "bad" suites, issuing warnings to the COs of squadrons causing problems and/or the elimination of all suites for one year. The minutes further reflected the following annotation:

RADM Service feels that unless these problems or behavior are solved he will not be able to support Tailhook, which would eliminate the use of the C-9s from AIRPAC Commands. He stated that VADM Martin (OP-5) has similar feeling.*

On October 15, 1985, another board meeting was held. Despite the concerns noted at the previous meeting, the minutes reflected that the board rejected all solutions discussed at the first board meeting. Instead, the minutes indicated that the board opted for the following:

*Rear Admiral (RADM) James Service, at the time of Tailhook '85, was the Commander, Naval Air Force, U.S. Pacific Fleet. VADM Edward H. Martin, at the time of Tailhook '85, was the Deputy Chief of Naval Operations, Air Warfare.

Rules to all COs prior to Vegas. Will not close suites
during symposiums, but will keep them low key.
Duty officers in all suites—adult supervision.

During the course of our investigation, we were informed by numerous attendees that many of the problems relating to the suites and
highlighted at Tailhook '85 were not resolved. Excessive drinking,
public nudity and various forms of entertainment (such as performances by strippers) in the hospitality suites continued through the
years, including Tailhook '91. Furthermore, the minutes of the Association's Board of Directors meeting of January 11, 1989, reflected the following concerns regarding behavior at Tailhook '88:

> Due to the large amount of ''Vegas Locals'' under the
> age of 21 who showed up in the suite area [name de-
> leted] suggest we check our liability to make sure we
> have the maximum protection to cover the underage
> and the behavior of some of our participants.

Prior to Tailhook '91, CAPT Ludwig issued separate letters directed
to the respective hospitality suite squadron commanders and hospitality suite coordinators. Both letters addressed issues regarding conduct and behavior in and around the hospitality suites and warned
against such things as ''gang mentality,'' underage drinking and
damage to Hilton property. When asked about the letters, CAPT
Ludwig told us, ''That has been the letter for several years, and I
don't know exactly when it first went in there. But my sense of this
is that it stemmed from what took place in '85.'' He went on to say,
''I felt that I understood what it was all about, and I felt that I understood it to mean what took place in '85, which is a group getting
totally blown away and running around destroying the hotel. That is
my sense of gang mentality.''

Although our investigation centered on misconduct occurring at
Tailhook '91, we also documented various instances of misconduct
that took place in the suites during the previous years. The third-
floor hospitality suites became the locale for the most notorious aspects of each year's convention.

B. TAILHOOK '91

The Las Vegas Hilton Hotel, one of the largest hotels in the city, is
a 30-story ''Y''-shaped structure with approximately 3,000 guest

rooms and suites, several restaurants, a large gambling casino, shopping arcade and convention area.

The Tailhook Association reserved approximately 1,000 guest rooms for Tailhook '91 attendees. Most of the misconduct discussed in this report occurred in or around the central and east tower hospitality suites located on the third floor. A number of the suites on the southern side of the third floor east tower open to a large patio area that has a pool, sunbathing deck, snack bar and shops. The pool patio, as it is generally referred to, gives the appearance of being on ground level. It is actually situated on the roof of the casino area and on the same level as the third-floor guest rooms. Some of the suites on the northern side of the third-floor east wing also open onto a patio area that is much smaller than the pool patio. Other suites on that side of the third-floor east tower are accessible only through the inside hallway. Those rooms have windows overlooking a parking lot three stories below.

There were 22 hospitality suites on the third floor of the Las Vegas Hilton during Tailhook '91. The same location within the hotel had been used by the Tailhook convention for several years.

Eleven of the suites* were adjacent to the pool patio deck level of the hotel and six suites† were located across the third-floor hallway. These 17 suites were bi-level—the upper section contained a bathroom and sleeping area, and the lower level a living room. The levels were separated by railings with the upper level two steps above the lower level. Access was gained through the third-floor hallway on the upper level and through sliding glass doors on the lower level that opened either onto the pool/patio deck or a small terrace. The remaining five suites‡ were single level, and access could be gained only through the third-floor hallway. The size of the suites varied depending on location and some suites adjoined other suites. Suite coordinators told us that, prior to the start of the convention, they either removed or rearranged furniture in the suites to maximize the available space.

Of the 22 hospitality suites, 19 were associated with Navy and Marine Corps squadrons and 3 were associated with Navy aviation training commands, schools or centers.§ More specifically, 17 suites

---

*Rooms 308, 307, 306, 305, 304, 303, 302, 357, 356, 355, and 354.

†Rooms 310, 315, 316, 318, 319, and 320.

‡Rooms 319, 360, 364, 371, and 373.

§Hereafter, all hosting commands or units will be referred to as squadrons.

were associated with Navy squadrons, 4 with Marine Corps squadrons, and 1 was hosted by former members of a deactivated Marine Corps squadron. Twenty of the squadrons were from naval bases located on the west coast of the United States and one each from the east and gulf coasts. Documentation revealed there were 24 hospitality suites hosted by various squadrons at Tailhook '90, many of which also sponsored suites at Tailhook '91.

According to the Tailhook Association, it "brokered" the suites with the Hilton on behalf of the respective hosting squadrons. Each squadron was directly responsible to the Hilton for paying suite rental charges and any damage occurring in its suite. CAPT Ludwig told us there was a procedure established to ensure that Tailhook committee members checked and inspected the suites and adjacent areas for damage prior to and after the convention. The Association was liable for damage to the common areas of the Hilton. He reported that the total damage bill for Tailhook '91 was approximately $23,000. Of that figure, $18,000 was for the installation of new carpeting on the third floor as a result of cigarette burns and drink stains. For the most part, the remaining damage occurred in the squadron hospitality suites, including one suite that was vandalized.

Regarding security in the hospitality suites, one Association committee coordinator informed us that, although the Hilton and not the Association was responsible for security on the third floor of the hotel, the squadron duty officers in the respective suites were expected to maintain order and prevent any damages.* During the course of our investigation, squadron COs and executive officers (XOs) explained that prior to Tailhook '91 they provided specific guidance to attending squadron members concerning behavior, conduct, damage to the suite and the responsibilities of the duty officers.

The COs and coordinators gave us various reasons for hosting a suite. Some suites such as the Fighter Squadron 126 were set up for the sole purpose of establishing a place for squadron members and their guests to meet and relax while at Tailhook. Other suites were administered to highlight the mission of a particular squadron or command, such as the Commander, Naval Air Reserve Force suite, which focused on attracting naval aviators into the Navy aviation reserve program. Finally there were suites organized to provide en-

---

*The issue of overall security responsibilities is discussed in Section IX of the report.

tertainment. Those suites featured activities as diverse as disk jockeys playing music for dancing; leg shaving;* and performances by strippers. Two suites featured phallic drink dispensers. One suite, Marine Corps Tactical Reconnaissance Squadron, featured a mural of a rhinoceros to which was affixed a dildo rigged by squadron members to dispense an alcoholic drink. The other suite, hosted by Marine All Weather Fighter Attack Squadron featured a statue of a "green knight" which also dispensed alcoholic drinks through a phallus.†

Members of the VA-128 squadron reportedly passed out business card–size "invitations" to people inviting them to visit the VA-128 hospitality suite in room 307. The "invitation" included a sexual double-entendre and encouraged people to visit the suite ". . . for an evening of imbibing, chicanery, and debauchery."‡

Our investigation determined that, for the most part, the hospitality suites were financed by individual assessments paid by attending squadron members. By most accounts, the assessment were voluntary and not considered excessive. In certain instances, the hosting squadron supplemented the funds by selling memorabilia or through other activities. Examples of suite financing range from $1,680 collected through individual assessments from the 24 officers of Fighter Squadron 1 who attended to the $19,000§ in available funding to support the Chief of Naval Air Training suite.

Witnesses reported that the suites had two things in common: the serving of alcohol and lengthy hours of operation. The hours in-

---

*This activity occurred on the third floor during Tailhook '91 and involved the shaving of women's legs and pubic area by male aviators.

†VMFA(AW)-121 is known as the Green Knight squadron. VMFP-3, known as the Rhino squadron decommissioned prior to Tailhook '91, but nonetheless former members of the unit hosted a suite.

‡Publisher's Note: The full text of the "invitation" was: "A-6 Tailhookers All-Weather Attack . . . 'We stay up *longer* . . . and deliver *Bigger Loads*.' Please join the Intruders for an evening of imbibing, chicanery, & debauchery. LAS VEGAS HILTON Suite 307." The invitation was widely distributed by A-6 aviators. Copies were handed out at local colleges as well as throughout the hotel area.

§Of that amount, $5,000 was the balance of funds left over from Tailhook '90 and the additional $14,000 was collected in individual assessments of $35 from each of the approximately 400 attending CNATRA members.

cluded the afternoon, evening and early morning hours of Thursday, Friday, and Saturday until early Sunday morning. Beer was served in every suite and 17 suites served mixed or "specialty" alcoholic drinks. It was common practice in the suites to provide alcohol free of charge to attending squadron members, their guests and any other visitors to the suite. The hosting squadron of one suite spent up to $8,500 for the purchase of alcoholic beverages.

Records reflected that the 22 hospitality suites spent a total of $33,500* on alcoholic beverages. However, this figure is not entirely accurate inasmuch as witnesses informed us that, as the initial supply of alcohol ran out, additional alcohol and beer were purchased using supplemental funds collected in Las Vegas from squadron attendees. In one case, squadron members' credit cards were collected and used to pay for additional liquor. A Las Vegas beer distributor stated he delivered 271 kegs, equating to 4,200 gallons of beer, to the suites over the course of the weekend. The total cost of the beer to the squadrons was $12,000. That figure does not include the cost of the 97 kegs of beer the Association ordered for consumption in the exhibition area.

One Navy commander compared the general conduct and consumption of alcohol in the suites to a "cruise party." The officer stated:

> Well, I don't think it's any secret that in times past, after we've been at sea for a long time and we've gone into port for the first time in some amount of time at sea, that we—that, traditionally, Navy aviation sets up an admin. suite, what we call an admin. suite in a hotel. And this is normally a common suite where guys can meet. It's kind of our living room ashore for a brief period of time.
>
> A lot of times it seems to serve two functions: It's one place where we can all congregate, and at other times it's a place of pretty—some good parties. You know, when I say the word "party," I mean somewhat similar—well, better not say similar—somewhat along the lines of what was happening up at Tailhook, not so much with nudity or women, that's usually not

*The figure does not include purchases of alcohol by two of the suites because their records for those purchases were not retained.

the case, but certainly a place to sit around and drink beer.

Well, this tradition of doing this on cruise is exactly what the suite thing at Tailhook is. It's the same thing. There's no difference, really, between the two, in terms of that, though Tailhook definitely is a lot rowdier than most of the parties on cruise get.

Evidence indicates that many officers consumed excessive amounts of alcohol during Tailhook '91. This may have been a contributing factor in the incidence of misconduct and other inappropriate behavior. The excessive consumption of alcohol at Tailhook '91 should be considered in light of two instructions issued by the Secretary of the Navy.

The Secretary's instruction on *Military Alcohol and Drug Abuse Prevention and Control* (SECNAVINST 5300.28B), issued in July 1990, defines alcohol abuse as the use of alcohol "to an extent that it has an adverse effect on performance, conduct, discipline, or mission effectiveness, and/or the user's health, behavior, family or community." The Secretary's instruction on *Alcohol Abuse and Drunk Driving* (SECNAVINST 5300.29), issued in April 1985, discusses three manifestations of alcohol abuse, including "public inebriation (i.e., 'drunken sailor') and its consequences. Brawls, public discredit to military service and injuries and deaths resulting from intoxicated driving are all examples of the adverse effects of that third form of alcohol abuse." Further, both instructions establish a policy that it is the goal of the Department of the Navy to be free of the effects of alcohol abuse. This policy was not complied with by many junior officers nor was it enforced by the senior officers in attendance during Tailhook '91.

Many naval aviators, their guests and other visitors recounted in detail various incidents of inappropriate or unbecoming conduct in the squadron hospitality suites and adjoining areas which were accessible by the public.* These incidents included a stripper performing oral sex on an aviator during her performance. Another account included an incident in which a woman, while getting her legs shaved by a male aviator, stripped off her clothes and had her pubic area shaved. There were additional accounts of women exposing

---

*Sections VII and VIII of the report briefly describe those activities. See Appendix E for detailed description.

themselves either to have squadron stickers applied to their breasts by aviators or to receive free squadron T-shirts. Other reports described male aviators who "ballwalked" or otherwise exposed themselves in the suites or in the third-floor hallway.* A number of ballwalking incidents were photographed. Finally, there were numerous descriptions of women performing simulated oral sex on the dildo attached to the rhinoceros mural in order to obtain a drink from it.

Nineteen indecent assaults occurred in various hospitality suites.† Those suites are identified as:

Hosting Squadron	Suite Number	Number of Assaults
VS-41	304	1
VMFP-3 (Rhino)	308	6
VMFAT-101	355	1
CNATRA	364	8
Unable to determine		3

Our investigation determined that naval aviators rented other rooms, in addition to the squadron hospitality suites, to sponsor private parties for groups of aviators. We were told that, in a number of those rooms, strippers performed or prostitutes were hired to engage in sexual activities with the attendees.‡

A number of contractors, including corporate members of the Association and exhibitors, sponsored hospitality suites at Tailhook '91. According to an Association employee, contractors made their own arrangements with the Las Vegas Hilton for those suites. By most accounts, the contractor suites were located on upper floors of the hotel. We found no instances of impropriety with regard to contractor-sponsored suites.

We were told by contractor personnel and naval aviators that there were a number of reasons for the suites. One contractor representa-

*Ballwalking was an activity engaged in by some aviators in which they publicly exposed their testicles. It is discussed at Section VII.C.

†The indecent assaults, along with information on the other reported assaults, are discussed in Section VI.

‡The issue of consensual sexual activity is discussed in Section VIII of the report.

tive explained their suite was used as a place for the company personnel to meet and plan their official activities at the convention.
One Navy officer described a suite, sponsored by an aircraft manu-
facturer, as a site for company representatives to socialize with naval
aviators and determine how the company might improve its aircraft.
In that suite, company representatives served alcohol and food to
guests. Token gifts of nominal value were available in the suite.*

*These gifts included such things as T-shirts and coffee mugs bearing a corpo-
rate logo.

SECTION VI
INDECENT ASSAULTS

A. GAUNTLET

Our investigation disclosed that the word "gauntlet," as applied in the context of Tailhook '91, was variously interpreted by the many people we interviewed. Some officers strongly disputed or denied even the existence of a gauntlet. One Navy lieutenant, for example, told us he thought the gauntlet was a "figment of someone's imagination" and he could not believe that a hundred guys would just stand around and allow someone to be assaulted. Other officers said they believed the gauntlet and Tailhook-related problems were created by the media. One Navy lieutenant simply asserted that "there is no such thing as the gauntlet." Another officer, a longstanding member of the Tailhook Association who attended numerous Tailhook conventions, said the gauntlet, as described in media reports as an organized effort by naval officers to grope females, "unequivocally does not exist."

Others told us the gauntlet existed, but did not involve assaultive behavior. Those witnesses defined the gauntlet as a very crowded hallway where people were drinking and socializing and where it was difficult to move without having drinks spilled on oneself. Yet others reported that the gauntlet consisted of "drunk" and "obnoxious" junior officers who pushed and shoved each other and anyone else in the hallway. Some described the gauntlet as a bunch of drunken male aviators who yelled catcalls, insults, and suggestive remarks to women as they passed through the hallway. Many people told us they understood the gauntlet to be a Tailhook tradition in which women willingly walked through columns of drunken aviators and were fondled, grabbed, groped, pinched, or otherwise consensually touched.

Numerous others told us the gauntlet involved uninvited, assaultive behavior against unsuspecting women entering the third floor hallway. Many of the witnesses and victims said they were alarmed and disturbed by the severity of the indecent assaults they either witnessed or had been subjected to at Tailhook '91. Finally, a substantial number of people we interviewed said that, although they had never heard the word *gauntlet* used in the context of the Tailhook conventions, they had observed assaultive behavior in the third-floor hallway at Tailhook '91 and earlier Tailhook conventions.

Our investigation confirmed that the gauntlet did indeed exist and at one time or another involved all of the behaviors described above. Based on the reports and descriptions we received, we found that the "gauntlet" evolved over the years from somewhat innocuous non-assaultive behavior to the assaultive acts that occurred in recent years. The gauntlet existed in some form for many years and was well known within the naval aviation community.

Literally hundreds of witnesses reported they either witnessed or were aware of behavior at past Tailhook conventions consistent with the descriptions of the gauntlet at Tailhook '91. Some of those people specifically referred to the gauntlet by name, while others simply described unruly behavior in the hallway. A Navy lieutenant who attended Tailhook for the first time in 1991 told us that while in the third-floor hallway he observed a crowd of men yelling and pinching women on the buttocks. A senior officer standing nearby told him that the activity was an "old Navy tradition called the gauntlet." A Marine Corps captain told us that participants at prior Tailhooks consisted of junior and senior officers, but a higher percentage of junior officers were involved. The same officer said the presence of senior officers did not inhibit the gauntlet activity.

A former Tailhook Association representative said that although he first heard the term "gauntlet" applied to Tailhook in media reports following Tailhook '91, he had observed and taken part in that type of behavior at Tailhook conventions 15 years earlier. He likened the yells of male aviators lining the hallway to construction worker catcalls at passing women. The earliest reported use of the term "gauntlet" in the context of Tailhook came from a Navy commander who said he heard the term in the early 1980s. He defined the gauntlet at that time as being a hallway filled with drunken officers who had overflowed into the hallway from the hospitality suites. The commander said that in the early 1980s there was no groping or indecent assault connotation to the gauntlet. A number of other naval officers provided similar descriptions of the gauntlet during Tailhook conventions through the early 1980s. One officer thought the practice started in 1983 but was not termed a gauntlet until 1986.

Regardless of when the term gauntlet was first applied to behavior at Tailhook, it is clear from the many interviews that the nature of the hallway activity changed over the years. Descriptions of early Tailhook conventions included aviators drinking and singing, standing against the wall and "cheering" as women walked through the most crowded parts of the hallway. There were also accounts that as women walked through the hallway, officers would call out ratings as to the women's attractiveness. Witnesses said that type of activity later changed to "horse-play" with aviators pushing, shoving and throwing beer on one another.

By most accounts, there were few women in attendance at earlier conventions. According to most descriptions, Tailhook conventions in earlier years were largely "stag" affairs. Reportedly, "unwritten" rules prohibited officers from bringing spouses or cameras to Tailhook. There are also reports that during earlier years, a large proportion of the women attending Tailhook conventions could be described as prostitutes or "groupies." However, in recent years, the number of women attendees, both in terms of female naval officers and the wives of male officers, increased.

The nature of the gauntlet activities apparently changed some time in the mid- to late 1980s when the gauntlet started to involve males touching women who walked through the hallway. Some witnesses suggested this was a progression from the cheering, catcalls, and ratings of women typical of earlier Tailhook conventions, to more physical contact in which officers would pinch and grab women's breasts, buttocks, and crotch areas as the women attempted to traverse the hallway. The descriptions suggested that, initially, touching was consensual and that the women involved were aware and tolerant of the consequences of walking through a hallway lined with drunken male aviators. Some accounts of prior Tailhook conventions described the women touching and grabbing men in response to the men's actions. Descriptions of the gauntlet in the mid- to late 1980s also included reports of women being passed overhead down the hallway, similar to a type of activity seen at some high school or college football games.

Witnesses reported they heard men in the hallway calling out "clear deck," "foul deck," "wave off" and "bolter." Those terms are normally associated with aircraft landings on carriers. Reportedly, the term "clear deck" was used as a signal to gauntlet participants that an attractive female was approaching. On the other hand, the terms "wave off," "foul deck," and "bolter" signaled the approach of unappealing females, senior naval officers, or security personnel. Other activities associated with the gauntlet included men pounding on the walls and repeatedly chanting "gauntlet" as they anticipated the approach of women in the hallway. Chanting and yelling has apparently been part of gauntlet activity for a long time. Some others reported chanting at Tailhook '91 or earlier Tailhook conventions included "abort, abort," used in the same context as "wave off" or "bolter." A few witnesses reported that the words "attitude," "bring back the bitch," and similar phrases were used whenever women showed anger at being subjected to the gauntlet.

Our investigation disclosed that gauntlet-related indecent assaults dated back to at least Tailhook '88. Ten women reported to us that they were assaulted when they attended Tailhook conventions between 1988 and 1990. The women reported they had been grabbed on the breasts, buttocks, and/or crotch area. None of the women are known to have reported their assaults to authorities until after Tailhook '91. A number of male aviators also reported that they witnessed assaults on women at Tailhook conventions in the 1980s.

During that time period, gauntlet participants were first observed acting in an organized fashion and using schemes apparently designed to lure women into the gauntlet. Witnesses told us that, as women approached the gauntlet, officers in the hallway pretended to be merely socializing in small groups. The witnesses described how the men would quiet down and create an opening in the crowd that unsuspecting women might think to use as a passageway. Witnesses went on to describe how women who entered the crowded portion of the hallway would then be suddenly surrounded by the gauntlet participants who groped them and prevented their exit.

Perhaps the best description of the gauntlet is contained in the testimony of a Navy commander:

Q. *During your interview . . . on October 3, 1992, you discussed incidents which occurred on the third floor of the Hilton Hotel late Saturday evening, September 7, after the hours of 2200 [10:00 p.m.].*

Could you explain what you witnessed? You had related an incident, I believe, regarding a woman who had passed through The Gauntlet, and if you could just briefly explain The Gauntlet.

A. Okay. My definition of The Gauntlet—it is a term that I've heard used at Tailhook or around Tailhook for several years. And I believe it comes from an old Clint Eastwood movie of the same name, about a street or an avenue that starts wide and narrows into a funnel area that's hard to get through. I think that's where the term "The Gauntlet" originated, in regards to Tailhook.

And The Gauntlet would be pretty much in progress on late Friday or late Saturday nights, and it would consist of again, my estimate, two to three hundred young people— young men. And that's just my estimate. I can tell you the hallway—probably as long as maybe 30 yards or so—is absolutely packed with bodies. And I would say the majority of them are between 21-to-26-year-old young men, mostly on the lower, probably the 21-to-24-year-olds and mostly, in my judgment, just by the attendance at Tailhook, mostly, young Naval officers, but also Marine officers and some Air Force guys; and I did see some people there in '91 that, by their dress and their hair, were not in the military at all. They were civilians that came from the local areas to attend the party.

The group mainly stands out there and drinks and chants and sings songs. And, on the occasion when a female would pass through the area, they would chant or, as it occurred on the late Saturday night, they would grab a girl's butt or breasts, apparently, as she went through.

That's, I guess, the best way I can describe The Gauntlet.

The third floor east wing hallway of the Las Vegas Hilton Hotel is approximately 6 feet wide, dimly lighted, and somewhat wider in the area of the guest elevators and service area. It narrows as it extends eastward into the suite corridor. By all accounts, the third-floor hallway was extremely crowded on Friday and Saturday evenings. Witnesses described the hallway as nearly impassable at times because of the large number of people standing, loitering, or attempting to walk through the hallway.

The hallway curves from the area of the main guest elevators to that straight section where gauntlet activity took place. Witnesses said that the curvature of the hallway, combined with the crowded conditions, made it very easy for someone to walk well into the third floor hallway before realizing that anything unusual was taking place.

Descriptions provided by most witnesses regarding the location of the gauntlet were generally consistent. The beginning of the gauntlet was frequently described as being in the hallway just beyond the hotel service area as one turned right out of the main guest elevators. The gauntlet started in the area of the HS-10 suite (room 315) and the VS-41 suite (room 304). It extended eastward and ended in the vicinity of the Rhino suite (room 308). Two civilian females and one civilian male described seeing a sign posted on the third floor which read "Gauntlet—Enter at your own risk" or some similar wording. One of the women specifically recalled that the sign was visible in the hallway area immediately on exiting the guest elevators.*

Witnesses used the analogy of a funnel to describe the mass of people in the gauntlet area. The area nearest the elevators was sparsely populated in comparison to the beginning of the gauntlet, beyond the elevator. The area was described as ". . . a million people per square inch." The crowd tapered off near the area of the VA-128 and Rhino suites.

Several people described the third-floor hallway as smelling of spilled beer, vomit, and urine at the height of the party on Friday and/or Saturday nights. One Navy squadron XO told us ". . . the hallway was gross . . . People—I'm sure they peed in the corners or wherever they happened to be standing, loss of bladder control. They puked there. It was terrible." Others said the hallway carpet was saturated with spilled beer to the point that it "squished" when walked on. Reportedly, the Hilton Hotel replaced or repaired and cleaned the third-floor hallway carpeting each year following the Tailhook convention because of the extensive damage.

The gauntlet operated intermittently, but most of the activity reportedly occurred between the hours of 9:00 p.m. and midnight on Friday and Saturday nights. Just as gauntlet activity escalated over the years, so too did the intensity and frequency of hallway assaults increase over the three nights of Tailhook '91.

Our investigation revealed that many women freely and knowingly participated in gauntlet activities. A significant number of witnesses reported that women went through the gauntlet and seemed to enjoy the attention and interaction with the aviators. Those witnesses, both men and women, generally stated they could tell the women were enjoying themselves because, despite being grabbed and pushed along through the crowd, they were smiling and giggling. Some of the women were observed going repeatedly through

*No other witnesses reported the existence of such a sign.

the gauntlet. Many women who went through the gauntlet told us they did so willingly and were not offended by the men touching them. A civilian woman employed by the Navy told us of a conversation she had with another young woman whom she met while on a commercial flight into Las Vegas to attend Tailhook '91. The young woman described the gauntlet and said that, at about 3:00 a.m., things get "real rough" and wild on the third floor. According to the Navy employee, the young woman implied that she enjoyed this type of activity and that was the reason she was going to Tailhook '91.

Our investigation also revealed a much more sinister aspect to the gauntlet at Tailhook '91 which involved assaults on unsuspecting women. Of those assaults which occurred in the hallway, 5 took place on Thursday, 11 on Friday, and 53 on Saturday. Individual witness descriptions best portrayed the assaults and related activities. The following are but a few of the many eyewitness accounts reported during the investigation.

A female Navy lieutenant described the spontaneous formation of the gauntlet. She said that squadron mates told her about the gauntlet prior to attending Tailhook and warned her ". . . don't be on the third floor after 11:00 p.m." Even though she was never told of the assaultive aspects of the gauntlet, she realized that something happened to women who walked through the gauntlet. She explained that in a matter of 30 minutes on Saturday night the hallway underwent a major transformation. At 10:00 p.m., it was a quiet place with 20 people. By 10:30 p.m., it had become an absolute mob scene. It was apparent to her that the gauntlet she had heard about was starting up, and she opined that people appeared to be exiting the suites into the hallway at a preplanned time for the gauntlet.

A male Navy lieutenant junior grade also described the transformation of the hallway, as well as an incident of indecent exposure in the gauntlet. He said that on Friday night he saw the third floor go from a "crowded hallway" where people were just laughing and joking to a "hallway where people started grabbing women" and exhibiting a "mob mentality." He observed a short male, whom he believed to be a Marine because of his short haircut, taking part in the gauntlet. He said the man was "half naked" and took a woman's hand and rubbed it against his exposed penis. This incident occurred near the end of the gauntlet. He added that he did not think the woman realized she had touched the man's penis, although she appeared to be distressed.

A male Navy lieutenant described one unsuspecting woman's passage through the gauntlet. He stated that on Friday night at approximately 11:00 p.m., while standing in the third-floor hallway in the area of the elevators, he heard people chanting and pounding on something in a rhythmic drumming manner. He observed approximately 200 men lined up along the hallway walls. He compared the activity to a high school football practice type of gauntlet. He saw a woman enter and it seemed to him that ''. . . she did not understand it was a gauntlet.'' As she attempted to walk through, he observed her being ''groped and molested.'' She was obviously ''not enjoying it [and] was pushing hands away from places she did not want them.'' As she approached the gauntlet he ''saw a look of fear in her eyes. She fought her way through the gauntlet and then busted out the side through a suite.'' He said the look of fear in the woman's eyes caused him to realize the gauntlet was not just a playful situation and he became concerned for other women in the hallway and vicinity of the gauntlet. He found a hotel security guard and advised him of the incident. He also warned some other women by telling them ''you don't want to go in there.''

A male Marine Corps captain told us that the gauntlet was operated in an organized manner. He said that on Saturday night between 10:00 and 11:00 p.m. he observed the gauntlet. It operated between the hotel service area and the VA-128 suite (room 307). He saw a group of about 30 men, whom he believed to be military personnel, milling around in the hallway. As he watched, women approached and someone yelled ''wave off,'' at which time the women walked through without being molested. On separate occasions, he saw two women walk into the group of men and, once inside, the men turned on the women and began jostling and pushing them along the hallway. When a woman entered the group, both ends of the gauntlet closed with men blocking any avenue of retreat. Once a woman escaped from the gauntlet, someone yelled, ''Mill about,'' which would then be repeated over and over in low voices by the men all along the gauntlet. In response, the men slowly shuffled their feet and faced at odd angles until the next woman approached, giving the appearance they were just standing along the hall socializing with each other.

The Marine captain also observed the group grab a woman who was accompanied by a man. The man yelled ''knock it off . . . that's my wife,'' and the man stepped in front of the woman to shield her. The group ignored the man and kept grabbing and jostling the woman until the husband started swinging his fists at the men who were assaulting his wife. At that point, the group stopped and allowed the couple to pass through. A Tailhook staff person later approached the group and yelled "knock this crap off." A couple of men attempted to argue with the Tailhook staffer, but the staffer did not back down and the group disbanded.

A male Marine Corps first lieutenant said that on Friday night he saw about a dozen women walk through the gauntlet, and approximately half of those appeared to be happy and enjoying themselves. The other half appeared displeased and at least one appeared seriously distressed. A crowd of about 200 males bunched together in the hall pounding the wall and shouting "gauntlet, gauntlet." Periodically, males shouted "mill about" at which time the people in the gauntlet would being feigning "milling about" and the general noise level would lower. When a female entered the gauntlet, the participants would surround her and touch, pat, and grab her while she was funnelled down the hall. He heard shouts of "shut the doors," which he deduced was intended to prevent women from escaping into the suites and to channel them through the length of the gauntlet. He said the general noise level increased substantially when an attractive female entered the gauntlet. He also heard shouts of "wave off," which he believed was a code indicating an older or "unattractive" female was entering the gauntlet. The participants did not touch women rated as "wave off."

Another male Navy lieutenant described how gauntlet participants treated women differently depending on how each woman reacted to being touched. He said he saw at least 15 women come through the gauntlet in a 2-hour period and estimated that a third of the women seemed to enjoy the gauntlet, another third were upset by it, and the remaining third were extremely resistant to the gauntlet. He noted that the more the women fought the men who were attacking them, the more the males attacked.

We received two independent accounts of a woman (or women) who walked through the hallway with electronic weapons. One male lieutenant said that on Saturday night he saw a woman come through the crowd carrying a "Tazer," which he described as a device similar to a small cattle prod and designed to foil attackers. He said the woman was waving the device, which was apparently recognized by the men in the hallway because they did not bother her. Another officer said he saw a woman on Saturday who looked "frazzled." He said that as the woman approached the elevators a man tried to grab her breasts. The woman pulled out a "zapper" (which he described as a stun gun) which she waved in the man's face.

A Navy enlisted man* stated that on Friday night, while standing in the hallway near the deck exit closest to the Rhino suite, he saw men lining up along the hallway. Several women pushed their way through and they emerged from the gauntlet near where he was standing. When they emerged, the women had squadron stickers on their bodies. The hallway scene looked "like a pin ball machine [with each] guy getting his shot in." He also saw a man near the elevators quieting the men in the hallway as unsuspecting women approached the gauntlet. He believed the gauntlet to be an organized event because the man quieting the crowd received a strong negative response from the men in the hall when, after successfully quieting the crowd, a man, rather than a woman, appeared at the gauntlet's entrance.

There were numerous accounts of how women were lured into the gauntlet. For example, some witnesses heard men in the gauntlet yell out that they needed more women, and men would then go down to the casino area to recruit them. A male civilian Navy employee told us that he observed the gauntlet on two occasions on Saturday night. Sometime between 9:00 and 10:00 p.m., he was standing in the hallway near the VX-4 suite (room 360). He could only see the end of the gauntlet because of the crowd. Although most women who exited did not appear upset and some were even laughing, he saw one woman crying and being consoled by two friends. About an hour later, he was standing near the HS-1 helicopter suite (room 315) where he observed the beginning of the gauntlet. As women entered, he saw hands reach out for their breasts, crotch areas, and buttocks. Two hotel security guards were standing near the service area advising women not to walk down the hall, but they took no steps to stop the gauntlet. During that same time, he watched a male walk up to women and escort them into the gauntlet. The male would walk up to the women, put his arm around them, and talk nicely to them, almost as if he were trying to disarm them and not let on that they were about to be thrust into a gauntlet. He heard participants whisper "shhhh" in an attempt to quiet everyone down. The noise level in the gauntlet decreased when new women approached and elevated once they were in the gauntlet.

A male Navy Lieutenant commander and his civilian spouse each

*We interviewed a total of 27 enlisted personnel who attended Tailhook '91.

described their observations of the gauntlet on Saturday night. The officer told us that he has attended four or five Tailhooks since 1982 and is familiar with the gauntlet, which occurred at every Tailhook convention. He said the term gauntlet is routinely used among naval aviators. It occurs at no established day or time and the hallway is lined with people who begin by chanting. He opined that, for the most part, the same people get involved in the gauntlet each year. The gauntlet varies in size depending on the time of the night. On Saturday night at Tailhook '91 his wife wanted to see the gauntlet in action. He was unsuccessful in dissuading her, so they went to the third-floor hallway where they stood about 5 to 6 feet away from the head of the gauntlet: they saw a very clear demarcation point where the gauntlet began. They watched for approximately 20 minutes and heard men yelling such things as "Clear deck," "Foul deck," "Wave off," and "Bolter." During that time, he saw a number of people enter the gauntlet. Men proceeded unmolested, however, several women were pinched or patted on the buttocks. All those women appeared to be laughing.

The lieutenant commander further stated that he also saw a couple who appeared to be in their mid- to late '60's enter the gauntlet area. As they walked through the gauntlet, a passageway opened up to let the couple through. His wife told him that she saw someone pat the woman's buttocks, but he did not see that himself. He recalled that one woman started down the gauntlet and became irate when she was apparently pinched. He said she turned around and threw a beer at a man standing 3 to 4 feet away, hitting him in the face and head with the beer. The man retaliated by throwing his beer on the woman. The woman hit the man on his jaw and the man then struck the side of the woman's head with a closed hand and the witness thought the woman might have fallen to her knees. He said the woman reversed course and "took off like a rocket."* At that point, his wife said she had seen enough and the couple departed. He noted that in previous years he also took part in the gauntlet. He opined that the gauntlet is more of a melee than an organized event and that no one individual organized it. He said that in the past, the gauntlet was a "promenade kind of thing" in which women went through for the express purpose of getting pinched. He added that it has been a rule for everyone involved in a significant gauntlet incident to leave

*This woman was not further identified during the course of our investigation.

as soon as the incident happened because that hinders identification of those involved.

The officer's spouse provided a somewhat different perspective of the same incidents. She said that when she and her husband entered the third floor hallway, people were screaming and yelling. She leaned against the wall so that her back was protected. Her husband stood in front of her to shield her from potential frontal assaults. She recalled that an unidentified male who was standing nearby, turned to her and said something like, "You probably will want to leave. You won't want to see what's about to happen." She said it appeared that some signal had been given that the "gauntlet" was about to start, and all the men in the hallway began lining the halls rather than milling about, as though suddenly organized. She said many of the men began drumming their hands on the walls. A clear passageway formed down the center of the hallway and women were pinched or patted on their buttocks as they walked through. Regarding the incident described by her husband in which a man and a woman struck each other in the gauntlet, she said that she was personally shocked by the force of the blow the man used. It appeared to her that the man put his full strength behind the blow. Unlike her husband, she did not see any women lining up to get pinched or patted, but rather it seemed to her that they were simply trying to get through the hallway.* She saw an older couple go through the gauntlet. It appeared to her that the crowd did not care about rank or age, as a number of men touched the woman's buttocks and the woman continuously tried to swat their hands away.

A vivid and detailed description of the gauntlet on Saturday night was reported by a male civilian Navy employee. He said, "I was probably 10 years older than the average age down here, and was just sort of being a fly on the wall, just observing." He said the men lining the hallway quieted and pressed their backs against the walls when females approached so as to give the appearance of a clear passage down the center of the hallway. He saw a white male who was standing in the hallway near the HS-1 helicopter suite (room 315) whom he described as the gauntlet "master of ceremonies." He said the "master of ceremonies" was moving about in a very animated fashion and appeared totally dedicated to getting all the women approaching the hallway to proceed down it. When unable to

---

*The officer's wife said she was "stone cold sober" at the time she witnessed the gauntlet, whereas she and her husband stated that he had been drinking.

coax women into entering the gauntlet, the "master of ceremonies" would "pick them up on his shoulders and carry them into the gauntlet area and deposit them and go out for more." He reported seeing four to six women carried into the gauntlet by the "master of ceremonies." On one occasion the "master of ceremonies" approached a woman from behind, squatted down, placed his head between her legs, and forcibly carried her on his shoulders into the gauntlet.

The Navy employee went on to describe how he happened to get caught in the middle of the gauntlet on Saturday evening:

> I had made my way down towards the training suites, the VF-121 (sic) suite, Room 373 and was then making my way back through the hallway—a very, very crowded hallway—very slow progress being made through the hallway. At about the Room 308 to 312 area there, there was some commotion in the hallway and some direction to make a hole, or clear the hallway.
>
> At this time all the people around me were getting up against the wall, they were clearing out of the hallway. So I did likewise. In about the area of Room 308, 307, on that side of the hallway. I then basically put my back to the wall and I had a beer mug with me, and awaited further instructions. I was just, once again, a fly on the wall.
>
> At this point, then, I noticed that there was one woman that had been behind me, obviously, and she was now to my right. She got accosted from both sides of the hallway. People were grabbing her. She was falling against the far side wall.

He further stated that the woman tried to protect herself as she was being grabbed high and low, both front and back, by all the men around her. He said that at least one of the men who grabbed the woman's breasts appeared to be a civilian. He said she was definitely not amused by the grabbing and she attempted to fight back.

Many eyewitness accounts described women who had articles of clothing ripped or removed as they went through the gauntlet. One particularly disturbing incident involved an intoxicated college freshman who was stripped from the waist down as she was passed overhead through the gauntlet and then left on the hallway floor.

Although she had not attained legal drinking age in Nevada, she was served a considerable amount of alcohol by the officers in the HS-1 hospitality suite. After becoming intoxicated, she was placed by those officers in the hallway in the vicinity of the gauntlet. Once in the hallway, she was lifted above the crowd of men and passed hand-over-hand down the hallway. As she was passed over the crowd, the men removed her slacks and underpants. At the end of the gauntlet, they dumped her on the floor, and cleared out of the hallway as hotel security officers came to the victim's assistance.

A Marine Corps first lieutenant who witnessed the same incident from the other end of the hallway described the reaction of gauntlet participants. He had just left the CNATRA suite and was in the hall-way walking toward the guest elevators and hotel service area. A mass of people was going in the same direction. Suddenly, there was a shift in the motion of the crowd and six to eight men rushed toward him, going in the other direction as quickly as possible, but laughing rather than fleeing in fear. The hallway suddenly cleared for several feet in front of him, and he saw a young female, naked from the waist down, seated in the middle of the hall.

The Executive Director of the Tailhook Association told us that he learned of this incident shortly after it occurred. When questioned about how he viewed the matter, he responded:

> I looked at it as a spontaneous incident, more along the line of a prank, not a prank in good taste, but I . . . that's my view of the situation at the time.

During the investigation, we obtained a photograph taken just after this incident occurred. It shows the victim, nude from the waist down, being escorted by security officials through the hallway as a group of aviators looks on. The hallway is littered with plastic drinking cups and the victim's pants. We chose not to publish the photograph out of consideration for the victim. However, we note that during several interviews we conducted in which the officer being interviewed expressed his belief that the events at Tailhook '91 were "no big deal," showing the officer a copy of the photograph had a dramatic effect. Several of the officers who viewed the photograph were visibly shaken.

The gauntlet was also vividly described to us by several victims. One female civilian victim, who was in Las Vegas on vacation with a female friend, told us she was walking through the third-floor hallway with her friend when a group of men in the hallway began chanting and yelling. The men reached out and began to grab at her breasts, buttocks, and crotch. They tried to lift her skirt and grabbed at her legs and buttocks while she desperately tried to hold down her skirt. As she looked back she saw that her friend was also being assaulted. The men also threw drinks on the victim, soaking her clothing with alcohol.

Another female civilian victim told us that, as she walked up the hallway, at least seven men suddenly attacked her. They pulled down her "tube top" and grabbed at her exposed breasts while she attempted to cover herself with her arms. She fell to the ground and the assault continued. She bit several of her attackers in an attempt to stop their assault. After a few moments, they stopped their attack and she was allowed to get up from the floor. She turned and looked back down the hallway and observed another woman screaming and fighting her way down the hallway as she too was attacked. The victim was crying profusely when she was approached by a Marine Corps aviator whom she had met earlier. He told her that it is an annual tradition at Tailhook conventions to harass women physically and verbally in the hallway and she should not worry about it. The victim later told her boyfriend, a Navy officer, about the attack but he advised her not to tell anyone about it because they would think she was a "slut."

In another incident, a 24-year-old female Navy officer told us that she entered the third-floor hallway and was immediately surrounded by five or six men who groped and grabbed at her breasts and buttocks. While she struggled to escape, she saw two male Navy officers she recognized standing in the hallway close to where she was being attacked. Although she believed the men witnessed her attack and failed to help her, both men denied having seen or heard anything unusual. The victim saw one of the Navy officers several months after Tailhook '91. He told the victim that men have been treating women like that "since caveman days," and that she had no business being there (Tailhook '91) in the first place because she was not an aviator.

One victim, a 32-year-old female, reported that she attended Tailhook '91 with her spouse, a Navy officer; her mother; and two of her mother's female friends. As the group walked through the hallway the victim, who was wearing a formal cocktail dress, was suddenly grabbed around the waist and lifted above the crowd by two men. The men lifted the skirt of her dress above her waist and pushed their hands between her legs in an attempt to get their fingers inside her panties. Our investigation revealed that the victim's mother as well as one of her mother's friends were also indecently assaulted as they walked through the hallway.

LT Paula Coughlin, the Navy officer who first publicly revealed allegations of impropriety at Tailhook '91, told us that she entered the third-floor hallway of the Hilton Hotel and, as she walked up the hallway and into a crowd of men, someone began to yell, "Admiral's Aide!" She was grabbed on the buttocks from behind with such force that she was lifted up off the ground. As she turned to confront the man, another man behind her grabbed her buttocks and she was pushed from behind into a crowd of men who collectively began pinching her body and pulling at her clothing. One man put both his hands down the front of her tank top, inside her brassiere, and grabbed her breasts. LT Coughlin told us that she crouched down and bit the man on his forearm and on his right hand. As the man released his grip on her breasts, another man reached up under her skirt and grabbed her panties. She then kicked out at her attackers. She stated, "I felt as though the group was trying to rape me." LT Coughlin told us that she saw one of the men in the group turn to walk away so she "reached out and tapped him on the hip, pleading with the man to just let me get in front of him." The man turned around to face her, raised both his hands, and placed them on her breasts.

Many witnesses stated there was nothing they could do to stop the assaults in the hallway and that the size of the crowd, the level of intoxication, and the noise would have made it impossible for them to put a stop to the gauntlet. One Navy lieutenant said that although he believed the actions of those in the gauntlet were inappropriate, he did not do anything to stop them simply because he is a junior officer. Others, however, stated that senior officers could have put a stop to the assaults if they had chosen to do so. A lieutenant commander opined that if a flag officer had elected to stop the gauntlet, it probably would have stopped. He added, however, the comment that "You get to a certain stage of drunkenness, you don't care."

We found one account to be particularly telling on the subject of whether anything could have been done to stop the gauntlet assaults. Apparently, the crowd comprising the gauntlet was capable of responding to direction. Two female victims told us that, after they were pushed and shoved through the gauntlet where they were grabbed on the breasts and buttocks, one of them realized she had lost her electronic pager. Both victims recounted that they were assisted by officers standing at the end of the gauntlet. One of the officers yelled to the gauntlet participants that the woman had lost a pager. According to one of the victims, the ". . . whole crowd stopped and began to look for the pager." The pager was located and returned to the woman without further incident.

Our investigation disclosed that, despite statements by many senior officers to the contrary, the fact that the gauntlet was in operation was well known. As previously mentioned, a large number of officers said they had witnessed or heard of the gauntlet at prior Tailhook conventions. Many others, particularly female officers, said they had been forewarned to avoid the third-floor hallway at certain times. Even many civilians who were in attendance at Tailhook '91 said they were aware of the gauntlet. Several witnesses described seeing similar gauntlet activity at settings other than Tailhook, such as at officers' clubs. A number of officers said they felt confident the gauntlet was common knowledge among military attendees at Tailhook. Several officers stated that anyone who spent time in the area of the third-floor hallway on Friday or Saturday night and said they were unaware of the gauntlet activity "must be lying."

Several witnesses mentioned that they heard references to the gauntlet while out on the pool deck. One lieutenant said that he recalled someone walking out onto the pool deck on either Friday or Saturday evening and saying "they've already run the gauntlet." There were accounts of other gauntlet activity. One gauntlet reportedly operated briefly on an upper floor of the hotel. Also, a witness described a "mini gauntlet" on the patio pool deck where several women repeatedly and consensually walked through a line of officers.

Of the many officers and civilian Tailhook attendees who admitted witnessing the gauntlet, only a few witnesses stated they were able to identify anyone else who was in the hallway at the time they witnessed the gauntlet in operation. In light of statements by most aviators that one of the primary reasons for attending Tailhook was to socialize with friends and former squadron mates, we found the inability of witnesses to identify gauntlet observers or participants to be incredible. The statements were also questionable in light of the fact that many of those same officers could identify persons in their company at other times during Tailhook '91.

When one Navy commander was queried as to the likelihood of an aviator being in the third-floor hallway without seeing anybody whom that person knew, the commander responded: "You couldn't have done that, I don't think . . . well, maybe in the morning and the afternoon, but, you know in the evenings. I don't think you could have done that." When asked, hypothetically, about witnesses who stated that they were in the hallway and did not see anybody that they knew, this witness stated: "I would say that the person would be lying, and I don't see how he could do that. I was an ensign the first time that I went there, and I knew people, even inside the air wing, okay? You would almost have to know somebody there. So I'm sure there's an isolated case, but I don't think so."

A T-shirt sold at Tailhook '91 and worn by many attendees serves to illustrate the expectations regarding the general atmosphere relative to the third floor.

B. VICTIMS

From Thursday, September 5, 1991, through the early morning hours of Sunday, September 8, 1991, at least 90 people were victims of some form of indecent assault while at Tailhook '91. Of that number, 83 were women and 7 were men.* Our investigation also disclosed information pertaining to 10 women who told us they were assaulted at previous Tailhook conventions. This report focuses on the Tailhook '91 assault victims.

Table 3 depicts various categories of victims by occupation or other affiliation.

The assault victims range from 18 to 48 years of age. Eight victims were assaulted more than once. Of those, four victims were assaulted on more than one evening and four were each assaulted at two different locations on the same night.

We divided the assaults into three separate nights. Those assaults indicated as occurring on Thursday include those that occurred in the early morning hours of Friday. Friday assaults include events in the early hours of Saturday morning, and Saturday includes early Sunday morning as well.

Eleven assaults, involving 10 women, took place on Thursday

---

*We are aware there are individuals, in addition to those discussed in this report, who were victims of indecent assault at Tailhook '91. That group includes five individuals who have been identified by us as assault victims, but who refused to be interviewed.

TABLE 3

Victims

Civilian Other (Female)	49
United States Navy (Female)	21
Government Employee (Female)	6
Military Spouse (Female)	6
United States Navy (Male)	5
United States Marine Corps (Male)	2
United States Air Force (Female)	1
Total Victims	*90*

evening. Five took place in the hallway, five in administrative suites, and one on the pool patio.*

Eighteen assaults occurred on Friday night. Eleven took place in the hallway, five in administrative suites, and two on the pool patio.

The greatest number of assaults occurred on Saturday evening, when there were a total of 68 assaults involving 63 victims. Fifty-three of those assaults took place in the third-floor hallway, eight in suites, six on the pool patio, and one victim was assaulted in one of the guest rooms on another floor. Of the assaults that took place in the third-floor hallway on Saturday night, 36 took place between 9:00 p.m. and 12:00 midnight. The assaults varied from victims being grabbed on the buttocks, to victims being groped, pinched, and fondled on their breasts, buttocks, and genitals.† Some victims were bitten by their assailants, others were knocked to the ground, and some had their clothing ripped or removed. Some of the victims confronted their attackers and felt they had handled the situation to their own satisfaction.

Few victims were able to identify positively their assailants. Typically, they attributed their inability to identify their attackers to several

*One victim was assaulted in the hallway and also in one of the administrative suites. Similarly two victims who were working as waitresses in an administrative suite were assaulted numerous times in the suite over the 3-day period.

†There were numerous accounts of lewd comments directed toward women, as well as accounts of women who were nonconsensually patted, touched, or "zapped" on various parts of their bodies. Those accounts were *not* included as assaults for purposes of this report.

factors, including poor lighting in the hallway, the confusion resulting from the crowded conditions, and their shock at being assaulted. The victims also said most of the men in the hallway looked alike in that they were young, physically fit, Caucasian males with short military-style haircuts, and typically dressed in T-shirts and shorts.

A complete summary of each of the assaults is attached as Appendix F. Of the victims, nine did not consider themselves to be a "victim" even though they have been subjected to indecent assault.*

C. OTHER ASSAULTS AND INJURIES

A number of assaults, other than indecent assaults, occurred at Tailhook '91. Several witnesses reported that fights occurred in the third-floor hallway and the pool patio area. Hotel security reported breaking up several such altercations on the third floor during Tailhook '91.

In one instance, a Marine Corps major was pushed over a clay planter by a Navy commander on the pool patio. The altercation occurred after the major, while intoxicated, deliberately splashed water onto the commander. The commander took umbrage and forcibly pushed the major over the planter. The major sustained back injuries and was transported to a local hospital.

In another incident, a 24-year-old male Air Force officer from Las Vegas, Nevada, walked into the hallway of the third floor of the hotel on Friday wearing his Air Force flight jacket. As soon as he exited the elevators, the naval aviators in the hallway yelled, "Hey boys, there's an Air Force guy." They then grabbed him, picked him up and passed him overhead about 80 to 100 feet down the hallway, spilling their drinks on him along the way. The officer subsequently escaped the area without sustaining any physical injuries.

Finally, a female student from the University of Las Vegas (UNLV) was on the pool patio talking with several other female UNLV students on Saturday evening when a sheet of glass from one of the upper-floor windows of the hotel was pushed out.† Glass shards from the window

---

*For the purposes of our investigation and report, we have used the term "victim" to describe any individual who was subjected to a nonconsensual indecent assault. If, however, an individual told us that he/she chose not to be classified as a victim, we so noted that fact in their individual assault summary.

†As discussed in Section VII.B of the report.

struck her on top of her head. She began to feel ill and went to the hospital where it was determined that she had suffered a concussion. According to several witnesses, the glass was pushed out of the window by people who were pressing their bare buttocks on the window while "mooning" the crowd on the pool patio below.

SECTION VII
INDECENT EXPOSURE

During our investigation, we received numerous reports of public nudity and indecent exposure in the third-floor hallway, in the hospitality suites and outside on the pool patio. This behavior falls into three general categories of "streaking," "mooning," and "ball-walking."

A. STREAKING

One form of indecent exposure that occurred at Tailhook '91 involved "streaking," a term used by most witnesses to describe the actions of males who removed their clothing and walked or ran nude past onlookers. Several streaking instances occurred during Tailhook '91. In each of the reported instances, males were seen running nude either through the suites or on the hotel pool patio. Some incidents involved a single streaker whereas others were reported to include as many as 10 individuals. Those instances occurred in the evening hours of Friday and Saturday or in the early morning hours Sunday.

Witnesses included numerous male and female naval officers, a Hilton Hotel security officer and civilians. Witnesses were able to provide information leading to the identification of six naval officers as streakers. Two of those officers are Navy flight surgeons.

Streakers were sometimes pursued by Hilton security officers. In those instances, other naval officers sought to delay or otherwise impede the security officers thus allowing the streakers to escape into the squadron hospitality suites. Several of the reported streaking incidents centered around the VAQ-129 and VS-41 suites. Witnesses, including officers assigned to VAQ-129, reported to us that they observed streakers in the VAQ-129 suite on numerous occasions. Witnesses told us that both men and women observed the streakers.

Other streaking incidents include a group of four or five males streaking across the patio early Sunday morning while being chased by security officers. These streakers were described as being naked except for their Rhino horn headgear (worn by many members of the former Marine "Rhino" squadron). A second instance involved a group of about 10 naked males who were seen winding their way through the patio crowd as they held hands. In yet another instance, a male aviator related that on Friday evening he entered the VS-41 suite and observed three males walking around the room naked despite the fact there were other male and female guests in the suite. A second officer stated that on Saturday night he observed six or seven streakers exit the VS-41 suite and run across the patio. The witness also noted that a group of fully dressed women preceded the men and appeared to be carrying the men's clothing.

Witnesses, including then Tailhook President, CAPT Ludwig, and the Executive Director acknowledged that streaking had been a persistent problem at Tailhook conferences. When interviewed, CAPT Ludwig stated that he saw five streakers run across the pool patio. CAPT Ludwig described the subsequent encounter as follows:

> And so I immediately go after them. And I get in a suite, look around and I'm—you know, I am absolutely astounded that these characters have disappeared. They are nowhere to be seen. The bathroom door is closed, so—you know, it is locked. I finally bang, and here is five guys huddled up, looking pretty sheepish in the bathroom . . . And so I chew the shit out of them, and tell them, "Get some towels on you, get your asses out of here and get yourselves dressed and don't ever let me see you again."

CAPT Ludwig stated that he did not inquire as to the officers names or specific unit but did note that the incident occurred in the VAQ-129 squadron suite. Our investigation identified the men involved in the incident. All were found to be Navy aviators.

No other action is known to have been taken either by the Navy or the Association in that or any of the other reported streaking incidents.

B. MOONING

Another form of indecent exposure, referred to as "mooning," involved individuals baring their buttocks within view of other attendees. An overwhelming number of attendees, including male and female military officers, Tailhook Association officers, civilians, contractor employees and hotel security staff acknowledged witnessing such instances. Mooning incidents occurred on every day and night of Tailhook '91 and were seen in various suites, in the third-floor hallway, on the pool patio and from the patio level while looking up at windows on many floors of the hotel. Evidence indicated that mooning was a common practice among naval aviators at Tailhook '91 and at previous Tailhook conventions.

Although most occurrences involved only males, some incidents involved only females while others included both males and females. Although a few male officers acknowledged or were reported by others to have participated in that activity, in most cases our investigation failed to identify individuals involved in specific mooning incidents.

Male officers, in some instances, posed for photographs while mooning at the request of female civilian attendees. Certain of those photographs were obtained as evidence during the course of our investigation. In the HS-1 suite (room 315), a few officers recorded over combat footage in a video camcorder to memorialize their mooning activities. They left the videotape in the camcorder to the later surprise of the squadron CO who owned the equipment.*

C. ''BALLWALKING''

The third form of indecent exposure engaged in by naval aviators at Tailhook '91 involved publicly exposing their testicles, commonly referred to in the naval aviation community as ''ballwalking.'' Eighty individuals reported to us that they witnessed ballwalking at Tailhook '91. Insufficient evidence was found to state with certainty exactly how many ballwalking incidents occurred at Tailhook '91. We identified 14 military officers who ballwalked during the convention.

*One mooning instance resulted in minor injuries and could conceivably have resulted in more serious injuries. Late Saturday evening, an unspecified number of individuals mooned the patio crowd from a window on the eighth floor of the Hilton Hotel. That apparently caused a large plate glass window to break and crash down onto the patio area, which at the time was crowded with guests. At least two individuals were cut by falling glass and required medical treatment.

Where and how the practice of ballwalking started is unclear, but several accounts serve to indicate how widespread the practice is within the Navy. Four officers told us that they observed ballwalking by naval officers in either Korea or the Philippines. One officer stated that he was first introduced to the practice of ballwalking at a squadron golf game. Those golfers who failed to reach the point of the women's tee, when teeing off, were required to play the remainder of the hole while ballwalking. The same officer stated he had observed ballwalking at various naval officers' clubs.

Another officer, who told us he declined an invitation by other officers to ballwalk at Tailhook '91, stated that ballwalking was commonplace at parties held by training squadrons at the NAS Meridian, Mississippi. The individual readily admitted to seeing and participating in ballwalking during those squadron parties. Still another officer, who was identified as a ballwalker at Tailhook '91, stated he had seen ballwalking at "wingings" when naval aviators are awarded their pilot's wings. He added that other male aviators had been caught ballwalking at the Officers' Club at NAS Kingsville, Texas, and that "nothing adverse happened to them."

One instance of ballwalking was reported to have occurred at the United States Naval Academy. An officer told us that while he was an Academy cadet, a senior cadet demonstrated ballwalking to him. After the demonstration, the senior cadet wanted the younger cadet to ballwalk in front of a female cadet. The cadet refused.

All but one of the reported instances of ballwalking took place on either the third floor or the pool patio deck area of the hotel on Friday and Saturday or very early Sunday morning. The exception involved two naval officers who, after leaving the Hilton early Sunday morning, ballwalked down the streets of Las Vegas. The ballwalkers were observed by a third officer and they even attempted to get him to ballwalk by stating, "It's a tradition, you've got to do this." The third officer refused to participate and distanced himself from them. The third officer added that, although it was early in the morning, there were people on the streets.

The incidents occurred primarily in three areas. The first area, the outside pool patio deck, was very large and could accommodate crowds with more ease than the other two. For that reason, many attendees preferred to spend time on the pool patio deck area, especially those who wanted to avoid the crowded hallway. There were 27 reported ballwalking sightings on the pool patio deck area.

The second area where ballwalking occurred was in individual suites. Specific suites in which ballwalking is known to have occurred include CNATRA, VT-24, VF-124, VA-128 and Naval Strike Warfare Center. Ballwalking apparently occurred in other suites but, in some instances, witnesses could not identify specific suites with certainty. One such incident involved either the VMFAT or the MAWTS suite (rooms 355 and 356) while another involved the VAQ-129, VAW-110 or the VS-41 suite (rooms 302, 303, 304). In short, ballwalking was not limited to a particular suite or otherwise confined in any one area.

The third area in which ballwalking incidents occurred was the hallway where the gauntlet took place. Thirteen people reported they observed ballwalking in the hallway. At least four specific incidents involved ballwalkers who went from the hallway into individual suites. Ballwalking was practiced by individual officers, in pairs, and in groups of three or more with about equal frequency.

A few aviators provided reasons why they ballwalked. One aviator described ballwalking as a "manly thing" to do with the guys. Another officer speculated that males do it for one-upmanship, "trying to be more rude and wild than the next person." The attitude of a ballwalker may best be illustrated by a T-shirt worn by a ballwalker at Tailhook '90. The T-shirt, which was sold at the convention, read, "HANG EM IF YOU GOT EM." Finally, a ballwalker at Tailhook '91 stated ballwalking is done as an "Act of Defiance."

We are aware of only three individuals who took corrective action with respect to ballwalking. In the first instance, a Naval Reserve commander told us that on Saturday night he saw a young white male whom he believed to be a naval officer on the pool patio deck area near the VR-57 suite. The commander noted that the individual was ballwalking and told him that ballwalking was not appreciated in his area. He told the officer to put his testicles back into his pants and act like an adult. The young man got very red in the face, followed the instructions, and then left the area.

The second action was also taken by a naval commander who observed two lieutenants ballwalking on the patio pool deck area. The commander said that it was the "most disgusting thing" he had ever seen and he immediately went over to the men and chastised them. He specifically told the ballwalkers to zip up their pants and that he did not want to see anything like that again. The commander stated that, in his view, he "handled the situation."

The only other individual we know to have taken corrective action was a hotel security officer who observed a male whose testicles were visible below the legs of his "short-shorts." The security officer told him to change into other clothes.

Ballwalking incidents reported at Tailhook '91 all occurred in the presence of male and female attendees. In at least one instance, a Navy captain was present and took no action. The civilian woman who related the events stated that she and a female Navy lieutenant were talking to a Navy captain when the civilian woman accidentally brushed up against a guy who was standing with his testicles exposed. When the captain informed the woman that the practice was called "ballwalking," she responded, "Oh, my God!" According to the woman, her shocked reaction caused the men, including the captain, to laugh. The captain then told her to ignore the activity. During our interview, the woman stated that she could not recall the identity of the ballwalker because she "was too embarrassed to look at his face." She did clearly recall there was more than one ballwalker and the captain took no action.

One admitted ballwalker stated to us that he ballwalked with five other aviators on a "dare." Initially the five aviators, after agreeing to ballwalk, stood in a corner of a crowded suite facing away from the other men and women. Subsequently, they began to mingle with the crowd individually introducing themselves to women in the room in an effort to see whether women would notice the ballwalking. The officer expressed to us his surprise that most of the people did not even notice that the men had their testicles exposed.

Another interviewee described a similar scene from an observer's viewpoint. He stated he looked into the VF-124 suite and was shocked to notice that about 10 of the men were exposing their genitals. The individuals were milling around the area as if nothing unusual was happening. There were numerous women in the suite at the time who were not paying any attention to the men exposing themselves. The witness stated he could not believe what the men were doing and was appalled at their behavior.

A Navy captain told us he witnessed male officers exposing their genitals while in the Philippines and Korea. He went on to say that "this activity is OK for officers to do as long as there are not enlisted or outsiders present." When questioned as to whether he thought the activity was appropriate for officers, he said, "yes" under the above circumstances. He added, "If done in public, then it would not be appropriate."

There were several instances in which individual aviators exposed their penises as well as their testicles at Tailhook '91. Those instances did not differ significantly from the ballwalking incidents except on one occasion. In that instance, three female university students entered a suite close to the elevator (either room 302, 303 or 304). A male exposed himself to the women while he was standing against a wall talking to two other males. When the women entered the suite, one of the males reached down and grabbed his friend's exposed genitals, shook them as he looked toward the women, and said, "Hey, ladies have you ever seen anything like this before?" One of the women stated she was shocked and could not believe what she had just seen and heard. She and her friends quickly left the suite. We determined that that type of exposure also occurred at Tailhook '90. One witness told us that during Tailhook '90 she saw a man in the patio area with his penis exposed and a "smiley face" drawn on his penis in red ink.

In several other instances, the investigators obtained photographs showing aviators posing for the cameras while they ballwalked. One female witness told us that her girlfriend coaxed several aviators to expose themselves so the girlfriend could get a picture. Later, the woman compiled a photograph album of Tailhook '91. There was also an instance where an officer asked to borrow a woman's camera. When the woman later had the film developed, she discovered a photograph of a penis among the pictures.

SECTION VIII
OTHER IMPROPER ACTIVITY

A. LEG SHAVING

Over 200 witnesses told us they observed leg shaving at the 1991 symposium. This activity occurred on the third floor during Tailhook '91 and involved the shaving of women's legs and pubic areas by male aviators. Our investigation disclosed that leg shaving has been an element of unit parties in the Navy for years, and that the "shaving booth" has been a fixture at Tailhook conventions. An estimated 50 women had their legs shaved during the 1991 weekend. We interviewed 10 of these women, 3 were naval officers.

Most of the leg shaving activity at Tailhook '91 occurred in the VAW-110 suite.* A banner measuring approximately 10 feet long and 2 feet wide reading, "FREE LEG SHAVES!" was posted on the sliding glass doors of the VAW-110 suite in plain sight of large portions of the pool patio.† The suite participants assembled their "booth" adjacent to the sliding glass doors so as to be visible from the patio. The "booth" consisted of a chair (for the woman being shaved), an equipment table, and a stool for the two male naval officers from the suite who performed the shaving. According to the witnesses and the officers involved, the leg shaving was a rather elaborate ritual that included the use of hot towels and baby oil, as well as the massaging of the woman's legs and feet. The entire process took between 30 and 45 minutes per shave. Other activities often accompanied leg shaving. For example, officers in the VR-57 suite reportedly licked females' legs with their tongues to ensure "quality control."

Several witnesses observed nudity in conjunction with leg shaving. Three instances were reported where women exposed their breasts while being shaved in the VAW-110 suite. Witnesses related

---

*Isolated instances of leg shaving were also reported to have occurred in the VR-57 suite.

†The banner was also used at the 1990 symposium.

that some women wore only underwear or bikinis during leg shaving, or pulled up their shorts or underwear to expose the areas they wanted shaved. Other witnesses reported that any woman who chose to have her legs shaved above her knees was offered a towel with which to cover her lap. One uncorroborated witness reported seeing a female naval officer having her legs shaved while wearing her "whites."

Women's pubic areas were sometimes shaved as well in what was referred to as a "bikini shave." In one instance, according to witnesses, a woman entered the VAW-110 suite on Saturday evening and requested a leg shave. As the woman was being shaved, she removed her top and told the officers that if the audience wanted to see more of her exposed, she wanted money. A few of the witnesses identified the woman as a stripper who performed in another suite. After she received money, she removed her shorts and requested a bikini shave. The woman was wearing no undergarments. The officer then shaved the woman's pubic area. After this the woman stood up in the chair, modeled the shave for the assembled crowd, dressed, and left the area.

These actions were witnessed by numerous onlookers within the suite, as well as those on the pool patio who were viewing the shaving through the sliding glass doors of the suite. Officers from nearby suites or those standing on the pool patio reported that a noticeable commotion was caused by the crowd peering into the suite, with screaming and banging on the windows when the officers inside the suite feigned closing the curtains.

None of the women who participated in the leg shaving claimed to have been forced into that activity, although two women, including a female Navy officer, reported being badgered repeatedly by suite occupants before consenting to have their legs shaved. An officer reported that naval officers loudly encouraged the women to have their legs shaved above the knees. One officer admitted asking women to have their legs shaved and identified another officer who was involved.

A number of senior naval officers, including several flag officers, knew of the leg shaving. The VAW-110 CO told us that he learned that leg shaving was to be featured in the suite just prior to the commencement of the symposium. He stated that he directed the officers performing the leg shaves to shave only legs. Although the CO's statements were corroborated by some witnesses, the officers involved in the leg shaving as well as some squadron members contend that the CO did not provide those instructions and, in fact, was aware that leg shaving would be featured in the VAW-110 suite.

B. "BELLY/NAVEL SHOTS"

The terms "belly shots" and "navel shots" describe the practice of drinking alcohol (typically tequila) out of people's navels. Incidents involving the exchange of belly shots between male and female officers and between male officers and female civilians at Tailhook '91 reportedly occurred in either the VF-124 or the VAW-110 suite.*

Witnesses and participants reported that three male officers drank belly shots from the navel of a female officer. This occurred in the VAW-110 suite on the same night the female officer had her legs shaved by two of the male officers. The female officer reported that a few of the women who participated in belly shots wore short dresses and no undergarments and exposed themselves while doing belly shots. Other witnesses reported male officers laying on a table while women drank alcohol from the men's navels.

C. PORNOGRAPHY

Several squadron hospitality suites featured pornography. Witnesses described various types of pornography ranging from "soft core" to "hard core" videos and slides. A few suites simply used the Hilton Hotel "pay for view" television to rent adult movies, which were then played on the suite's television set. Other squadrons used adult videotapes and, in at least one instance, adult-oriented slides. The VF-124 suite was reported to have displayed hard core pornographic movies on the walls of the suite at various times, including during a live strip show performed by two paid strippers on Saturday night. Other squadrons known to have shown adult-oriented videos were VX-4 and Top Gun. The MAWTS-1 squadron reportedly interspersed a few adult-oriented slides throughout its squadron's aviation slide show.

*Witnesses reported that drinking alcohol from a member of the opposite sex's navel occurred more often at the 1990 Tailhook convention. In 1990, belly shots were reportedly exchanged in the VAW-110 suite and on the pool deck. In fact, one officer reported seeing 12 to 20 men drink alcohol from a particular female officer's navel at the 1990 convention.

Films and slides were not shown on a continuous basis but, rather, intermittently by squadron members. Additionally, some squadrons displayed wall posters of nude or scantily clad females.

D. CHICKEN FIGHTS

Dozens of witnesses stated they observed "chicken fights" in the Hilton Hotel pool. These chicken fights involved women sitting on the shoulders of male aviators in the swimming pool and attempting to remove the bathing suit tops of other women. By all accounts, the activity was totally consensual. Although witnesses related that the breasts of several women were exposed, no evidence was found that any of the women were naval officers. Similarly, no evidence was found that any of the male aviators removed women's bathing suits. We also noted that many of the witnesses' accounts appear to involve two women who were civilians from the San Diego area.

E. "BUTT BITING"

Another type of assaultive behavior that occurred on the third floor of the Hilton Hotel during Tailhook '91 involved individuals biting attendees on the buttocks. That activity was commonly referred to by witnesses as "butt biting," or "sharking." The origin of butt biting at Tailhook is unknown, but one Marine major reported that, in his squadron, "sharking" was a common activity between males and females dating back about 20 years. He further explained the activity was normally consensual and if the activity was not consented to by an individual, that individual was no longer subjected to the butt biting. The major opined that butt biting is no longer widely practiced because it is now considered socially unacceptable. Three officers and one civilian stated that butt biting is sometimes engaged in on a consensual basis at naval officers' clubs. Two of those officers acknowledged they had personally participated in such activity. Those and other witnesses referred to butt biting as "butt rodeo," whereby the biter clasps onto another person's buttocks until he or she is shaken loose by the person bitten.

In regard to nonconsensual, assaultive behavior, eight individuals (seven females and one male), including four officers, a suite cocktail waitress, a Tailhook Association employee, an aviator's girlfriend, and a UNLV student, reported they were forcibly bitten on the buttocks at Tailhook '91. For the most part, male officers at the Tailhook convention bit the buttocks of female officers and civilians. However, at least three instances of civilian females biting males on the buttocks were reported. At least two of the individuals bitten reported they were bitten twice by the same individual. Some of the women bitten reported that the bites resulted in bruises to their buttocks.

The majority of the butt biting incidents reportedly occurred on Thursday night, although a few incidents reportedly took place on Friday and Saturday nights. Those assaults occurred in various locations on the third floor, including the pool patio, the VMFAT-101, the VA-128, the VFA-125, and the CNATRA suites, and outside the MAWTS-1 suite.

With respect to individuals responsible for that activity, a foreign exchange officer assigned to the VMFAT-101 was described and identified as the most frequent perpetrator. When interviewed, the officer said that he was heavily intoxicated while at Tailhook '91 and that he did not recall biting women on the buttocks. However, he noted that he received formal counseling and a letter of reprimand from his embassy as a result of his activities at Tailhook '91.

Our investigation disclosed that two Navy commanders and two Navy flight surgeons also engaged in butt biting. One of the commanders and both flight surgeons had reportedly bitten people on the buttocks while streaking through crowded areas.

Three other types of biting incidents were also reported. A woman was bitten on the ankle and two male officers were bitten by other male officers during fights. In one fight, an officer was bitten on the neck. In the other, the officer was bitten on the ear. Witnesses reported that both officers required medical attention.

F. "ZAPPING"

"Zapping" is an activity often associated with the gauntlet in the third-floor hallway at Tailhook '91. That activity involved placing stickers imprinted with a squadron logo on people (usually women) to symbolize the presence of a particular squadron. A retired officer explained that zapping originated years ago and that Marine Corps and Navy officers zapped aircraft from different squadrons visiting their respective bases. According to the retired officer, that ultimately led to indiscriminate zapping. Zapping women at Tailhook has reportedly occurred since 1985.

Almost 240 Tailhook '91 attendees reported they were familiar with the practice of zapping. Those individuals either engaged in, witnessed, or heard about zapping. Many, though they did not witness zapping firsthand, were aware of it as a result of observing stickers affixed to people. Eleven male officers and one male civilian admitted placing squadron stickers on women at Tailhook '91. Most of the officers who admitted zapping women maintained that the activity was consensual and the women either asked for the sticker or the officer had asked for the women's permission prior to zapping. Some reported they zapped women over their clothing and in areas of the women's bodies other than the breasts, buttocks, or crotch. One officer told us he was initially directed to zap a woman on the buttocks by an unknown superior officer, and he subsequently zapped several women.

Dozens of women, including a commander, a lieutenant commander, two lieutenants, an ensign, an Air Force captain, and a staff sergeant, as well as a male hotel security officer, reported they were zapped. A majority of the attendees who were zapped reported they were not offended or upset by the ''zaps.'' They were either zapped by friends, were asked for permission prior to the zapping, or were not even aware they had been zapped until they later found stickers on clothing.

Three women, however, including a female commander, reported they were zapped in private areas while traversing the hallway. One of the women stated that when she took umbrage at the attempts to zap her on the breasts and buttocks, the men in the hallway then started throwing the stickers at her. Another woman reported that as she was passing through the gauntlet, men lifted her skirt, ripped her blouse, and zapped her in the crotch and on her breasts. Two suite waitresses reported that men in the suite continued to zap them even though they repeatedly asked them to stop.

Several incidents of indecent exposure in conjunction with zapping were reported. All of the instances involved women exposing either their breasts, buttocks, and/or pubic areas for the purpose of collecting stickers. One of the more notable incidents occurred out on the pool patio on Friday night. A witness reported that a male aviator walked up to a female who was sitting on another male's lap and asked if he could put a zapper on her breast. The woman responded, "Sure," lifted up her top, and was zapped on her breast by the male. According to the witness, another male aviator then approached the same woman and asked to place a zapper on her other breast. The woman agreed and a sticker was applied to her other breast.

In another incident, a civilian Government employee reported that, while he was standing on the pool deck Saturday with a zapper in his hand, he was approached by a woman who asked him to zap her anywhere he desired. The man placed the sticker on her breast, over her clothing. Another man with a sticker then approached the woman. The woman pulled up her skirt, revealing her pantyhose, and told the other man to zap her in the crotch. The other man obliged. After zapping her, the second man said that was the place to zap women and the woman agreed. The first man then asked if the woman wanted him to also zap her in the crotch. The woman responded affirmatively and the man removed the sticker he had earlier affixed to her breast and placed it on her crotch.

Additional accounts of women exposing their "already zapped" breasts were reportedly witnessed in the hallway, in some of the suites (VA-128, MAG-11/Rhino, VAQ-129), and on the pool deck and patios. Officers related that a woman walked into the VA-128 suite, lifted her shirt to reveal the five or six zappers covering her bare breasts, and asked officers in the suite to rearrange the stickers for her. Witnesses also reported a few instances on the pool patio of women exposing their buttocks for zaps. Similarly, it was reported that strippers displayed zaps while performing in the VF-124 and the VMFA(AW)-242 suites. A photograph taken during a stripper's performance in the VMFA(AW)-242 suite depicts a nude stripper with a VMFA(AW)-242 squadron zapper on her buttocks. The stripper is shown straddling a squadron member as he lies on the floor looking up toward the stripper.

In a separate incident, an officer admitted paying a stripper $20 to display a VF-126 decal on each breast. A few witnesses reported seeing women wearing zappers over their clothing and opined that the women were collecting the zaps. Most witnesses agreed that many women did not object to the zaps, and, in some instances, even solicited zaps or applied zaps to themselves. In one instance, an officer told us that his CO instructed him to bring the zappers to Tailhook '91.

G. PUBLIC AND PAID SEX

While consensual sexual activity was not the focus of the investigation, such information was revealed during questioning about other areas under investigation. There were a number of reported instances of public or paid sex. In all instances, the activities were willingly engaged in by the participants.

Prostitution, while legal in some counties in Nevada, is not legal within the city limits of Las Vegas. Several of the suites engaged strippers to perform during the evening hours on Friday and Saturday night. In some instances, the strippers engaged in paid oral sex with members of the squadron. In other cases, strippers were hired to perform at bachelor parties or other "private" parties in which sexual acts were performed with suite members.

Witnesses described incidents in which couples had consensual sexual intercourse or oral sex in the suites, with other persons watching. Other witnesses observed oral sex or sexual intercourse in the pool patio area or near the tennis courts.

Such activities serve to illustrate the general atmosphere of debauchery prevailing in the area of the third floor at the time the indecent assaults occurred. Further, certain activities such as sodomy and conduct unbecoming an officer violate the UCMJ.

SECTION IX
SECURITY

In light of the many indecent assaults and other inappropriate behavior at Tailhook '91, we reviewed the issue of hotel security as well as the role played by the Tailhook Association.

A. LAS VEGAS HILTON HOTEL

The Tailhook Association coordinated security requirements directly with the Las Vegas Hilton Hotel. The coordination was effected in preparation of each year's symposium. The Hotel Security Department is comprised of a director, various levels of supervisors, and approximately 100 security officers. Each of the three shifts needed to provide round-the-clock security is manned by approximately 23 officers. Those officers wear distinctive dark blue uniforms and are normally posted in the hotel's casino and elsewhere within the hotel property.

We found that security personnel had extensive knowledge relating to Tailhook '91 and had provided coverage at previous Tailhook conventions.* Two security officers are associate members of the Tailhook Association.

Hotel management recognized from past experience that additional security officers would be needed on the third floor, pool patio and hallway areas to control crowds and limit damage to hotel property. The additional coverage was achieved by paying overtime to existing security staff. Officers assigned to those duties were not, however, committed exclusively to Tailhook and frequently responded to other calls for assistance throughout the hotel.

Twelve hotel security officers identified as having patrolled the third-floor area were interviewed. Interviews were conducted with the cooperation of the Las Vegas Hilton Hotel.† The hotel also pro-

---

*Tailhoook conventions have been held at the Las Vegas Hilton on an annual basis for 18 years.

†Throughout our investigation, the Hilton Hotel cooperated fully with us in

vided us copies of the officers' written incident reports and security blotters. From those sources we determined that several Tailhook related incidents had been reported, including the following:

1. Security officers stopped three aviators from carrying off a wall lamp they had torn from a wall.

2. Security officers broke up a large crowd of aviators who were chanting at a woman in an attempt to encourage the woman to expose her breasts.

3. Security officers stopped an intoxicated naked male who had walked out of room 302* onto the pool patio. They returned him to the room but made no effort to identify the individual or take further action.

4. Security officers responded to incidents involving public urination, physical altercations, and aviators expectorating ignited alcohol. No effort was made to identify the individuals involved in those activities.

5. A security officer reported that while he was walking with a woman on the pool patio, the woman was grabbed on the buttocks. The woman verbally confronted her attacker but the security officer, at the woman's request, took no action.

6. The most significant incident reported by security related to an intoxicated female in the third-floor hallway. According to two of the security officers, they heard a commotion, witnessed a pair of pants being thrown up in the air from a crowd of men in the hallway, and saw the crowd quickly disperse into various squadron suites. They observed a female naked from the waist down and lying on the floor of the hallway. The security officers assisted her and advised the Chairman of the Tailhook Association Committee of the incident warning him that improper conduct by attendees

---

arranging interviews of hotel staff and in providing all required hotel records relating to Tailhook '91.

*Room 302 served as the VAQ-129 hospitality suite.

had to cease or the hotel would be forced to close down all activities in the hallway.

7. The only other assault-related incident reported by hotel security involved two women who had reported they were assaulted in the third floor hallway.* The security officers told us the women reported the matter to the Las Vegas Police but had been referred back to hotel security because the women refused to return to the third floor and attempt to identify their attackers.

The security officers told us that, excluding the aforenoted incidents, no women reported being assaulted nor did any of the security officers witness any assaults. Relatedly, no victims, with the exception of victim 64, told us they were helped by security during or after their assaults. The security officers did, however, express their belief that their efforts to maintain order and to act effectively had been impaired as a result of code words and hand signals used by the aviators to announce the approach of security officers.

Security officers told us they heard radio messages from officers patrolling the third floor advising that gauntlets were forming in the hallway and one security officer defined the gauntlet as men "grabbing women in the hallway." Security officers assigned to the third-floor area told us they cleared the hallway whenever they saw that type of activity.

Witnesses told us that many assaults occurred in the presence of the hotel security staff and those officers failed to act in the absence of a specific complaint by the victims. One witness stated that men lined the hallway against the walls and closed ranks around women attempting to traverse the corridor. The witness observed women being grabbed on the buttocks and being picked up by the crowd. The witness told us he observed "two Hilton Hotel security guards standing against the wall near room 317, who appeared to be just observing the events in the hallway." The witness, who also saw the attack on the 18-year-old, as described previously, further stated, "The security guards made no attempt to come to the assistance of any of the women who were being subjected to the gauntlet" except for the young woman who was partially disrobed.

*These are the only two women who stated they had reported their assaults to hotel security.

Similarly, another witness told us he witnessed several women being attack in the gauntlet and that a man in uniform, whom he believed to be a hotel security officer, was "watching the gauntlet and doing nothing other than talking on the radio."

Yet another witness reported she saw approximately 10 women attacked in the gauntlet over a short period of time. He noted that although the women were protesting their treatment, "There were two security guards or police officers standing there laughing while watching the assaults."

Finally, several witnesses reported seeing hotel security officers in the hospitality suites watching strip shows and pornographic movies. One Navy civilian employee noted that he found it ludicrous that hotel security officers chased streakers on the pool patio but did not intervene during the gauntlet.

B. TAILHOOK ASSOCIATION

The Tailhook Association maintains a committee to work with hotel staff. In part, they coordinate security issues relating to Tailhook attendees. As agreed between the hotel and the Association, committee members were provided radio pagers by the Association. Pager numbers as well as respective guest room telephone numbers of committee members were furnished to the hotel security staff to ensure that committee members could respond quickly to any problem or situation detected by the hotel security staff.

Committee members wore blue shirts imprinted with the Tailhook Association logo. When interviewed, the Tailhook Association committee members generally denied knowledge of any assault and stated they were reasonably effective in controlling third-floor activities.

Witnesses told us the committee members did not intercede on behalf of the assault victims and were frequently seen watching strip shows in the suites. Hotel security officers told us the committee members were ineffective and did not respond to calls for assistance by the hotel security staff. One hotel security officer told us he overheard a senior Tailhook committee member comment that he was going to turn off his pager and make himself unavailable if inappropriate activity occurred.

We found the relationship between the Tailhook Association committee members and the hotel was such that both parties approached the security function simply as an issue of containment. Neither party sought to control improper activities unless severe bodily harm or significant property damage appeared imminent. The attendees paid for damages to hotel property.

The general opinion stated by countless witnesses was that, within the confines of the Tailhook convention, the aviators could act with impunity.

SECTION X
OFFICER ATTITUDES AND
LEADERSHIP ISSUES

A. OFFICER ATTITUDES

A discussion of the attitudes of the officers in attendance is central to an understanding of the misconduct at Tailhook '91. Until this point, we have focused on "what" happened with little discussion or commentary as to "why" events at the convention degenerated to a point where indecent assaults, indecent exposure, and excessive alcohol consumption became commonplace.

Navy and Marine Corps aviation officers are well educated, physically fit, technically proficient and well trained. Many are Naval Academy graduates or alumni of other top colleges and universities and certainly have the education and background to recognize societal issues such as sexual harassment. Yet some of these individuals acted with disregard toward individual rights and failed by a wide margin to conduct themselves as officers and gentlemen in the Armed Forces of the United States.

Although there were approximately 4,000 naval officers at Tailhook '91, and significant evidence of serious misconduct involving 117 officers has been developed, the number of individuals involved in all types of misconduct or other inappropriate behavior was more widespread than these figures would suggest. Furthermore, several hundred other officers were aware of the misconduct and chose to ignore it. We believe that many of these officers deliberately lied or sought to mislead our investigators in an effort to protect themselves or their fellow officers. On the other hand, there were hundreds of other officers who, when questioned, gave full and truthful accounts of their actions and observations while at Tailhook '91. Similarly, there were several hundred officers who spent their time at Tailhook '91 attending symposium events, visiting tourist sites, and otherwise occupying themselves in places other than the third floor. Unfortunately, the reputations of those officers, who are guilty of no wrong-doing, have been tarnished by the actions of their fellow officers.

Officers who engaged in misconduct gave a variety of reasons for their behavior at Tailhook '91. Perhaps the most common rationale was that such behavior was "expected" of junior officers and that Tailhook was comprised of "traditions" built on various lore.* Another reason given by many attendees was that their behavior was somehow justified or at least excusable, because they were "returning heroes," from Desert Storm. Many attendees, especially younger officers, viewed Tailhook as a means of celebrating the United States' victory over Iraqi forces. Numerous officers expressed their belief that Tailhook was a type of "free-fire zone" where they could celebrate without regard to rank or ordinary decorum. As one Navy officer opined, "It was condoned early in some of the senior officers' careers. It was probably condoned back when Tailhook started . . . And I imagine at one time, when this first—the thing started, they were the elite, they thought they could [do] anything they wanted in Naval aviation and not have to answer the questions we're answering today about it."

Many officers told us they believed they could act free of normal constraints because Tailhook was an accepted part of a culture in some ways separate from the main stream of the Armed Forces. They stated that the career progression for naval aviators is such that most do not bear the leadership responsibilities of commanding a unit until they approach the 10-year point in their careers. (Aviation officers do not follow the career progression of command of increasingly larger units from the outset of their Military Service. Unlike Army ground units, where the newest second lieutenant is trained to be a unit leader, aviators for the most part are viewed as unit members for the initial portion of their careers.)†

*Throughout our investigation, witnesses told us remarkable incidents at past Tailhook conventions. Incidents related by witnesses included a high-ranking Navy civilian official dancing with strippers in hospitality suites, the throwing of flaming mannequins from rooftops, food fights, earlier gauntlets and strip shows, an admiral taxiing an aircraft to the hotel, another admiral entering a banquet on horseback and the use of a chainsaw to demolish a wall separating two suites. While some of these incidents were more prankish than improper, they combined to form the aura of "anything goes" which was the predominant attitude expressed by naval aviators regarding the annual Tailhook conventions.

†Indeed, during our interviews of them, many senior officers repeatedly re-

Some senior officers blamed the younger officers for rowdy behavior and cited a "Top Gun" mentality. They expressed their belief that many young officers had been influenced by the image of naval aviators portrayed in the movie "Top Gun." The officers told us that the movie fueled misconceptions on the part of junior officers as to what was expected of them and also served to increase the general awareness of naval aviation and glorify naval pilots in the eyes of many young women.

One female Navy commander opined that the 1991 Tailhook convention was different in some ways from previous years, in part because of the recent Gulf War and the congressional inquiries regarding women in combat.

> The heightened emotions from the Gulf War were also enhanced with the forthcoming . . . downsizing of the military, so that you had people feeling very threatened for their job security and to more than just their jobs, their lifestyle. So you had people worried about what was coming down with the future. You had quite a bit of change. You had people that had been to the Gulf War. You had alcohol. You had a convention that had a lot of ingredients for any emotional whirlwind of controversy.

She went on to say that these potentially explosive ingredients combined at Tailhook '91, and resulted in ". . . an animosity in this Tailhook that existed that was telling the women that 'We don't have any respect for you now as humans.' " The animosity, in this officer's opinion, was focused on women:

> "This was the woman that was making you, you know, change your ways. This was the woman that was threatening your livelihood. This was the woman

---

ferred to the aviation lieutenants and lieutenant commanders as "the kids." To us, their use of this term, in context, symbolized an attitude where irresponsible behavior and conduct were accepted manifestations of high-spirited youth. The attitude is a major departure from the traditions of the ground forces, where newly commissioned second lieutenants control the lives of their platoon members and are expected by their superiors to demonstrate the personal qualities of a leader.

that was threatening your lifestyle. This was the
woman that wanted to take your spot in that combat
aircraft.''

We found that all those factors were at play among the Tailhook
'91 attendees. One rationale, that of the returning heroes, empha-
sizes that naval aviation is among the most dangerous and stressful
occupations in the world. During Desert Storm, for example, the
U.S. Navy suffered six fatalities, all of whom were aviation officers.
We also found that the ''live for today for tomorrow you may die''
attitude expressed by many officers is a fact of life for many aviation
officers. Over 30 officers died in the one-year period following Tailhook '91 as a result of military aviation–related accidents. Others
were found to have died in nonmilitary plane accidents, in vehicle
crashes and, in at least one incident, by suicide. Although none of
these factors justify the activities at Tailhook, they help illuminate
the attitudes of many attendees.

Many officers likened Tailhook to an overseas deployment, ex-
plaining that naval officers traditionally live a spartan existence
while on board ship and then party while on liberty in foreign ports.
Dozens of officers cited excessive drinking, indecent exposure, and
visits to prostitutes as common activities while on liberty. That was
acknowledged by virtually all interviewees, from junior officers
through flag officers. The most frequently heard comment in that
regard was ''what happens overseas, stays overseas.'' Officers said
that activities such as adultery, drunkenness, and indecent exposure
which occur overseas are not to be discussed or otherwise revealed
once the ship returns to home port.

A similar attitude carried over to the annual Tailhook conventions.
Countless officers told us it was common knowledge that ''what happened at Tailhook stayed at Tailhook'' and there were unwritten rules
to enforce the policy. Frequently cited was the ''no wives, no cameras'' rule, which dated back to the earliest Tailhook reunions. Reportedly few officers took their wives and only a small number of
women attended. Witnesses told us that at earlier Tailhooks many of
the women in attendance were prostitutes. As years went by, however, women began to play a larger role as officers in naval aviation.
Civilian women also began attending Tailhook conventions as a
means of meeting naval pilots. The increase in the number of women
attendees is supported by the fact that we were able to identify over
470 female attendees, many of whom were interviewed. Officers

told us that the improper activity discussed in this report was nothing new but had merely come to light as a result of the influx of female attendees. The officers frequently opined that gauntlet participants could not or would not differentiate between the groupies and prostitutes who had been a part of Tailhook for many years, and other women who attended Tailhook '91.

Despite the "no cameras" policy, our investigation collected more than 800 photographs, some of which depict indecent exposure. It is interesting to note that approximately two-thirds of the photographs were provided to us by female civilians and that nearly half of the remaining pictures were furnished by female naval officers.

One disturbing aspect of the attitudes exhibited at Tailhook '91 was the blatant sexism displayed by some officers toward women. That attitude is best exemplified in a T-shirt worn by several male officers. The back of their shirt reads "WOMEN ARE PROPERTY," while the front reads "HE MAN WOMEN HATER'S CLUB." The shirts, as well as demeaning posters and lapel pins,* expressed an attitude held by some male attendees that women were at Tailhook to "serve"† the male attendees and that women were not welcome within naval aviation.

During the course of our investigation, an incident involving sexual harassment came to our attention. One of the squadron hospitality suites provided the forum for an informal job interview between a Navy captain and a civilian female. The woman had applied for a

---

*Some officers wore pins stating "NOT IN MY SQUADRON." This is an apparent parody of the Navy's "Not in My Navy" slogan which is intended to express the Navy prohibition of sexual harrassment against women. Some officers told us that the pins signified contempt for women in naval aviation and, specifically the desire to maintain the combat exclusion with respect to women. Other officers told us that the pins merely expressed the desire to keep the F-14 aircraft rather than the F-18 replacement planned by the Navy.

†One squadron called a UNLV official and requested the telephone numbers of all UNLV sorority sisters. When she refused to furnish the information, the officer told her that she was "denying" the girls the "opportunity to serve their country." The UNLV official reported that the officer was rude, resulting in her abrupt termination of the call. She also reported that "fliers" soliciting girls to attend Tailhook '91 were later placed in all UNLV sorority mailboxes. The official identified the invitation described in Section V of this report as a copy of one of the fliers.

GM-15 position within the captain's command. The captain was the hiring official for the position. Our investigation determined that the captain made numerous sexually oriented comments to the woman, questioned her sexual preferences and also directed her to stand up and turn around in front of him so as to enable him to view her buttocks. The incident was witnessed by other naval officers, as well as a civilian. Details of this matter have been referred under separate cover to Navy authorities.

B. THE FAILURE OF LEADERSHIP

One of the most difficult issues we sought to address was accountability, from a leadership standpoint, for the events at Tailhook '91. The various types of misconduct that took place in the third-floor corridor and in the suites, if not tacitly approved, were nevertheless allowed to continue by the leadership of the naval aviation community and the Tailhook Association.

The military is a hierarchical organization, which requires and is supposed to ensure accountability at every level. As one moves up through the chain of command, the focus on accountability narrows to fewer individuals. At the highest levels of the command structure, accountability becomes less dependent on actual knowledge of the specific actions of subordinates. At some point, "the buck stops here" applies. In the case of Tailhook '91, the buck stops with the senior leaders of naval aviation.

Tailhook '91 is the culmination of a long-term failure of leadership in naval aviation. What happened at Tailhook '91 was destined to happen sooner or later in the "can you top this" atmosphere that appeared to increase with each succeeding convention. Senior aviation leadership seemed to ignore the deteriorating standards of behavior and failed to deal with the increasing disorderly, improper, and promiscuous behavior.

Throughout our investigation, officers told us that Tailhook '91 was not significantly different from earlier conventions with respect to outrageous behavior. Most of the officers we spoke to said that excesses seen at Tailhook '91 such as excessive consumption of alcohol, strippers, indecent exposure, and other inappropriate behavior were accepted by senior officers simply because those things had gone on for years. Indeed, heavy drinking, the gauntlet, and widespread promiscuity were part of the allure of Tailhook conventions to a significant number of the Navy and Marine Corps attendees.

In seeking to identify the measure of responsibility properly borne by senior officers, it would be unfair to focus solely on the senior officers who attended Tailhook '91. Some measure of responsibility is also borne by other senior officers, some still on active duty and others now retired who attended previous Tailhook conventions and permitted the excesses of the annual conventions to continue unchecked.

As we reported in Tailhook '91, Part 1, the nature of the misconduct at the annual conventions was well-known to senior aviation leaders. However, although aware of the activities and atmosphere, they were incapable of dealing with the increasingly indulgent behavior. The efforts taken to control their subordinates at Tailhook, through the years, were sometimes effective but only for limited periods. In our view, by September 1991, both individually and collectively, the senior leaders of naval aviation were unwilling to take the kinds of measures necessary to effectively end the types of misconduct that they had every reason to expect would occur at Tailhook '91.

Moreover, the misconduct at Tailhook '91 went far beyond the "treatment of women" issues for which the Navy had enacted new policies in the years preceding Tailhook '91. The Tailhook traditions (the gauntlet, ballwalking, leg shaving, mooning, streaking, and lewd sexual conduct) so deviated from the standards of behavior the nation expects of its military officers that the repetition of this behavior year after year raises serious questions about the senior leadership of the Navy. We found a great disparity between espoused Navy policies regarding consumption of alcohol and treatment of women and the actual conduct of significant numbers of those officers at Tailhook '91.

We were repeatedly told that such behavior was widely condoned by Navy civilian and military leadership. Some senior officers themselves had participated in third-floor improprieties in previous years when they were junior officers to the extent that certain offensive activities had become a matter of tradition. For example, we found that officers, including some field-grade officers, engaged in improper conduct such as indecent exposure and physial contact with strippers.

In that regard, one Navy lieutenant told us, ". . . I don't think that anybody saw anything that they felt hadn't happened in the past. And so . . . if it had been allowed to happen in the past, they'd just let it go. They felt there was no reason to stop anything that they hadn't *(sic)* seen before." Relatedly, a lieutenant commander stated: "And I think you have to say that aviators emulate those who preceded them, and that Tailhooks that preceded them have legends of their own, and young aviators are going to try to mimic those people who are in a position to teach them and train them.''

Another junior officer, who admitted to participating in the gauntlet, told us, ''If I thought that going around and goosing a few girls on the breasts was going to create a national incident, do you think I would have done that? We only did it because the party atmosphere seemed to promote that. Admiral Dunleavy and the rest of his cronies who go to Hook every year, man, they must be wearing some blinders, because it has been happening every single year that I know of.''

Senior officers, on the other hand, referred to their perception that the third floor was somehow the domain of the younger officers. Senior officers, including an admiral, told us there was a lack of respect exhibited toward older officers by some junior officers and noted their belief that they would have been powerless to act successfully in attempting to stop third-floor improprieties.

An example of the lack of respect is illustrated in an anecdote related by a Navy lieutenant. He told us that on Saturday night at about 10:00 p.m. he and two other lieutenants were waiting in line to use a suite rest room. An admiral tried to cut in front of them. The lieutenant challenged the admiral who reminded the officers that he was an admiral (O-8). The lieutenant (O-3) objected to the admiral's attempt to pull rank and told the admiral that the three O-3s added up to an O-9 and the admiral should go to the back of the line.

Many factors contributed to a feeling of resentment by junior officers toward higher ranking officers. One aspect related to a perception that, despite their success in Desert Storm, junior officers would be adversely affected by the anticipated drawdown of troops. Yet another factor related to us was the squadron officers' use of their personal funds to pay for the suites, alcohol, and entertainment. Flag officers and many of the Navy captains and Marine Corps colonels in attendance did not help fund the third-floor activities. That fact, together with the lack of uniforms and absence of any official Navy participation with regard to squadron hospitality suites contributed to a perception held by many attendees that the party was a private one hosted by junior officers.

Numerous officers attributed the perception that they could act with impunity to the uniqueness of the naval aviation community.*

*We found that aviation officers view themselves as unique. The perception is based not only on their occupation but also on such matters as progression in

They explained that aviators are used to working in a rank-neutral environment, frequently addressing more senior officers by their pilot "call signs" rather than by their rank. The witnesses also noted that aviation officers are less rank conscious and, therefore, less intimidated by the presence of more senior officers.

The demarcation between junior and senior officers was further blurred by the abundance of alcohol and nearly everyone's dressing in T-shirts and shorts as opposed to Navy or Marine Corps uniforms. As told to us by one officer, ". . . the more you drink, the less noticeable any ranks would be, from looking upward and looking downward, you know."

FIELD-GRADE OFFICERS

We interviewed 331 field-grade officers who attended Tailhook '91.*

A number of those officers were the commanders of squadrons that hosted suites at the convention. Others had responsibility over groups of squadrons represented at Tailhook '91 or had previously commanded or been members of those squadrons. The field-grade officers typically had completed more than 12 years of service and many had more than 20 years of experience in naval aviation. A large portion of the field-grade officers had attended prior Tailhook conventions.

As indicated throughout the report there were isolated instances in which field-grade officers sought to remedy or prevent acts of misconduct; while in other instances, field-grade officers themselves engaged in misconduct.

With respect to the squadron commanders who attended Tailhook '91, we found similar patterns of behavior. Prior to Tailhook '91, the squadron commanders had received letters from the Tailhook Association president warning them about underage drinking and the "late-night gang mentality" that had occurred at prior conventions.

Some squadron commanders enforced proper conduct within their

---

rank and even their uniform. Aviation officers can frequently progress to the rank of lieutenant commander without ever having been in command of a unit. They are also distinguishable from other naval officers by their aviation wings insignia and brown, rather than black, uniform shoes.

*This group consisted of 85 Navy captains, 7 Marine Corps colonels, 218 Navy commanders, and 21 Marine Corps lieutenant colonels.

suites. Others chose to ignore events in their suites under the premise that Tailhook '91 was a private function rather than an official Navy activity. Several commanders told us they had difficulty in ensuring proper decorum despite prohibitions they issued. In one instance, a commander closed his unit's suite because of damage done to the suite.*

The commanders who sought to forestall improper conduct at Tailhook '91 nevertheless were unwilling or unable to take actions to determine those responsible for the misconduct that actually took place at Tailhook '91. We found no evidence that any commander initiated any inquiry or took any disciplinary measures in the month between the Las Vegas convention and the initiation of the NIS investigation into the assault on LT Coughlin. Further, even those commanders who later told that their subordinates had violated their orders regarding operation of the hospitality suites did nothing to address the misconduct that they acknowledged to us.†

THE FLAG OFFICERS

We interviewed each of the 30 active duty admirals, 2 active duty Marine Corps generals and 3 Navy Reserve admirals who attended Tailhook '91.‡ We believe a discussion of the activities of the flag officers at Tailhook '91 is necessary and relevant, as was the discussion of the participation of Secretary of the Navy H. Lawrence Garrett III, which was included in Tailhook '91, Part 1, in order to provide the backdrop against which the misconduct of junior officers occurred, as well as to assess their accountability.

*The details regarding activities in each of the 22 squadron hospitality suites are set forth at Appendix E.

†This failure is consistent with the inaction of many officers who told us they witnessed assaults, indecent exposure, and other improprieties at Tailhook '91 and elected at that time not to intervene.

‡By rank, this group consisted of 2 admirals, 6 vice admirals, 1 lieutenant general, 4 rear admirals (upper half), 1 major general and 18 rear admirals (lower half). These numbers include officers selected for promotion prior to Tailhook '91 (see Appendix G). A significant number of retired flag officers also attended Tailhook '91. During our investigation, we spoke with 41 retired admirals and 1 retired Marine Corps general who attended. Together, there were nearly 80 flag officers, active, Reserve, and retired at Tailhook '91.

In interviewing the flag officers who attended Tailhook '91, we attempted to determine which of them had specific knowledge of any misconduct. For the most part, the flag officers participated in or attended the scheduled symposium activities such as seminars, sporting events, and dinners.* Of the 35 flag officers we interviewed, 28 told us that they visited the third floor on Friday or Saturday night, or both nights, shortly after the conclusion of the evening dinner. Most of the officers stated that they arrived on the third floor between 9:30 and 10:00 p.m. Some flag officers told us they remained only briefly while others stayed for up to several hours. According to their testimony, with the notable exception discussed at length below, none of the flag officers, including those who spent several hours on the third floor and adjoining patio, witnessed any nudity or indecent exposure (including ballwalking, streaking, or mooning), nor any activity occurring during the gauntlet.

We interviewed VADM Richard M. Dunleavy, then the Assistant Chief of Naval Operations (Air Warfare) during the investigation.† In his initial interview, VADM Dunleavy denied having observed both leg shaving and the gauntlet, even when confronted with information we had obtained alleging that he observed leg shaving at Tailhook '90, had made favorable comments about leg shaving to the officers engaged in the activity, and had observed it again at Tailhook '91.

When we interviewed VADM Dunleavy the next day, he acknowledged that he had encouraged leg shaving at Tailhook '91 based on his favorable impression of the activity during the previous year's convention. Further, he acknowledged knowing that strippers performed during Tailhook '91 and prior conventions. Most significantly, he acknowledged to us that he was aware of the existence of the gauntlet and observed the activity that occurred during the gauntlet at Tailhook '91.

*A few of the flag officers did not attend the entire convention. For example, the major general arrived at 12:00 noon on Thursday and left at 5:00 p.m. that same day.

†During the Navy's initial investigations of Tailhook '91, the Assistant Secretary of the Navy (Manpower and Reserve Affairs) suspected that VADM Dunleavy may have had knowledge of the existence of the gauntlet. The interview of VADM Dunleavy by the Navy was discussed in Tailhook '91, Part 1, p. 17. VADM Dunleavy retired on July 1, 1992. A nomination for his retirement in the grade of Vice Admiral was not acted on by the Senate prior to its adjournment.

VADM Dunleavy told us that after the 1990 convention, he learned that the term "gauntlet" was being used to identify a group of young aviators who gathered along the walls in the third-floor hallway where they groped women who passed through the corridor. On Saturday night of the 1991 convention, he was on the third floor and became aware that the gauntlet was forming. He further told us that when he went into the third-floor hallway, he saw that it was crowded and a commotion was occurring as the men "hooted and hollered." He stated he heard men yelling "Show us your tits!" but that he did not intervene because he believed he would not be heard above the commotion and because the activities "appeared to be in fun, rather than molestation." He stated that it was his impression at the time that no one was upset and he believed that "they [women] would not have gone down the hall if they did not like it."

We believe that VADM Dunleavy's attitude toward leg shaving—which was one of approval and encouragement—and, more significantly, toward the gauntlet—which was one of tolerance—represents a serious, individual failure to recognize the impropriety of these activities and to take action to stop them.

We find ourselves in a serious dilemma with respect to what the flag officers did not see. Although we obtained significant evidence that misconduct occurred at Tailhook '91 on a widespread basis, flag officers, according to their testimony, seemed to be relatively unaware of it. We are of the opinion that the majority of them are being truthful in stating their lack of knowledge with respect to specific acts of sexual misconduct. While we have reservations about the categorical denials of some of the flag officers that they were completely unaware of any specific misconduct, especially when viewed in light of their past experiences at prior Tailhook conventions, it would be unfair for us to question the credibility of any one of them in the absence of controverting evidence on this matter.

In addition to whatever specific knowledge any of the flag officers may have had, it is our opinion that there was general knowledge among the Navy's senior aviation leadership of the inappropriate behavior that had become commonplace on the third floor during annual Tailhook conventions. In part, we base this opinion on the fact that 33 of the 35 flag officers who attended Tailhook '91 had attended prior Tailhook conventions; that 2 of the flag officers were past Tailhook Association Presidents; and that all of the aviation flag officers were former squadron commanders. Further, concern was expressed by flag officers over the excesses at prior Tailhook conventions as early as 1985. Many of the junior officers we interviewed told us that knowledge of the type of misconduct which occured at Tailhook '91 was widespread throughout the aviation community. Finally, we obtained eyewitness testimony that one former high-ranking Navy civilian official engaged in inappropriate activity with a stripper in front of junior officers at a prior Tailhook convention, indicating that, at least in one instance, a senior official was aware of and participated in the type of activities for which junior officers are now being criticized.

SECTION XI
CONCLUSIONS

There was a serious breakdown of leadership at Tailhook '91. Misconduct went far beyond the "treatment of women" issues for which the Navy had enacted new policies in the years preceding Tailhook '91. Tailhook "traditions" such as the gauntlet, ballwalking, leg shaving, mooning, streaking, and lewd sexual conduct significantly deviated from the standards of behavior that the Nation expects of its military officers. The disparity between the espoused Navy policies regarding officer conduct and the actual conduct of significant numbers of officers at Tailhook '91 could not have been greater. Officers who assaulted women, as well as those who engaged in improper sexual behavior, knew that their actions would not be condoned under any objective standard. These officers needed no "policemen at the elbow" to warn them of the wrongful nature of their actions and they, therefore, must bear a major portion of the blame.

Leaders in naval aviation, ranging from the squadron commanders to flag officers who tolerated a culture that engendered the misconduct also bear a portion of the blame. The damage suffered by the Navy as a result of Tailhook cannot be fully repaired until the integrity of the Navy is restored, which, in turn, depends on the integrity of each of its members. The senior officers must lead the way in that endeavor. For the credibility of the Navy and Marine Corps as institutions, each senior officer who attended Tailhook '91, or previous Tailhook symposia, should consider the extent to which he bears some personal responsibility for what occurred there and how he can best serve the Navy and the Marine Corps in the future.

Navy Department leadership, military and civilian, will face many difficult decisions as it comes to grips with the issues raised in this report and the individual misconduct referrals that accompany the report. Personal friendship, knowledge of past service and sacrifice by the officers involved, and a general reluctance to end or adversely impact otherwise promising military careers will further complicate the matter.

The Acting Secretary of the Navy has appointed two convening authorities, a Marine Corps lieutenant general and a Navy vice admiral, who we expect will deal with the disciplinary and military judicial aspects of this matter with dispatch, equality, and compassion. The next Secretary of the Navy, the Chief of Naval Operations, and the Commandant of the Marine Corps are left with the more difficult problem of determining how to resolve and correct the long-term failure of leadership that characterized Tailhook '91.

We have every expectation that the Navy will address the causes and conduct that combined to produce the disgrace of Tailhook '91, and therefore, we offer no recommendations.

APPENDICES

Appendix A
Tailhook '91 Agenda

35th Annual
Tailhook Symposium
5, 6, 7 & 8 September 1991

Las Vegas Hilton
Las Vegas, Nevada

THE TAILHOOK ASSOCIATION

PRESIDENT
CAPT Frederic G. Ludwig, Jr. USN

VICE PRESIDENTS

Industrial Affairs
G. C. "Buddy" Gilman

Corporate Development
CDR Howard E. Ruggles, USN(Ret)

Reserve Affairs
LCDR William McKinnon, USNR

Marine Affairs
COL M. A. Rietsch, USMC

Educational Activity
LCDR David W. Cully, USN

BOARD OF DIRECTORS

Chairman Emeritus
CAPT F. A. W. Franke, Jr., USN(Ret)

Chairman
CAPT W. D. "Bill" Knutson, USN(Ret)
CAPT R. F. "Skip" Braden, USN
CAPT Michael J. McCabe, USN
CAPT "Cal" Swanson, USN(Ret)
CAPT Wynn F. Foster, USN(Ret)
CAPT Terry E. Magee, USN
LCOL C. L. "Chuck" Zangas, USMC(Ret)
LCDR James P. Usbeck, USN

Advisor, Naval Aviation Matters
RADM James D. Ramage, USN(Ret)

Executive Director
Ron Thomas

General Counsel
J. Wesley Fry

Treasurer
CAPT "Cal" Swanson, USN(Ret)

EDITOR
CAPT Stephen T. Millikin, USN(Ret)

MANAGING EDITOR
Jan C. Jacobs

ASSOCIATE EDITORS
CAPT Wynn F. Foster, USN(Ret)
Barrett Tillman
CW04 Carl W. Snow, USN(Ret)

CARRIER EDITOR
Robert J. Cressman

EDITORIAL COMMITTEE
RADM James D. Ramage, USN(Ret)

CONTRIBUTING EDITORS
CDR Doug Siegfried, USN(Ret)
CDR Pete Clayton, USN
Hal Andrews

CONTRIBUTING PHOTOGRAPHERS
Douglas D. Olson
Michael L. Grove
Bruce R. Trombecky
Keith Snyder

Information regarding Tailhook Symposiums is available from the Tailhook Association. Editorial matters only are handled at The Hook address.

Articles and news items are welcomed. Submit material for THE HOOK to: Editorial Offices, The Hook.

THURSDAY, 5 SEPTEMBER 1991

0900 READY ROOM AND EXHIBITS
OPEN .... BARRON ROOM
ALL SYMPOSIUM PROGRAMS WILL BE HELD
IN PAVILLION AREA
1600-1630 TAILHOOK ASSOCIATION MEETING
1630-1700 AVIATION SAFETY .... RADM J. B. FINNEY
(COMNAVSAFECEN)
1700-1730 ADVANCE AIRCRAFT
TECHNOLOGIES ....MR. T. MORGENFELD
(LOCKHEAD NAFT TEST PILOT)
1800 EXHIBITS CLOSED
1900-2100 NO HOST COCKTAIL PARTY/EXHIBITS
OPEN .... BARRON ROOM
2100 REGISTRATION BOOTH CLOSED

FRIDAY, 6 SEPTEMBER 1991

0730 GOLF AND TENNIS TOURNAMENTS
0900 REGISTRATION AND EXHIBITS
OPEN .... BARRON ROOM
ALL SYMPOSIUM PROGRAMS WILL BE HELD
IN PAVILLION AREA
1030-1045 SYMPOSIUM INTRODUCTION ..... VADM R. M.
DUNLEAVY (OP-05)
CAPT F. G. LUDWIG (TAILHOOK PRESIDENT)
1045-1245 DESERT STORM NAVAL OPERATIONS

—MASTER COORDINATED STRIKE
PLAN .... CAPT L. G. BIEN
—PERSIAN GULF ....CAPT J. BURIN (CVW-5)
—RED SEA .... CAPT W. J. FALLON (CVW-8)
—BAHRAIN/SAUDI
ARABIA ......COL D. BEAUFAIT (MAG-11)

1245-1300 HOOKER HOTDOGS

1300–1400 NAVAL AIR SYSTEMS DESERT STORM
MUNITIONS EFFECTIVENESS BRIEFINGS

–TOMAHAWK .... LCDR B. JOHANSON
(STRIKE U)
–AIR-GROUND
PROGRAMS .. CAPT B. RAMSAY (PMA-201)
–AIR-AIR PROGRAMS ...CDR T. MCKENZIE
(OP-501)

1400–1515 DESERT STORM RECONNAISSANCE/
SURVEILLANCE/INTELLIGENCE OVERVIEW

–INTEL/JOINT-
STARS .... CAPT. C. JOHNSON (SPEARS)
–TARPS ....LDCR D. PARSONS
(VF-32)/LT P. MONGER (VF-2)
–RPVs ...... CAPT A. C. AUER (3rd RPV CO)
1515–1545 MIG KILLER DEBRIEF ...... LT N. MONGELLO
(VFA-81)
1545–1630 PRISONER OF WAR
EXPERIENCES .... CAPT C. BERRYMAN
LT R. SLADE
LT R. WETZEL
1630–1700 DESERT STORM STRIKE RESCUE
OPERATIONS ..... CDR M. MCCARTY (OP-503F)
MR. R. MASTRONARDI (SIKORSKY AIRCRAFT)
1700–1730 F-18 E/F .... CAPT C. STRIDLE (PFA-265)
1730–1800 AX: NAVAL STRIKE
FIGHTER .... RADM J. TAYLOR (OP-05)
1800–1830 RESERVE OFFICER
MEETING ....RADM R. K. CHAMBERS
(COMNAVAIRESFOR)
1800 EXHIBITS CLOSED
1900–2100 COCKTAIL PARTY AND BUFFET (NO HOST
AFTER 2000) .... BARRON ROOM

SATURDAY, 7 SEPTEMBER 1991

0700	5K FUN RUN
0900	EXHIBITS OPEN .... BARRON ROOM
0900–0930	AVIATION PERSONNEL ISSUES .... RADM J. L. JOHNSON (BUPERS)
0930–1000	CARRIER PLANS/NAVAL AIR STATION PLANS .... RADM R. P. HICKEY (OP-05)
1000–1030	CARRIER AIR WING PLANS .... RADM R. D. MIXSON (OP-05B)
1030–1100	NAVAL AVIATION BUDGET OVERVIEW .... RADM J. TAYLOR (OP-50)
1100–1200	STATE OF NAVAL AVIATION ADDRESS ..... VADM R. M. DUNLEAVY (OP-05)
1200–1400	AWARDS LUNCH—PAVILLION
1400–1405	FIGHTS ON, FIGHTS ON IV .... CUBIC CORP
1405–1420	ASSOCIATION OF NAVAL AVIATION .... VADM W. P. LAWRENCE
1420–1435	TAILHOOK ASSOCIATION BUILDING FUND UPDATE .... CAPT W. KNUTSON
1435	FLAG PANEL .. VADM R. M. DUNLEAVY (OP-05) VADM J. B. FETTERMAN, JR. (CNET) VADM E. R. KOHN (CNAP) VADM A. A. LESS (CNAL) LGEN D. A. WILLS (HQMC) VADM W. C. BOWES (CNASC) RADM R. K. CHAMBERS (CNARF) RADM W. R. MCGOWEN (CNATRA) RADM J. L. JOHNSON (BUPERS) CAPT F. G. LUDWIG (MODERATOR)
1500–1800	EXHIBITS CLOSED
1800	NO HOST COCKTAIL PARTY/EXHIBITS OPEN .... BARRON ROOM
1900	BANQUET—PAVILLION .... HONORABLE H. LAWRENCE GARRETT, III, SECRETARY OF THE NAVY

SUNDAY, 8 SEPTEMBER 1991

AM	BUFFET BRUNCH—PAVILLION
1200	CHECK OUT

APPENDIX B
TAILHOOK ASSOCIATION
SUBMITTAL

RECEIVED FROM TAILHOOK
ASSOCIATION
(NOVEMBER 30, 1992)

TAILHOOK 1991 SYMPOSIUM

The 35th annual Naval Aviation Symposium, held at the Las Vegas Hilton 5–9 September 1991, was more than the latest "Tailhook convention." It was the largest, most dynamic meeting of its type, drawing 2,100 active, reserve, and retired aviators who registered either in advance or at the convention itself for a three-day evaluation of Navy and Marine Corps aviation in Operation Desert Shield/Desert Storm. An estimated 2,500 additional active or retired aviators and civilians attended the symposium, but were not registered.

SYMPOSIUM ORIGINS

The fleet aviators, naval and government leaders, and aerospace industry representatives who gathered at "Tailhook '91" represented a purpose and a professionalism entirely beyond the Tailhook Association's early meetings. Founded in 1956, the Association grew from a socially oriented group to a California-chartered nonprofit organization in 1968. After early meetings in Rosarito Beach, Mexico and San Diego, annual symposiums have been held in Las Vegas continuously since 1963.

The symposium aspect of Tailhook gatherings began in the late-1960s with a series of briefings by naval aviation units and contractors concerning developments in the war in Vietnam and weapon systems developments. Briefings at that time were relatively short and not central to Tailhook gatherings.

However, during the Vietnam War aviators attending the convention capitalized upon the opportunity to exchange information on tactical trends and developments—a rare opportunity not otherwise available to aircrews from both Pacific and Atlantic Fleets. Upon recognizing the value of professional "cross-talk" among naval aviators that led to more effective performance in the cockpit, the structure of the symposium changed. Participation by the Deputy Chief of Naval Operations for Air Warfare (OP-05) increased steadily to the point where, in recent years, symposium events have been directly planned by the Navy in conjunction with Association planners.

T A I L H O O K   ' 9 1

Tailhook '91 was typical of many symposiums held in recent years. Months before the event, an organizational committee consisting of approximately 25 male and female naval aviators began preparations for the event. Many on the committee had served for as many as eight years previously and were highly valued for their skills and "corporate knowledge" in staging this complex event.

Therefore, when Tailhood '91 convened in Las Vegas, the stage was set not only for the largest meeting in the group's history, but a highly professional debrief and victory celebration following the war with Iraq. Additionally, the exhibit hall housing defense contractor exhibits and Navy informational booths (provided at no cost to the Navy) numbered a record 172 booths in what has become one of the largest aerospace industry trade shows in the nation. The exhibitors' displays were open virtually from the opening of the symposium to well into the evening hours. Symposium visitors typically spent hours viewing the displays and exchanging informaiton with contractor representatives.

T H U R S D A Y ,   5   S E P T E M B E R

Attendance at Tailhook '91 symposium events averaged almost 1,100 personnel. The formal symposium program began in the late afternoon of Thursday, 5 September, with the Association's annual business meeting, followed by an aviation safety discussion and a contractor's presentation on advanced aircraft technologies. Both events had an audience of 300 or more.

FRIDAY, 6 SEPTEMBER

Friday's events were keynoted by VADM Richard M. Dunleavy, Assistant Chief of Naval Operations for Air Warfare (Op-05). VADM Dunleavy was aided by CAPT Frederick G. Ludwig, Tailhook Association president, who in turn introduced the first of the program panelists.

By the time the Operation Desert Storm naval operations symposium began at 10:45 AM, attendance in the Hilton ballroom had grown to more than 1,400 with standing room only. CAPT Lyle G. Bien, an air wing commander during the Desert Storm operation, described the master coordinated strike plan for the air war against Iraq, and noted that "Saddam won the toss—and elected to receive." Navy and Marine Corps roles in the air plan were described in detail, with emphasis as how carrier- and land-based units fit into the overall picture.

Tactical operations were next described by air wing commanders CAPT Jim Burin, and CAPT W. J. Fallon together with COL Don Beaufait of Marine Air Group Eleven who addressed the successes and problems with carrier operations conducted from the Persian Gulf, Red Sea, and Bahrain/Saudi Arabian areas. The series of briefings was one of the more popular of the symposium.

Other topics discussed that day included munitions effectiveness in Operation Desert Storm, the use of Tomahawk Land-Attack Missiles in the conflict as well as problems and successes in ordnance logistics.

Missile effectiveness in air-to-air combat next drew the attention of attendees. The success ratios of AIM-7 Sparrow, and AIM-9 Sidewinder air-to-air missiles were examined, though carrier aviators logged only three of the 45 aerial victories credited to Coalition pilots during the war.

Later in the series of briefings, attendees were told of recent trends in tactical and joint-service information gathering. Discussions of the F-14 reconnaissance program and the use of Israeli-built drones followed.

Two of the most heavily attended, most enthusiastically received briefings that afternoon involved LT Nick Mongello of VFA-81 and

Marine CAPT Chuck McGill, who described their MiG shootdowns during Desert Storm. At one point, McGill, serving at the time as an exchange pilot with the Air Force, commented on the aerodynamic beauty of the MiG-29 he had downed. During the question period that followed, a listener arose in the audience to express similar sentiments and to state that he was formerly a Soviet Air Force captain who had in 1989 defected from the USSR to Turkey in a MiG-29 Fulcrum. Alexander Zuyev was known to many attendees for his invaluable briefings at Navy and Marine Corps tactical units over the previous year. Many pilots in the audience quickly took full advantage of an unexpected and unique opportunity to talk face to face with a former adversary.

The standing-room-only crowd remained and was riveted in place for the POW debrief that followed. Three of the eight Navy or Marine fliers captured by Iraq and imprisoned from January until March reported that their knowledge of how other Tailhookers had endured captivity during the Vietnam War helped to sustain them. The group received a thunderous ovation from 1,300 of their comrades in the audience who recognized that any one of the veterans of Desert Storm present could have themselves been captives.

Following the prisoner of war briefing, between 600 and 700 symposium attendees heard plans for future naval aircraft and Navy plans for a carrier-based attack aircraft projected to follow in the wake of the failed A-12 program.

Friday's program was a long one, lasting from 9:00 a.m. to well after 6:30 p.m. The annual president's dinner was held later that evening with some 250 industry and military dignitaries in attendance. The featured speaker was ADM Frank Kelso, Chief of Naval Operations.

S A T U R D A Y ,   7   S E P T E M B E R

Saturday's program began at 9:00 a.m. with discussion of aviation personnel issues in which listeners were told that the Navy could expect a 14 percent reduction in manpower by 1996. Plans for the retirement of several current aircraft carriers and the closure of various naval air stations also was addressed in later briefings.

About 600 individuals who attended listened next to a discussion of plans for future carrier air wings. The optimum mix of attack, fighter, anti-submarine, and supporting aircraft on carrier decks over the next decade or more was evaluated in light of current and possible acquisitions plans. An overview of naval aviation's likely budget situation followed in which listeners were told that the Navy is able to purchase only about three-quarters of the aircraft needed. The briefer urged the fleet, including active naval aviators present at the briefing, to make suggestions to planners in Washington.

An annual awards luncheon featured VADM Dunleavy's "state of naval aviation" address. Numerous honors were presented at the luncheon, including industry-sponsored awards by numerous industry contractors. Most of these trophies are awarded annually to leading squadrons in the various aviation communities, but individual awards were bestowed as well upon outstanding pilots, naval flight officers, landing signal officers, and Marines.

Finally, following a tradition established in 1986, three new fliers chose to receive their Wings of Gold at the Tailhook symposium. Senior Navy officers and family members joined the over 1,000 in the audience in looking on during the ceremony.

FLAG PANEL

The major event of the Tailhook '91 symposium convened following the luncheon. The Flag Panel is one of the truly unique aspects of Tailhook and the armed services. In this forum, Navy and Marine flag and general officers assemble as a panel to respond to tough questions posed by the audience. Leaders in virtually every aspect of the naval service are represented and each receives his share of questions.

The Flag Panel is a forum that is open and free of often stifling aspects of military protocol. As the questioner is in civilian clothes, his or her identity or rank is unknown to the flag officer. It is impossible for the officer questioned to duck or evade in the answer. The candor and sophistication of questions and answers is to be found in no other place in naval aviation, if not the military. It is here that flag and general officers learn of decisions or policies that sound good in Washington but have unexpected or adverse impact upon those in the fleet. Here new ideas emerge from junior officers, many of which represent a fresh perspective. Ideas are discussed and, in several noteworthy cases, implemented. In all discussions, the exchange of views is accompanied with a directness but mutual respect that otherwise is impossible.

This type of senior-officer "reality check" is invaluable to those leaders who are genuinely open-minded and receptive to the concerns of their subordinates, and more than a few flag officers have emphasized the value of this unique forum to the Navy. It is in the Flag Panel discussions that Tailhook and naval aviation, over the years, has become stronger and more progressive.

VADM Dunleavy presented the Tailhook '91 Flag Officer Panel to an estimated 1,500 people jammed into the hall. Other panelists were VADM J. H. Fetterman (Naval Education and Training), VADM E. R. Kohn (Naval Air Forces, Pacific), VADM A. A. Less (Naval Air Forces, Atlantic), VADM W. C. Bowes (Naval Air Systems Command), LGEN D. A. Wills (Headquarters Marine Corps), RADM R. K. Chambers (Naval Air Reserve), RADM W. R. McGowen (Naval Air Training), and RADM J. L. Johnson (Naval Personnel).

One of the continuing questions posed to the flag panel over the years has been the subject of women in combat aircraft. The matter arose again in 1991, as reported on the CBS Evening News by Pentagon correspondent David Martin. CBS had obtained a videotape of the flag panel and showed VADM Dunleavy as a feminine voice asked off-camera when women might receive combat assignments. Dunleavy, already on record on the subject, first gave a "Hoo-boy" reaction that was followed by faint laughter in the room. At that point the CBS segment ended. However, five seconds later Dunleavy told the audience, supporters and detractors of the position alike, "If Congress directs SecNav to allow qualified women to fly combat aircraft, we will comply." He repeated those words later in the symposium, adding that female pilots already fly helicopters in the fleet and are most likely to appear first in E-2s and S-3s aboard carriers. It is important to note, however, that VADM Dunleavy's complete response was not reported in the press.

Additional subjects addressed at Flag Panel discussions included adversary aircraft, class scheduling at the Naval Fighter Weapon School, composition of S-3 squadrons, replacement airframes for various types, budgetary and personnel matters. The symposium briefings for Saturday, 7 September, concluded at 6:30 p.m.

EVENING BANQUET

The evening banquet began with presentation of the "Tailhooker of the Year" award to CAPT Jay Campbell, honored for his leadership of Air Wing Two aboard USS *Ranger* during Operation Desert Storm. For twenty years the accolade had been bestowed almost automatically upon senior admirals. But beginning in the 1980s, emphasis shifted to honoring air wing commanders and carrier captains who demonstrated innovative methods or exceptional competence at the operational level of naval aviation.

Highlight of the banquet was the presence of ADM Kelso and the main address by Secretary of the Navy H. Lawrence Garrett III. It marked the second symposium for each, recalling ADM Kelso's remarks that he wished the surface and submarine communities had a professional forum comparable to that of Tailhook. Secretary Garrett stated in his address that the Navy faced difficult times—especially in the area of reduced budgets and force levels—but stressed that naval aviation had survived such challenges before.

SUMMARY

By the time the event ended with a farewell brunch on Sunday morning, the Tailhook Association knew to a certainty that the Naval Aviation Symposium had realized its full potential. With a varied, objective assessment of the first victory in a full-scale war in half a century, America's fleet aviators departed with enhanced pride in their profession and in themselves.

At no time in the Association's 35-year history had there been a better illustration of the unique triumvirate that is Tailhook: a symbiotic relationship among aviators, admirals, and industry, each giving and receiving information from the other.

For nowhere else is so objective and relaxed an atmosphere possible in a military context. A lieutenant (jg) can tell a vice admiral what's wrong with a piece of equipment, and five minutes later that admiral can ask an industry representative how to fix it. Conversely, the admirals can explain policy directives or tactical changes to junior officers with a directness that otherwise probably would be impossible. And simultaneously, an aircraft designer or ordnance engineer can tell a Navy program manager what to expect from a new procurement item without an onerous paperwork burden.

In summary, if the United States Navy did not already have access to a Tailhook Association, there would be every good reason to create one.

Appendix C
Navy Submittal

Department of the Navy
Office of the Chief of Naval
Operations
Washington, D.C. 20350-2000

In Reply Refer To
15 Dec. 1992

Memorandum for The Inspector General,
Department of Defense

Subj: TAILHOOK '91 PROFESSIONAL EVENTS

1. Annual Tailhook Conventions have provided a unique professional exchange between Navy leadership, industry, and the largest
assembled group of rank and file Navy aviators. Over 3,000 active,
reserve, and retired aviators registered for the convention. An estimated 2,000 additional persons attended the convention, but were
not registered. Tailhook success has always depended on the quality
of presentations and the rapport and mutual credibility between presenters and audience. The Tailhook '91 program began on Thursday,
5 September '92, with a presentation by the Navy Safety Center on
current trends in aviation safety. The Lockheed Corporation followed with a symposium on advanced aircraft technologies.

2. On Friday, the presentations had a strong emphasis on the lessons
learned during Desert Storm operations. The senior naval aviator on
the staff at Riyadh during Desert Storm described joint planning for
the air war and the effectiveness the allies had in dismembering the
Iraqi command and control system. The air wing commander on
USS MIDWAY briefed combat air operations from the Persian Gulf.
He covered the air threat encountered, strike profiles for the aircraft,

intensity of operations, targets, and weapon loadouts and effectiveness. The air wing commander on USS ROOSEVELT described naval air operations from that vessel. He covered the difficulties of long range strikes, including tanking, naval targets, use of electronic counter-measures and weapons, weapons loadout, coordination with the Air Force, and intelligence and reconnaissance support. The Marine air group commander described Marine Corps air operations from Bahrain and Saudi Arabia. He covered composition of the air wing, tactics, integration with electronic warfare, and targets. The Naval Air Systems Command gave an hour presentation on the effectiveness of Tomahawk, air-to-ground ordnance, and air-to-air ordnance. Specific comments were made on improvements to each system made as a result of combat performance. A presentation was given on reconnaissance, surveillance, and intelligence support in the war. The discussion covered the lessons learned in combat as to the effectiveness of intelligence support, F-14 reconnaissance missions and information, and remotely piloted vehicles. The two most popular presentations were given by aviators that had engaged Iraqi aircraft and on the POW experiences of three aviators. Additional presentations were given on strike rescue by the Chief of Naval Operations (OPNAV) staff and representatives of the Sikorsky Corporation, the development of the F/A-18E/F aircraft, and the development of the AX aircraft.

3. On Saturday, the symposium began with a presentation by the Bureau of Navy Personnel on personnel issues facing naval aviators, including the expected 14 percent manpower reduction by 1996. This was followed by a presentation by the OPNAV staff on the future of naval air stations and future carrier air wing composition. The optimum mix of attack, fighter, anti-submarine, and support aircraft on carrier decks was evaluated in light of current and possible acquisition plans. An overview on naval aviation's likely budget constraints followed. The audience was told that the Navy is able to purchase only about three-quarters of the aircraft needed. VADM Dunleavy, Assistant Chief of Naval Operations for Air Warfare, gave the ''state of naval aviation'' at an awards luncheon. Awards were given to leading squadrons as well as outstanding pilots, naval flight officers, landing signal officers, and Marines. That afternoon, the Flag Panel, composed of nine flag officers, answered questions from the 2,000 plus aviators in attendance. This forum (a town hall meeting) allows frank exchange of views between Navy leadership and

the audience of mostly junior officers that is not possible under normal military protocol. The audience raised questions specifically on the design of the F/A-18E/F and AX, service life of the A-6 aircraft, effectiveness of the AV-8B aircraft, and weapons development—including various air-to-ground and air-to-air needs, adversary aircraft, class scheduling at Naval Fighter Weapons School, and composition of S-3 aircraft squadrons. The status of women in combat was raised by the audience and discussed by the panel. The conclusion of the panel was that, if Congress directs the Secretary of the Navy to allow women to fly combat aircraft, the Navy will comply. That evening, the Secretary of the Navy spoke on the state and future of naval aviation.

4. The frank exchange of ideas at Tailhook continued to assist Navy leadership in planning for and resolving a variety of issues facing Navy aviation. Immediate positive results of the professional exchange during the convention were realized in new studies on the types of aircraft and training required for combat search and rescue. In addition, as a result of the shortcomings identified during the seminar on prisoners of war, Navy aviators flying over Southern Iraq in Operation Southern Guard are now carrying the hand-held Global Positioning System.

R. D. MIXON
Director, Air Warfare

APPENDIX D
GLOSSARY OF SQUADRON
DESIGNATORS

CAG	Carrier Air Group (USN)
CNATRA	Chief of Naval Air Training (USN)
COMNAVAIRRESFOR	Commander, Naval Air Reserve Force (USN)
CVW	Carrier Air Wing (USN)
CVWR	Carrier Air Wing Reserve (USN)
HS	Helicopter Anti-Submarine Squadron (USN)
MAG	Marine Air Group (USMC)
MAWTS	Marine Aviation Weapons & Tactics Squadron (USMC)
NFWS	Naval Fighter Weapons School (USN)
NSWC	Naval Strike Warfare Center (USN)
STRKFIGHTWINGPAC	Strike Fighter Wing Pacific (USN)
TOP GUN	Naval Fighter Weapons School (USN)
VA	Attack Squadron (USN)
VAQ	Tactical Electronic Warfare Squadron (USN)
VAW	Carrier Airborne Early Warning Squadron (USN)
VF	Fighter Squadron (USN)
VFA	Strike Fighter Squadron (USN)

VMA	Attack Squadron (USMC)
VMA(AW)	All Weather Attack Squadron (USMC)
VMAQ	Tactical Electronic Warfare Squadron (USMC)
VMAT	Attack Training Squadron (USMC)
VMAT(AW)	All Weather Attack Training Squadron (USMC)
VMFA	Fighter Attack Squadron (USMC)
VMFA(AW)	All Weather Fighter Attack Squadron (USMC)
VMFAT	Fighter Attack Training Squadron (USMC)
VMFP	Tactical Reconnaissance Squadron (USMC)
VMFT	Marine Fighter Training Squadron (USMC)
VR	Fleet Logistics Support Squadron (USN)
VS	Anti-Submarine Squadron (USN)
VT	Training Squadron
VX	Air Test and Evaluation Squadron (USN)

Appendix E
Individual Squadron Suite
Summaries

Tactical Electronic Warfare Squadron 129 (VAQ-129)
Naval Air Station, Whidbey Island
Oak Harbor, WA

Hilton Suite Number: 302

Commanding Officer: CDR Richard H. Porritt, Jr.,
                                    USN (attended Tailhook '91)

Executive Officer: (did not attend Tailhook '91)

Contributing Squadrons: VAQ-129 and other VAQ
                                    squadrons (EA6B) at NAS
                                    Whidbey (12 squadrons)

Squadron Members Attending: Unable to determine

Suite Financing: Individual officer contributions
                                    of $25 and excess funds from
                                    the Prowler Ball, an annual
                                    all-VAQ squadron event.

Hours of Operation: Thursday, 11:00 a.m. to
                                    Friday, 2:00 a.m.; Friday,
                                    11:00 a.m. to Saturday, 2:00
                                    a.m.; Saturday, 11:00 a.m. to
                                    Sunday, 2:00 a.m.

Type of Alcohol Served: Beer and vodka/lemonade
                                    punch

Total Cost of Alcohol: $1,325.02

Total Cost of Suite Damage: $124 maid service, cleaning, and damages

The VAQ-129 was the host squadron at Tailhook '91 for all the Tactical Electronic Warfare squadrons. The suite was the first suite on the right side of the hallway that people would come to as they exited the main bank of elevators and turned right into the main part of the third-floor hallway. The VAQ-129 suite was located in the area where the gauntlet and most crowded portion of the hallway started.

Prior to Tailhook '91, the VAQ-129 CO did not provide formal instructions or guidance to the squadron members other than posting two letters, both dated August 15, 1991, from CAPT Ludwig, the Tailhook Association President, on the "all officers read board." According to the squadron CO the duty officers were instructed to check identification of anyone they thought might be under the legal drinking age. They were also instructed to confront and, if needed, escort anyone intoxicated or unruly from the suite.

The suite coordinators and duty officers reported their duties consisted mostly of making certain there was an adequate supply of ice, food, and beverages on hand at all times. The primary suite coordinator said he hired two waitresses from a Las Vegas restaurant to serve drinks on Friday and Saturday nights. He paid each woman $100 per night. One Navy commander described the waitresses he saw in the suite as being scantily dressed.

The primary suite coordinator estimated the VAQ-129 purchased and served between 16 and 20 kegs of beer and at least 4 cases of vodka. By most accounts, the suite was quiet on Thursday and Friday nights. However, the party atmosphere increased on Saturday night.

Nineteen Navy and Marine Corps officers reported there was a strip show in the VAQ-129 suite. The majority of their accounts were consistent in detail. The witnesses stated there were two strippers who performed on Saturday night at approximately 11:00 p.m. Most of the officers said the strippers solicited tips, which the men placed in the strippers' G-strings. By most accounts, the doors were closed and window shades were drawn during the strippers' performance. One of the suite coordinators recalled that one stripper wore a G-string and the other was eventually completely naked. Another suite coordinator said he paid the strippers approximately $100 each for their performance. One officer recalled that some male officers danced with the strippers while another officer said one stripper accepted a tip by lifting her breast and allowing an officer to place his money there. Yet another officer recalled seeing males tipping the strippers and giving them "hugs."

Eight naval officers and one Hilton Hotel security officer stated there were streakers in the VAQ-129 suite. Although the witnesses' specific recollections were not entirely consistent, the general version was that on Saturday night four or five naked males ran across the pool patio area and into the suite. The men were being chased by Hilton Hotel security officers and Tailhook Association officials. People on the pool patio and in the suite intentionally hindered the security officers by bumping into them, blocking their path, and closing and locking the suite patio doors after the streakers entered the suite. As described elsewhere in this report, CAPT Ludwig reported that he found the streakers hiding together in the bathroom of the VAQ-129 suite and he verbally reprimanded them but did not seek to identify the officers by name or specific squadron. Two other officers recalled they witnessed CAPT Ludwig also reprimanding the suite duty officers who were present at the time. Although few witnesses could or would identify any of the streakers, they were ultimately identified during the course of our investigation.

There were two reports that women were grabbed or pinched by males who were standing in the doorways of the suite. One person said that it occurred in the doorway leading to the third-floor hallway while another person described it as taking place in the door leading to the pool patio. A Navy lieutenant admitted that he and three or four other males pinched women who were entering the VAQ-129 suite from the hallway. The lieutenant said that if a woman voiced objections he would stop. He also told us he could not recall the faces or names of the other men who were taking part in that activity.

Another naval officer said at one point he saw some girls in the VAQ-129 suite who appeared to him to be minors. With regard to consensual activity, one officer stated he witnessed a woman in the suite who asked a male to "zap" her. The male then "zapped" the woman on the buttocks. There was also one officer who said he witnessed an incident in the VAQ-129 suite in which a woman came up to a group of men who were standing around talking and reportedly pulled down the pants of at least one of the men and bit him/them on the buttocks. The witness said the men laughed about the incident.

CARRIER AIRBORNE EARLY WARNING SQUADRON ONE HUNDRED
TEN (VAW-110)
NAVAL AIR STATION, MIRAMAR, SAN DIEGO, CA

Hilton Suite Number: 303

Commanding Officer: CDR Christopher John
Remshak, USN (attended
Tailhook '91)

Executive Officer: (did not attend Tailhook '91)

Contributing Squadrons: VAW-120, VAW-114, VRC-30,
CAEWWS

Squadron Members Attending: Approximately 50 from VAW-
110 and an undetermined
number from the contributing
squadrons

Suite Financing: Contributions from squadron
wardroom funds totaling
approximately $3,200

Hours of Operation: Thursday, 3:00 p.m. to Friday,
2:00 a.m.; Friday, 3:00 p.m.
to Saturday, 2:00 a.m.;
Saturday, 9:00 a.m. to
Sunday, 2:00 a.m.

Type of Alcohol Served: Beer and mixed drinks

Total Cost of Alcohol: $900

Total Cost of Suite Damage: $1,316

The VAW-110 suite had pictures of naval aircraft hanging on the
walls of the suite; however, its featured attraction was the "leg-shaving booth." The suite was arranged and organized for two purposes:
as a place to socialize with other squadron members and also to
entertain guests with the "leg-shaving booth." According to one of

the officers in charge of leg shaving, the booth was initiated at the 1990 symposium as a "scam" to attract guests to the suite. In conjunction with the 1991 leg-shaving booth, there were reports of "belly shots" and displays of nudity in the suite.*

The CO told us that prior to the symposium, in more than one all-officers meeting, he discussed CAPT Ludwig's August 15, 1991, letter with the suite coordinators and other squadron members. The CO felt all the officers knew his position; the suite was to be run in a "respectable" manner and that he would not allow any disrespectful actions or activities toward females. Only two squadron members we interviewed, however, could recall attending any all-officers meetings prior to the convention where expected conduct was discussed.

In two separate interviews, the CO stated that prior to the symposium he was not aware that the suite would have a "leg-shaving booth" as its entertainment. However, two squadron members provided information that directly conflicted with the CO's statements. One member recalled that before leaving for Tailhook '91, the CO told his assembled officers that since the unit had women in its command, the leg shaving had to be kept aboveboard. The other member stated he believed the CO was fully aware that leg shaving was planned.

According to the CO, the first time he became aware of the leg shaving was when he arrived in the suite on Thursday afternoon as the booth was being set up. The CO told us that after discovering what the booth was for, he immediately told one of the officers in charge of the booth that there would be no underage participants, leg shaving would be done by consent only, and only legs would be shaved. The two officers who administered the leg shaving told us that the CO never provided them any such instructions. One of the suite coordinators also told us he was not aware of the CO giving any instructions to the two officers in charge of the booth. The primary officer in charge of the booth recalled that when he and the CO were introduced to each other,† the CO said, ". . . I've heard a lot about you."

There were at least four instances of partial or complete nudity in the suite, most of which were related to the leg shaving. Three instances involved women exposing their breasts, while the fourth in-

---

*Details of leg-shaving activities and belly shots are provided in Section VIII of this report.

†The primary officer responsible for the leg-shaving booth was from VAW-120, Norfolk Naval Air Station, and had not previously met the CO of VAW-110.

stance involved a woman removing all her clothing and having her pubic area shaved.

The CO and squadron attendees told us the suite was vandalized on Thursday night and, as a result, the door to the hallway was closed for the remainder of the symposium. The only access to the suite was through the patio doors. Those squadron members who saw the vandalism stated that it consisted of graffiti painted on the walls, grenadine-stained carpet, and torn and scratched wallpaper. There were words on the walls that appeared to be call signs and a squadron slogan. At least four squadron members suspected the culprits of the vandalism were members of the VFA-151 squadron at Miramar Naval Air Station, as the call signs and slogan were associated with that particular squadron.

Two civilian women told us that an older male, approximately 70 to 85 years of age, was in the suite giving away stickers in the shape of Navy wings. The male told one of the women that if she wanted Navy wings, he would put them over her navel. She told him to put them near her shoulder instead. The second woman allowed the man to place the wings on her navel, and then gave the man the kiss that he requested in exchange for the wings.

Regarding the indecent assaults, one squadron member told us that while he was in the suite, he heard yelling and screaming coming from the hallway through the closed door. Another squadron member recalled a woman coming into the suite and appearing to be upset. The squadron member attempted to ask her what was wrong, but she would not answer or speak with him.

AIR ANTISUBMARINE SQUADRON FORTY-ONE (VS-41)
NAVAL AIR STATION, NORTH ISLAND, SAN DIEGO, CA

Hilton Suite Number: 304

Commanding Officer: CDR Glenn A. Main, USN
(did not attend Tailhook '91)

Executive Officer: CDR John William Winkler, USN (attended Tailhook '91)

Contributing Squadrons: VS-21, 22, 24, 27, 28, 29, 30, 33, 35, 37, 38, 174, and 294; VQ-5 and 6

Squadron Members Attending: Unable to determine

Suite Financing: Squadron wardroom
contributions totaling $5,050

Hours of Operation: Thursday, 3:00 p.m. to Friday,
1:00 a.m.; Friday, 10:00 a.m.
to Saturday, 2:00 a.m.;
Saturday, 10:00 a.m. to
Sunday, 1:00 a.m.

Type of Alcohol Served: Keg beer and cubi specials

Total Cost of Alcohol: $2,208

Total Cost of Suite Damage: $257

The VS-41 suite was commonly referred to as the "Viking" suite or the S-3 "Hummer Hole." By most accounts, it was organized and administered as an entertainment-type suite. The suite served complimentary beverages and food to its guests. The suite coordinator and a Lockheed representative told us that Lockheed gave approximately 500 "Hook" T-shirts to squadron members or affiliates. The suite coordinator told us 17 squadrons contributed money to the funding of the suite. He collected $5,050, which was used to pay for the cost of the suite rental ($800), two hostesses ($300), two stripper performances ($550), suite damage ($257), and the balance ($3,143) was for food, beer, rum, vodka, and sodas. According to the suite coordinator, the east coast squadrons were responsible for providing duty officer assignments and security of the suite.

The CO told us that prior to Tailhook '91, he conducted a meeting at which he addressed the conduct he expected from his officers while at the convention. He read to the squadron members the August 15, 1991, letter issued by CAPT Ludwig and added his guidance regarding underage drinking, rowdiness, excessive drinking, and accountable conduct while in the suites.

The CO and XO told us the suite's traditional form of entertainment at past Tailhook conventions had been strippers, and, in that regard, they were aware there would be strippers performing in the suite at the Tailhook '91. The CO stated he informed one of the suite coordinators the show was to be professional and aboveboard with the doors closed and the curtains drawn.

The suite coordinator told us he hired two strippers to perform on Friday night. They performed for two shows: one 45-minute show from 9:15 to 10:00 p.m. and another 1-hour 15-minute show from 10:15 to 11:30 p.m. One squadron member described the strippers as being very attractive and very young, approximately 17 years of age or younger. Three squadron members recalled they had to pay a $1 fee before they could enter the suite and see the show; that upset one squadron member because he had already contributed money for alcohol and would be denied access to the drinks because of the stripper performance if he did not pay the entrance fee. More than half the squadron members indicated that the doors to the suite were locked during each performance; at least 10 Tailhook attendees, including the VS-41 XO, were unable to get into the suite to see the show because the doors were locked. One squadron member recalled all women present in the suite were requested to leave prior to the strip show.

The XO told us in addition to the CO's rules regarding the stripper, he also gave the suite coordinators two of his own rules: there would be no touching of the stripper, and no one would be allowed in the suite once the strip show had started. Information provided by eight squadron members indicated that there was physical contact between the stripper and the audience. One squadron member recalled there were two strip acts, with an intermission where the strippers went into the suite bathroom while the suite was cleared for the next group of people coming in. During the first performance, a large group of aviators on the patio and in the hallway were clamoring to get into the suite. The same squadron member recalled that the strippers rubbed against the men in the suite and sat in their laps in a provocative manner attempting to elicit tips while the men touched the strippers' breasts, buttocks, and pubic areas. The other seven witnesses who told us about the strippers recalled a variety of activities engaged in by the strippers and the audience. One witness said that if one of the officers tipped the stripper, she would come over, sit on his lap, and rub her breasts in his face. Another witness remembered seeing guys put rolled bills in their mouths, and the strippers retrieved the bills by pressing them between their breasts or by clenching them with their vagina. One witness identified a squadron member who laid on the floor, at least once, if not twice, holding money in his mouth and touching the stripper's buttocks and vaginal area as she squatted over his face to retrieve the money with her vagina. When the squadron member was questioned about his activity, he stated he had done that sort of thing in the past and would probably do it again in the future, but that he could not remember if he did it at Tailhook '91. Another witness recalled that a lieutenant commander started dancing with the stripper, hovering over her, touching and grabbing her hips. The stripper appeared irritated with the officer. One of the junior officers in the audience asked the lieutenant commander to get out of the way because he was blocking the junior officer's view of the stripper. The lieutenant commander "pulled rank" on the junior officer and nothing else was said. Shortly thereafter, a "chem light" was broken, and the chemical inside the stick was handed to the lieutenant commander, who then rubbed the chemical on the stripper. At least four witnesses recalled that the stripper appeared to have green glowing handprints all over her body. When questioned about his behavior, the lieutenant commander stated that he "dressed down" the junior officer for confronting him. He denied putting the chemical on the stripper's breasts, buttocks, or pubic area and stated he put the chemical only on the stripper's shoulders and back.

One of the hostesses told us that the VS-41 suite was one of the most popular suites as it was known to "go through the most beer"; she opined that about 37 kegs of beer were consumed in the suite during the 3 days of the convention. The other hostess stated she was one of the poster girls for the squadron. She said a suite coordinator had taken photographs of her next to squadron aircraft, and the pictures were on display in the suite. She recalled that while serving drinks, various aviators told her about the gauntlet that would take place on Saturday evening. They described that the halls would be lined with officers chanting and harassing women as they went down the hallway. Most of the squadron members recalled that the two bartenders were scantily clad in bikinis, lacy bras, or black bras stuffed with dollar bills; however, no information was developed that indicated either hostess was assaulted in the gauntlet.

There were several instances of nudity displayed in the VS-41 suite in addition to the stripper performances. One witness recalled on Friday evening he entered the suite and observed three males walking around the room naked despite there being females present. Another witness told us that late Saturday night, six to seven male streakers came out of the VS-41 suite and ran through the patio. Preceding the streakers by a few moments were five or six women who appeared to be carrying the

---

*"Chem light" is a term commonly used to refer to a stick-light device that can be chemically activated to glow and thereby emit colored light.

streakers' clothing. Another display of nudity occurred when a woman who was wearing no bra removed her shirt to replace it with a Tailhook T-shirt. The XO told us he observed a female enter the suite restroom, remove her blouse and bra, return to the suite area, display her breasts, and then exit the suite.

Regarding the gauntlet, three squadron members recalled that on Saturday evening while in the suite, they heard guys in the hallway banging on the walls and shouting, "Foul deck" and "Clear deck." Another squadron member recalled he heard a loud commotion out in the hallway and, as he peered out the suite doorway to see what was going on, he saw males running down the hallway ducking into suites very quickly as if they were trying to clear the hall. He then saw two security guards assisting a female who was disrobed from her waist down. Yet another squadron member said he was with a woman in the hallway when she was grabbed all over her body. He attempted at the time to identify the individuals that grabbed her, but the victim did not want him to get involved. The female refused to be interviewed during our investigation.

NAVAL STRIKE WARFARE CENTER (NSWC)
NAVAL AIR STATION, FALLON, NV

Hilton Suite Number:	305
Commanding Officer:	CAPT David V. Park, USN (attended Tailhook '91)
Executive Officer:	(did not attend Tailhook '91)
Contributing Squadrons:	None
Center Members Attending:	29
Suite Financing:	Initial voluntary contribution by attending center members of $50 and an additional $20 after the convention

Hours of Operation: Thursday, 9:00 a.m. to Friday,
                             3:00 a.m.; Friday, 9:00 a.m.
                             to Saturday, 3:00 a.m.;
                             Saturday, 9:00 a.m. to
                             Sunday, 3:00 a.m.; alcohol
                             was served from 3:00 p.m. to
                             3:00 a.m.

Type of Alcohol Served: Keg beer

Total Cost of Alcohol: $1,160

Total Cost of Suite Damage: $138

The NSWC suite was referred to as the "Strike University" or
"Strike U" suite as the mission of the NSWC is to provide instruction and training on the planning and execution of naval air strikes.
The CO told us the purpose of the suite was to afford those NSWC
officers, civilian employees, and their guests with a place to meet
and relax while at Tailhook '91. Although the suite did not offer any
organized entertainment, it did feature videos of various aircraft and
weapon systems.

Attending officers said that prior to Tailhook '91, they agreed, as
in previous years, to sponsor a hospitality suite at the convention. It
was further decided that duty officers would be present in the suite
while it was in operation to ensure "calm conditions" and to mini-
mize damage. Other officers explained that arrangements were also
made to hire two civilian women from Fallon, NV, and San Fran-
cisco, CA, to act as bartenders during the afternoon and evening
hours and to sell NSWC T-shirts at the bar as a means of raising
additional monies to support the suite. The NSWC attendees paid the
women's transportation and lodging expenses while they were in Las
Vegas in exchange for their bartending services. The CO told us that
he gave instructions to the suite coordinator that the duty officers
were not to allow any activity in the suite that would embarrass the
Navy, the NSWC, or the CO. The NSWC officers stated they had a
recollection of receiving instructions from the CO before departing
for Tailhook '91. The CO informed us that while at the convention
he frequented the suite to ensure the instructions were being followed. The CO acknowledged that he received CAPT Ludwig's
letter of August 15, 1991, regarding various problems at previous

Tailhooks and told us he provided copies of the letter to the XO and the suite coordinator.

The CO said that, after returning from the convention, he spoke with the suite coordinator and duty officers and was assured that no questionable conduct occurred in the suite at Tailhook '91. The CO did tell us that during the course of the weekend several intoxicated aviators were asked to leave the suite.

Regarding the assaults that occurred at Tailhook '91, both bartenders explained that while in the suite they did not observe any improper conduct, but one stated that during Saturday evening a number of women entered the suite from the third-floor hallway and complained about being grabbed by the aviators out in the hall. She described the women as being irritated and angry at what had happened to them. We were told by NSWC officers that at some point on Saturday evening the entrance door to the hallway was closed and locked. Women entering the suite by way of the patio were warned not to enter the hallway. According to one of those NSWC officers, that was done so the women would not be subjected to the gauntlet.

Several Tailhook attendees told us that on Saturday evening there was one incident of sexual harassment in the suite. The incident involved verbal abuse in the form of sexual innuendos directed toward two female civilian guests.*

FIGHTER SQUADRON 126 (VF-126)
NAVAL AIR STATION, MIRAMAR, CA

Hilton Suite Number: 306

Commander: CDR Peter C. Chisholm, USN
                              (attended Tailhook '91)

Executive Officer: (attended Tailhook '91)

Contributing Squadrons: None

Squadron Members Attending: 20

*This incident is detailed in Section X.

Suite Financing: Voluntary payment of
                                    approximately $70 per
                                    attendee

Hours of Operation: Thursday, 12:00 noon to
                                    Friday, 4:00 a.m.; Friday,
                                    12:00 noon to Saturday, 4:00
                                    a.m.; Saturday, 12:00 noon to
                                    Sunday, 4:00 a.m.

Type of Alcohol Served: Keg beer

Total Cost of Alcohol: $411

Total Cost of Suite Damage: $131 for carpet and sofa
                                    cleaning

The VF-126 suite, according to the CO, was booked to have a central
and convenient meeting place available at the convention for the attending squadron members. The suite served as a "locator" so that other
aviators at Tailhook '91 could locate the VF-126 squadron members in
attendance. The suite also afforded the squadron attendees a place to
store their luggage, change, and shower while at the convention. The
CO further said that the suite did not offer any form of entertainment
and only keg beer was available for consumption. No information to the
contrary was developed during the investigation.

The CO told us that prior to Tailhook '91, he discussed hosting a
hospitality suite at a squadron officers' meeting. He also discussed
the ground rules regarding the operation and use of the suite, as well
as officer conduct in general. The CO acknowledged receiving
CAPT Ludwig's letter of August 15, 1991, regarding various problems at previous Tailhook conventions and had each officer attending
the convention read the letter. The XO confirmed that such issues
were discussed at the all-officers meeting.

One squadron member in attendance, a female naval officer, was
the victim of an assault on Saturday evening, September 7, 1992, in
the gauntlet. The assault occurred as the officer approached the VP-
126 hospitality suite from the third-floor hallway. The incident was
reported to the XO who subsequently contacted a Hilton Hotel security officer and asked if additional security officers could be stationed on the third floor. After the convention, the XO personally

contacted CAPT Ludwig and notified him of the assault. He further suggested to the victim that she file a formal complaint with the Tailhook Association.

No derogatory information was developed regarding specific activities within the suite.

ATTACK SQUADRON 128 (VA-128)
NAVAL AIR STATION, WHIDBEY ISLAND
OAK HARBOR, WA

Hilton Suite Number:	307
Commanding Officer:	CAPT Bernis H. Bailey, USN (attended Tailhook '91)
Executive Officer:	(did not attend Tailhook '91)
Contributing Squadrons:	VA-128, VA-155, VA-165, VA-52, VA-145, and VA-196
Squadron Members Attending:	Approximately 50 from VA-128
Suite Financing:	Individual assessments of $40 from 135 participating squadron members
Hours of Operation:	Thursday, 11:00 a.m. to Friday, 2:00 a.m.; Friday, 11:00 a.m. to Saturday, 2:00 a.m.
Type of Alcohol Served:	Frozen margaritas and draft beer
Total Cost of Alcohol:	$895.13 for beer; $1,685.25 for margarita machine rental, mix, and tequila; $2,580.38 total
Total Cost of Suite Damage:	$124.55 for cleaning charges; $500 for carpet replacement

In sponsoring the administrative suite, the VA-128 squadron served as the Tailhook '91 host for all the Navy A-6 Intruder attack squadrons. The two suite coordinators and eight suite duty officers reported that the conduct in the VA-128 suite was professional and the decorum in accordance with strict instructions of the squadron CO.

Investigation disclosed that when CAPT Bailey took command of the VA-128 in August 1991, a decision had already been made that the squadron would host an administrative suite at Tailhook '91. The primary suite coordinator said the new CO was not in favor of hosting the suite but went along since the decision had already been made to do so. The other suite coordinator recalled that the CO said the VA-128 would not hire any women to serve drinks in the suite.

The VA-128 CO held an all-officers meeting on Monday, September 2, 1991, in which he addressed appropriate behavior and the general decorum in the suite. One Marine Corps captain, who served as a duty officer, recalled that the CO told the squadron members to cancel any strip shows or similar entertainment they may have planned for the suite. The Marine captain also recalled that was not well received by some of the men in the squadron.

The CO was very specific and strict in his rules and conditions for the operation of the suite. He directed that the guidelines be written and posted in the squadron ready room prior to Tailhook '91. The written guidelines were also posted in the suite during Tailhook '91. The written guidelines covered the responsibilities of the duty officers, including security and safety in the suite, and specifically stated there would be "no lewd or lascivious acts."

The suite was funded by collecting $40 from each of the VA-128 and other A-6 squadron members who indicated they were planning to attend. There were a total of 135 persons from mostly west coast A-6 squadrons who were on record as contributors. That included 47 VA-128 squadron members. According to CAPT Bailey, there were 54 VA-128 squadron members listed on the manifest for a C-9 flight from Whidbey Island to Las Vegas for Tailhook '91. An invitation was extended to the east coast A-6 squadrons as well.

The suite served beer, frozen margaritas, and on Friday evening served a 6-foot hoagie sandwich. There was no entertainment provided in the suite. Much of the furniture was removed from the suite and there were posters of A-6 aircraft on the walls. Some officers said they used the suite as a safe place to temporarily stow their belongings. One duty officer commented that most people came into the suite to get a drink and then would quickly leave because there was no place to sit down. Two of the duty officers described the atmosphere inside the suite as "boring." Of the many other persons who said they visited the VA-128 suite, there were no particularly remarkable or noteworthy comments about the activity in the suite. One Navy lieutenant recalled that he saw a female bartender in the VA-128 suite who wore a vest with no shirt underneath. That account was uncorroborated.

Some of the VA-128 squadron members wore caps with a replica of an A-6 Intruder in-flight refueling probe in front. The caps were also reportedly sold in the suite. One civilian described the refueling probe replica as being black with a grey tip, and about 6 to 8 inches long.

One VA-128 squadron member said that at about 10:00 p.m. on Friday he witnessed a woman walk into the suite, lift her shirt, and invite men to place zappers (squadron stickers) on her bare breasts. If the men had no zappers, she invited them to rearrange the zappers already placed on her breasts. The officer recalled that five or six men accepted the woman's invitation. The suite coordinator stated that as soon as he became aware of that activity, he asked the woman to leave.

Investigation disclosed that the VA-128 suite was located in the area of the hallway where the gauntlet activity ended. Ten naval officers and one Hilton Hotel security officer gave descriptions of being in the hallway in the vicinity of the VA-128 suite when they witnessed women exiting the gauntlet. Two other naval officers said that while they were in the suite they heard chanting and pounding on the walls coming from the hallway. One of the suite coordinators said that he occasionally closed the suite/hallway door to cut down on the noise when it became too loud.

Three gauntlet victims, two civilians and LT Paula Coughlin, stated they went into the VA-128 suite immediately after they were assaulted in the gauntlet. In each case, there were male naval officers who confirmed the victims came into the suite on Saturday night and that they saw or spoke with the women, who appeared to be upset or stated they had been assaulted in the gauntlet.

One female naval officer, who was not herself assaulted in the gauntlet, reported she was in the A-6 suite when a senior officer, whom she could not further identify, suggested that she join the activities in the hallway. She said that the comment infuriated her because the officer was condoning what was going on in the hallway.

The primary suite coordinator said he was absolutely certain that none of the CO's directions or orders were violated during Tailhook '91. The results of our investigation were consistent with that statement insofar as the activities in the suite. However, investigation disclosed that individual VA-128 squadron members engaged in improper conduct elsewhere in the Hilton Hotel.

Three individuals reported that VA-128 squadron members rented a suite or suites in the Hilton Hotel, described variously as being on the sixth, seventh, and/or eighth floors. The room(s) were used by squadron members for lodging and, by one account, as a hospitality suite. One naval officer said he attended a private bachelor's party for a VA-128 squadron member in one of those rooms on Friday night. He estimated there were about 20 to 30 VA-128 squadron members in attendance at the bachelor party and there were 2 female strippers performing. He recalled there were some verbal altercations between the strippers and the squadron members because the women wanted better tips and the crowd did not want to pay them more money.

Another Marine officer, a VA-128 squadron member, said he attended a bachelor party for another squadron member on Saturday night. He said the party was held in a private room on the seventh floor and that a stripper performed. He said when the stripper arrived at about 9:30 p.m. or 10:00 p.m., he made arrangements with the stripper to perform oral sex on the bachelor for whom the party was being held after the strip show ended. The Marine officer said he collected about $25 from each attendee and gave the stripper about $150 to perform fellatio. After the strip show ended, everyone left except for the stripper and the guest of honor. The Marine officer left the bachelor party and went to the VA-128 suite in room 307. After about 30 minutes the stripper and the bachelor came into the VA-128 suite also. The Marine said the bachelor told him the stripper had performed fellatio on him.

MARINE CORPS TACTICAL RECONNAISSANCE SQUADRON 3 (VMFP-3)
DEACTIVATED 1990

Hilton Suite Number: 308

Commanding Officer: N/A

Executive Officer: N/A

Suite Coordinator(s):   CAPT David Prudhomme,
                                   USMC

Contributing Squadrons: None

Squadron Members Attending: Unable to determine

Suite Financing: Proceeds from the sale of the
                                   squadron automobile
                                   amounting to $3,000; proceeds
                                   from the sale of squadron T-
                                   shirts; and a $50 charge to all
                                   former squadron members
                                   attending Tailhook

Hours of Operation: Thursday, 11:00 p.m. to
                                   Friday, 2:00 a.m.; Friday,
                                   11:00 p.m. to Saturday, 2:00
                                   a.m.; Saturday, 6:00 p.m. to
                                   Sunday, 2:00 a.m.

Type of Alcohol Served: Beer, "Rhino Spunk" (rum,
                                   Kahlúa, milk/cream, and ice),
                                   and rum and Coke

Total Cost of Alcohol: Unable to determine

Total Cost of Suite Damage: $530, to include damage to
                                   suite and carpet cleaning

The VMFP-3 suite was called the "Rhino" room or suite, as the rhinoceros was the squadron mascot. In addition, we were told that former squadron members in attendance at Tailhook '91 could be identified as such as they wore headgear in the form of a rhinoceros horn at various times throughout the weekend.

By most accounts, the suite was organized and administered as an entertainment suite. Although the VMFP-3 squadron was deactivated in 1990, former squadron members sponsored the suite at Tailhook '91. Since the squadron had been deactivated, no squadron commander or XO was present at the convention. However, the former CO and XO (both active duty) did attend Tailhook '91. They told us they participated in the planning of the hospitality suite and visited the suite throughout the weekend of the convention. Suite activities centered around a hand-painted mural of a rhinoceros (approximately 5′ × 8′) to which was affixed a dildo rigged by squadron members for use as a drink-dispensing mechanism. The dildo dispensed an alcoholic-based liquid referred to as "Rhino Spunk" by attendees. A squadron member acted as bartender and operated the dispensing machine. By way of background, witnesses told us that the original "Rhino" mascot was made of papier mâché and was displayed by the squadron at the 1989 and 1990 Tailhook conventions. The original "Rhino" also had a large phallus device from which drinks were dispensed. Women received a drink by kissing the papier mâché "Rhino" on the lips.

As the original "Rhino" had been given to a bar in Pensacola, FL, after the Tailhook '90 convention, a decision was made by a number of former senior and junior officers to create a new mascot (the mural) for Tailhook '91. During Tailhook '91, some women would kiss, suck, or stroke the dildo to obtain a drink.

A number of aviators told us that while in the suite they observed a "deep throat" contest during which women would simulate performing oral sex on the dildo. The crowd would chant, "Beat the line . . . beat the line." The chant referred to a line that was placed on the dildo to indicate how much of the dildo the previous woman was able to take into her mouth.

Former squadron members stated that women were not forced, coerced, or intimidated in any way to drink from the dildo. However, many witnesses informed us that women were certainly encouraged to drink from the "Rhino" and various organized chants were used to accomplish that, such as "Kiss the Rhino," "Do the Rhino," or "Suck the Rhino." Women's names were also used in the chants. If a woman drank from the "Rhino" or refused to drink, she would be cheered or booed accordingly by the crowd. A number of women told us they found the behavior to be unnerving. One Navy commander stated he was concerned that women were being coerced by former squadron members into drinking from the "Rhino." He approached one Marine who was attempting to get women to enter the suite from the third-floor patio area of the Hilton. The commander instructed him to be careful and not to force any women into the suite or to intimidate them into drinking from the dildo. The commander further stated that the Marine just "blew him off."

During the course of our investigation, five women told us that on entering the suite, they were physically restrained from leaving. During one of those incidents, a woman noticed that an unknown individual was behind the mural. That individual removed the dildo and replaced it with his exposed penis. Another woman explained that she was escorted through the suite to the mural and as the crowd started to chant her name she was surrounded. An individual whom she believed to be an aviator grabbed her arms. She perceived that she would be prevented from leaving until she drank from the rhinoceros' penis. She was eventually escorted from the suite by a friend and another aviator not associated with the suite. The third woman, whose husband was an aviator, told us of being grabbed in the hallway, dragged into the suite, and verbally harassed when she refused to drink from the "Rhino." The fourth woman, a naval officer, described being shoved and pushed up to the mural whereupon her head was forced toward the dildo.

The fifth woman, a student from UNLV, entered the suite in order to get out of the hallway. Once inside the suite, she was grabbed and pushed up to the mural by four aviators. She screamed and struggled and was eventually escorted from the suite by her friends from whom she had been separated upon first entering the suite.

Other activities reported to have taken place in the suite included women exposing their breasts to obtain squadron T-shirts. Additional incidents that were detailed by witnesses included "mooning," consensual sex, and one episode in which a former squadron member had his pants pulled down by two women visitors to the suite. Reportedly, men who were wearing "Rhino" horns and believed to be aviators were "butting" women with their horns in the third-floor hallway on Saturday evening.

COMMANDER NAVAL AIR RESERVE FORCE (COMNAVAIRRESFOR)
NEW ORLEANS, LA

Hilton Suite Number: 310

Commander: CAPT John P. Hazelrig, USN
                              (attended Tailhook '91)

Chief of Staff: (attended Tailhook '91)

Contributing Squadrons: Carrier Air Wing Reserve 30
                                   (CVWR-30)

Squadron Members Attending: 6 CVWR staff officers and an
                                   unknown number of squadron
                                   officers

Suite Financing: Voluntary payment of
                                   approximately $10 per
                                   CVWR-30 attendee

Hours of Operation: Thursday, 5:30 p.m. to 12:00
                                   midnight; Friday, 2:00 p.m. to
                                   Saturday, 2:00 a.m.; Saturday,
                                   2:00 p.m. to Sunday,
                                   2:00 a.m.

Type of Alcohol Served: Keg beer and mixed drinks

Total Cost of Alcohol: $750

Total Cost of Suite Damage: $81.66 for carpet cleaning

The COMNAVAIRRESFOR was the host command for the suite. The CVWR-30, located at NAS Miramar, CA, and its seven subordinate squadrons were responsible for funding and administering the suite at Tailhook '91. According to one suite coordinator, those responsibilities alternated every other year between his wing, CVWR-30, and the east coast Reserve wing, CVWR-20. The wing commander told us the primary purpose of the suite was to afford all Reserve officers attending Tailhook '91 with a place to meet and relax. In addition, the suite served as an informal recruiting center for the Navy Reserve program. The wing commander also told us the suite was further used to "play up" the 75th anniversary of the Naval Reserve. The wing commander stated that keg beer, mixed and soft drinks were served in the suite. No "specialty" drinks were served and no entertainment was sponsored in the suite. No information to the contrary was developed during the investigation.

The wing commander told us that prior to Tailhook '91, he had a specific recollection of discussing suite administration and conduct during at least three staff meetings. During our interviews of staff officers and squadron members, a number of them confirmed receiving such instructions. Although the wing commander could not recall receiving CAPT Ludwig's letter regarding behavior at Tailhook '91, at least one of the suite coordinators recalled seeing the letter. He further noted that the contents of the letter were discussed with the wing squadron commanders. The wing commander informed us that he attended Tailhook '91 because his wing was hosting the hospitality suite and one of the wing squadrons was receiving an award at the convention.

No derogatory information was developed regarding specific activities in the COMNAVAIRRESFOR suite.

HELICOPTER ANTISUBMARINE SQUADRON ONE (HS-1)
NAVAL AIR STATION, JACKSONVILLE, FL

Hilton Suite Number: 315

Commanding Officer: CAPT Christopher Warren Cole, USN (attended Tailhook '91)

Executive Officer: (attended Tailhook '91)

Contributing Squadrons: HS-2 through HS-12, HS-14, 15, 17, 75, & 85

Squadron Members Attending: Unable to determine

Suite Financing: Contributions of $100 from stateside squadrons; contributions of $50 from overseas squadrons

Hours of Operation: Thursday, 12:00 noon to Friday, 2:00 a.m.; Friday, 12:00 noon to Saturday, 2:00 a.m.; Saturday, 12:00 noon to Sunday, 2:00 a.m.

Type of Alcohol Served: Beer and frozen margaritas

Total Cost of Alcohol: $500

Total Cost of Suite Damage: $470

The HS-1 suite functioned as a meeting place for the squadron members to see old friends and promote the naval helicopter community. Several squadron members told us that, traditionally, helicopter units did not attend Tailhook conventions, and having a hospitality suite was a means to get the helicopter community better integrated with the rest of the naval aviation community. Squadron members told us they felt it was important to portray a positive image and there were no "gimmicks" or unusual forms of entertainment in the suite.

By several accounts, the HS-1 suite was described as a "safe haven" and appeared to some people to be the most calm of all the suites. Several females had taken "refuge" in the suite to get out of the third-floor hallway. Occasionally, people came into the suite to get promotional cards or helicopter posters signed by the squadron members.

The CO and another squadron member told us that on Friday and Saturday afternoons, a group of 6 to 15 females in their 30s and 40s performed an unsolicited aerobics routine similar to a Jane Fonda workout. The group of women, who said they were from Arizona, provided their own music and before they left they thanked everyone for watching their routine. One squadron member recalled that over the course of Saturday, the women wore "upgraded" outfits as they continued to visit the suite. They started out wearing aerobics outfits, later changed to jeans, and, in the evening, returned to the third floor wearing dresses. During their later visits at 2:00 a.m. to 3:00 a.m. on Sunday morning, the women* "package checked" some of the men and put chemically lighted glow sticks down the men's shorts.

In spite of the aforementioned contention regarding the lack of inappropriate activity in the suite, our investigation did disclose that squadron members may have been involved in at least one major assault. By the accounts of most squadron members, the "hooping

*Witnesses decribed a practice known as "package checking" whereby attendees fondled the genitals of members of the opposite sex. Reports of that activity included witness accounts of a male and female who took turns fondling each other's exposed genitals in front of a large number of suite attendees.

[*sic*], hollering, and yelling" in the hallway could be easily heard from within the suite. The door to the suite was eventually closed because of the loud noise coming from the hallway. Most squadron members were aware of the "gauntlet" activities in the hallway, and several of the squadron members tried to help women by encouraging them not to go down the hallway. However, during the course of our investigation, information was developed that indicated a female who was underage,* and was known to be underage by some of the squadron members, spent some time in the suite dancing and conversing with several squadron members. No one attempted to prevent her from obtaining alcohol and she became severely intoxicated. Squadron members told us that to avoid embarrassing the squadron or placing responsibility for her intoxication on its members, the woman was removed from the suite and placed against the hallway wall opposite the suite by squadron members who were aware of the existence of the gauntlet and the potential consequences of the woman being placed in the hallway. One squadron member told us that after he and others placed the woman in the hallway, they again shut the door to the suite. The woman was assaulted in the gauntlet.

Other information and evidence developed through our investigation indicated that one of the squadron members videotaped other members hanging a stolen VF-114 squadron flag on the wall of the HS-1 suite and then "mooning" the camcorder.

FIGHTER SQUADRON 1 (VF-1)
NAVAL AIR STATION, MIRAMAR, CA

Hilton Suite Number:	316
Commanding Officer:	CDR Steven C. Gaylor, USN (attended Tailhook '91)
Executive Officer:	(attended Tailhook '91)
Contributing Squadrons:	None
Squadron Members Attending:	24

*Persons under the age of 21 are classified as underage under Nevada State law; thus, they are not legally able to purchase or be served alcohol in that state.

Suite Financing: Voluntary payment of $70 per
                                    attendee

Hours of Operation: Thursday, 5:00 p.m. to 12:00
                                    midnight; Friday, 5:00 p.m. to
                                    12:00 midnight; Saturday, 5:00
                                    p.m. to 6:00 p.m.

Type of Alcohol Served: Keg beer and limited mixed
                                    drinks

Total Cost of Alcohol: $88

Total Cost of Suite Damage: $70 for carpet cleaning

The VF-1 suite, by most accounts, was intended to afford squadron
attendees and their guests a central and convenient meeting location,
as well as a place to relax while at the convention. According to
squadron members, it was not an "entertainment"-type suite and
only limited quantities of alcohol and food were available for consumption. No information to the contrary was developed during the
investigation.

The CO and XO told us the decision to host the suite as well as
the arrangements for operating the suite, duty officer assignments,
and general behavior requirements for those members participating
in Tailhook '91 were discussed at an officers meeting at the squadron
prior to the convention. That information was basically confirmed by
a number of officers during our interviews of squadron members at
the Naval Air Station, Miramar; however, not all the officers recalled
receiving such instructions relative to their conduct at the convention. The CO acknowledged receiving CAPT Ludwig's letter of
August 15, 1991, regarding various problems at previous Tailhook
conventions. The CO stated that he attended Tailhook '91 specifically to ensure there were no such problems associated with the operation of the VF-1 suite.

With respect to the hours of operation of the suite on Saturday
evening, September 7, 1991, the CO noted that he "closed" the
suite at approximately 6:00 p.m. after finding the suite unattended
by the duty officer. This information was confirmed, in other interviews, although the time of closure as reflected in the interviews
ranged from 6:00 p.m. to 10:00 p.m.

No derogatory information was developed regarding specific activities within the suite. However, one photograph provided during the investigation and believed to have been taken in the VF-1 suite on Saturday evening depicts two males assisting two females in exposing themselves. Specifically, one officer is shown pulling down a woman's tube top blouse, thus exposing her bare breasts. The second officer is shown lifting the other woman's dress, exposing her buttocks and bikini panties. All four people depicted in the photographs are seen smiling while posing for the picture. The two males have been identified as Navy officers, but were not members of the VF-1 squadron. When interviewed, the two officers told us that they did not recall engaging in the activity shown in the photograph and attributed their lack of recall to having been intoxicated.

MARINE ALL WEATHER FIGHTER ATTACK SQUADRON 12
1 (VMFA[AW]-121)
MARINE CORPS AIR STATION, EL TORO, CA

Hilton Suite Number: 318

Commanding Officer: LTC Stephen F. Mugg, USMC
                               (attended Tailhook '91)

Executive Officer: (did not attend Tailhook '91)

Contributing Squadrons: VMFA (AW)-121 and VMFA
                               (AW)-314

Squadron Members Attending: 25

Suite Financing: Money deposited in Officers'
                               Fund

Hours of Operation: Friday, 12:00 noon to
                               Saturday, 4:00 a.m.; Saturday,
                               12:00 noon to Sunday,
                               3:00 a.m.

Type of Alcohol Served: Bloody Marys in the a.m.,
beer and margaritas in the
p.m.

Total Cost of Alcohol: Beer total $655; liquor and
food totals $782

Total Cost of Suite Damage: No damage; cleaning charge of
$76

The VMFA-121 suite, by most accounts, served as a central meeting place for the squadron attendees. The only entertainment provided in the suite were [*sic*] videos of the Gulf war with F-18 aircraft shooting rockets.

The CO stated that 6 weeks prior to the convention, he held an all-officers meeting to "talk up" the convention and give instructions to the attendees regarding their conduct there. He circulated the August 15, 1991, letter from CAPT Ludwig regarding the convention and reiterated to his squadron members that there would be "no gauntlet and no stupid stuff." He instructed them to ensure that refreshments, condition of the suite, and squadron members' property were appropriately maintained.

According to the CO, the mascot of VMFA(AW)-121 is a green knight. On Friday night, a 4-foot-high sheet metal statue of a green knight was used to block open the door to the suite. On Saturday night, to attract attention to the suite, the "green knight" was endowed with a rubber dildo, which was then modified to dispense margaritas. The CO told us that the dildo on the "green knight" was not offensive nor harmful to anyone and, in fact, caused more people to come through the suite. The CO told us that if the dildo had been offensive to anyone, he would have told those individuals to leave the suite rather than remove the dildo. The dildo was described by most Tailhook attendees who saw the "green knight" as "no big deal" and not offensive in nature.

The CO stated he would not let people put their mouths on the dildo to receive drinks because that would have violated health regulations. However, military and civilian Tailhook attendees who were interviewed, stated people did, in fact, put their mouths on the dildo to receive drinks. One Marine attendee stated that people were drinking directly from the dildo, while a Navy attendee said he watched a woman massage the dildo to obtain a drink. Two civilian attendees witnessed people sucking on the dildo, some of whom while down on their hands and knees. A Navy attendee noted that at some point on Saturday night, the dildo was covered with a condom.

The CO and two former squadron members told us the concept of the "green knight" dildo originated with a former squadron member's wife. In 1988 or 1989, while the former squadron member was on a long-term cruise, his wife was presented with a dildo as a gag gift during a squadron wives' club meeting. When the squadron member returned from the cruise, his wife gave him the dildo and he, in turn, gave it to the squadron so it could be placed on the "green knight."

No one that we interviewed reported seeing any strippers in the VMFA(AW)-121 suite. However, the NIS interviewed at least six officers who reported that they personally observed or heard of stripper(s) in the suite. Four of those officers recalled that it was on Friday night that they specifically saw the stripper(s).

Information provided by one officer indicated that one squadron member was with a woman in the hallway when she was assaulted in the gauntlet. While the woman was being grabbed, swatted on the buttocks, and disrobed, the VMFA(AW)-121 squadron member was encouraging her to continue on through the crowd. When the woman got to the end of the gauntlet, she was dropped on the floor wearing just her brassiere* and panties. The VMFA(AW)-121 squadron member and others in the hallway "dashed" into the suites as security guards came to the woman's rescue.

FIGHTER SQUADRON FIFTY-ONE (VF-51)
MIRAMAR NAVAL AIR STATION, SAN DIEGO, CA

Hilton Suite Number: 319

Commanding Officer: CDR Thomas George Sobieck, USN (attended Tailhook '91)

Executive Officer: (attended Tailhook '91)

Contributing Squadrons: None

*The officer could not identify the victim by name nor was she further identified during the course of the investigation.

Squadron Members Attending: 25

Suite Financing:	Individual assessments of $25 and wardroom funds of $100
Hours of Operation:	Open to squadron personnel 24 hours, Thursday–Saturday
Type of Alcohol Served:	Beer, wine, and liquor
Total Cost of Alcohol:	$200
Total Cost of Suite Damage:	None

Investigation disclosed that the VF-51 administrative suite served as a central meeting place for squadron members. It was not an open-door hospitality suite like many of the others. The suite was located at the extreme far end of the third-floor hallway away from where the majority of the gauntlet-related assaults occurred.

The only entertainment provided in the suite was a bachelor party for one of the squadron members where two strippers performed on Friday night. By most accounts, the party was a closed-door event for only VF-51 members and friends of the bachelor. There were approximately 30 people in attendance. One civilian Tailhook attendee recalled trying to enter the suite but the door was locked; behind the door was an unidentified male who was preventing the entry of any uninvited guests.

The squadron member in charge of hiring the strippers said he paid the strippers $150 to $200 for the performance. The strippers wore G-strings and only removed their tops. One squadron member told us the strippers removed the bachelor's clothing, to include his underwear, which embarrassed the bachelor. Two other squadron members recalled that the strippers attempted to remove the bachelor's underwear, but he resisted. Also, a former squadron member told us that prior to the strippers' performance, as a joke, he paid one of the strippers $20 to put VF-126 stickers on each breast so they would be visible for all the VF-51 squadron members to see when she removed her clothes.

By the accounts of all VF-51 members interviewed, there was no touching of the stripper by anyone in the audience. However, information to the contrary was provided by a witness not connected with

VF-51. The witness was a naval officer and a friend of the bachelor. The witness indicated that the bachelor laid [*sic*] on the floor with dollar bills in his mouth and was stripped down to his underwear while the women were dancing; the bachelor then placed money inside his underwear, and the women retrieved it. Other details provided by the witness indicated that the witness's recollection was quite vivid. It should be noted that detailed information was not provided by the VF-51 squadron members, and that the witness providing the information was interviewed at a different location approximately two months after the squadron members were interviewed.

MARINE ALL WEATHER FIGHTER ATTACK SQUADRON 24 2 (VMFA[AW]-242)
MARINE CORPS AIR STATION, EL TORO, SANTA ANA, CA

Hilton Suite Number:	320
Commander:	LTC Daniel Driscoll, USMC (attended Tailhook '91)
Executive Officer:	(attended Tailhook '91)
Contributing Squadrons:	None
Squadron Members Attending:	17
Suite Financing:	$60 individual assessment
Hours of Operation:	Thursday, 3:00 p.m. to Friday, 1:00 a.m.; Friday, 3:00 p.m. to Saturday, 1:00 a.m.; Saturday, 3:00 p.m. to Sunday, 1:00 a.m.
Type of Alcohol Served:	Draft beer
Total Cost of Alcohol:	Unable to determine
Total Cost of Suite Damage:	$69.50 for standard carpet/sofa cleaning bill

The VMFA(AW)-242 hosted the hospitality suite as a place for the squadron members, commonly called the "Bats," to meet and relax. The only entertainment that the suite sponsored for the public were videos of F-18 Hornet flights. On all three nights of the symposium, there were "private" parties for squadron members during which strippers performed.

The CO told us that prior to the symposium, he held two all-officers meetings during which he briefed the squadron officers on what he expected from them concerning their conduct and deportment. He used the August 15, 1991, letter from CAPT Ludwig as a guide to instruct the officers there would be no minors or intoxicated officers allowed in the suite and offensive behavior or "gang mentality" would not be tolerated.

The CO stated he had numerous meetings with the XO concerning the operation of the suite. The XO told us that he appointed duty officers to keep order in the suite at all times. Through interviews of several squadron members, we were able to determine that the responsibilities of the suite duty officers were to "police" the suite, ensure there was no damage to the suite itself, and maintain general order.

The CO and XO told us that prior to the symposium they granted permission to the junior officers to host a bachelor party in the suite. The bachelor party included the hiring of professional strippers. The CO said that he saw nothing wrong with having a private party in the suite as long as it did not include any "sex acts."

The suite coordinator told us that he was tasked by the XO with providing the entertainment, including a stripper, for the bachelor party. He located a stripper in an advertisement of erotic dance companies. On Thursday night the stripper who was to perform at the bachelor party gave a preview performance to several squadron members in the suite. Some of the junior officers present for the preview unsuccessfully attempted to procure oral sex for the XO. Neither the stripper nor the XO complied. After the preview, the stripper presented her ground rules on how the men in attendance at the Friday night bachelor party should conduct themselves. According to the suite coordinator, the stripper said she would dance in her panties; no one would be allowed to touch her breasts, groin area, or buttocks; she was to be paid $150 for dancing; and she would leave at any time she became uncomfortable. The suite coordinator asked her to bring a second "dancer" with her on Friday night since there would be two bachelors for which the party was being held. On Friday night, two strippers performed.

According to those persons attending the Friday night performance, a crowd of between 40 and 70 people was present. By most accounts, the doors were shut and the curtains were drawn. The strippers began their performance at about 9:00 p.m., which lasted approximately 45 minutes to 1 hour. The two strippers performed by completely undressing themselves, undressing the two bachelors down to their shorts, rubbing their bodies against the bachelors, and collecting tips from the onlookers. The bachelors laid [*sic*] down on the floor between the strippers' legs and held dollar bills in their mouths; the strippers picked up the bills with various parts of their bodies. Money was collected from the crowd to purchase sex for the bachelors; however, our investigation failed to substantiate any related sex acts.

For Saturday night, the suite coordinator arranged another stripper performance by a different dancer than the prior two nights. One of the squadron officers told us that to "liven up the party," he laid [*sic*] down on the floor below the stripper and between her legs. He and other squadron members placed bills on various locations of his body to include between his teeth, in his mouth, in his nose, and in his zipper/crotch area; the stripper picked them up with her buttocks, crotch, and hands, just as the strippers had done on Friday night. In addition to the "tips," the stripper was paid a $150 fee. We obtained candid photographs of portions of the performance which include pictures wherein the XO and other officers are shown having nonsexual physical contact with the stripper.

Through interviews of persons who attended the Friday and Saturday night performances, we obtained information that directly conflicted with the CO's testimony regarding the party. According to the CO, his orders were that no one was allowed to attend the party who was not a member of the squadron; however, we interviewed several attendees of the parties who were neither former nor current squadron members. Interviews of several squadron members confirmed that the CO of the Marine Aircraft Group 11 was also present during the stripper performances.

During the interview process, it became evident that the squadron members were not being completely candid with investigators.

AIR TEST AND EVALUATION SQUADRON FIVE (VX-5)
NAVAL WEAPONS CENTER, CHINA LAKE, CA

Hilton Suite Number: 354

Commanding Officer: CAPT R. Kellet, USN (did not attend Tailhook '91) CAPT Garth A. Van Sickle, USN (attended Tailhook '91) NOTE: CAPT Kellet was the CO of VX-5 at the time of Tailhook '91. CAPT Van Sickle took command of VX-5 in late September 1991, several weeks after the Tailhook '91 symposium.

Executive Officer: (attended Tailhook '91)

Contributing Squadrons: VX-5

Squadron Members Attending: Approximately 30

Suite Financing: Individual assessment of wardroom funds.

Hours of Operation: Thursday, 2:00 p.m. to Friday, 2:00 a.m.; Friday, 10:00 p.m. to Saturday, 2:00 a.m.; Saturday, 10:00 p.m. to Sunday, 2:00 a.m.; Sunday, 8:00 a.m. to 12:00 noon

Type of Alcohol Served: Beer

Total Cost of Alcohol: $719

Total Cost of Suite Damage: $63 cleaning charge

Investigation disclosed that the VX-5 administrative suite was, by all accounts, managed professionally and operated with decorum. The suite served as a central meeting place for squadron members and had a quiet, uncrowded atmosphere where people could talk and relax. The VX-5 suite was on the far end of the third-floor hallway from the other hospitality suites. The location is on the other side of the elevators and at the extreme far end of the crowded portion of the hallway away from where the gauntlet activity occurred.

The only alcoholic beverage served in the VX-5 suite was beer. The suite was popular because it showed videotapes of aircraft flight operations, to include footage of Operation Desert Storm and aircraft testing. By many accounts, the pool patio area just outside the VX-5 suite was a popular gathering place because it was relatively un-crowded and convenient to obtain beer in the VX-5 suite. CAPT Van Sickle, the CO, stated that prior to Tailhook '91, the VX-5 squadron members were instructed they were not to drink while assigned as suite duty officers. They were also instructed to keep the suite clean and stocked with food and beverages, to guard against rowdy behavior, and not to serve alcohol to minors. The CO advised that CAPT Ludwig's letter of August 15, 1991, was referenced in passing the instructions to the squadron members. The interviews of the squadron members generally corroborated the information.

There was no derogatory information developed regarding specific activities within the suite.

Marine Fighter Attack Training Squadron 101 (VMFAT-101)
Marine Corps Air Station El Toro
Santa Ana, CA

Hilton Suite Number: 355

Commanding Officer: COL George C. Tullos, USMC
                              (attended Tailhook '91)

Executive Officer: (attended Tailhook '91)

Contributing Squadrons: VMFAT-101

Squadron Members Attending: Approximately 50

Suite Financing: Individual assessments of
                                    VMFAT-101 officers

Hours of Operation: Thursday, 2 p.m. to Friday, 2
                                    a.m.; Friday, 2 p.m. to
                                    Saturday, 2 a.m.; Saturday, 2
                                    p.m. to Sunday, 2 a.m.

Type of Alcohol Served: Draft beer and hard liquor
                                    mixed drinks

Total Cost of Alcohol: $600

Total Cost of Suite Damage: Unable to determine; charges
                                    assessed for cleaning only; no
                                    damages reported

The VMFAT-101 suite was located in a remote area from the main, crowded area of the third-floor hallway. Investigation disclosed there was no inappropriate entertainment sponsored by the squadron. By most accounts, the atmosphere in the suite was subdued and unremarkable. The suite had beer and hard-liquor mixed drinks, but did not serve any specialty drinks.

The VMFAT-101 CO stated that prior to Tailhook '91 he instructed his squadron as to their expected conduct at the convention and cited CAPT Ludwig's letter of August 15, 1991. The CO said he told his subordinate officers they were to act appropriately as they would in any social setting or military event. The CO also told us he instructed the suite duty officers and other squadron members they were not to get involved in drinking contests or allow underage drinking. Further, they were told not to allow any damage to occur to the suite and they should all help to police the suite.

A junior officer assigned to the VMFAT-101 squadron recalled attending numerous "all officers meetings during which there were general discussions among the officers that good judgment and common sense should be exercised at Tailhook '91. However, despite the CO's contentions, the junior officer did not recall any specific formal guidance offered by his command and said he never saw CAPT Ludwig's letter of August 15, 1991. The officer said, although he did not receive specific cautions from his command, he was aware from previous attendance at Tailhook conventions that behavior could get out of control. The junior officer said he recalled that most of the official discussion at the all-officers meetings involving Tailhook related to the logistics of transportation and purchasing of alcohol for the squadron hospitality suite. He stated that in addition to serving drinks, the VMFAT-101 also supplied squadron stickers (zappers) and T-shirts as liaison gifts. He emphasized that all the items were paid for by the squadron members.

The VMFAT-101 chartered a bus using money from the officers' coffee fund. An estimated 30 to 40 squadron members traveled to Tailhook '91 on the bus.

Most witnesses who told us they visited the VMFAT-101 suite described it in terms such as "quiet" and "uneventful." There were, however, a few reported events that bear mentioning.

At one point, a butt-biting episode took place in the suite. A foreign exchange officer assigned to the VMFAT-101 bit a woman on the hip and buttocks. The woman involved in the incident said that while she did not find the incident amusing, neither did she consider herself a "victim." She said that she and the Marine Corps officers who were with her when the incident occurred handled it at the time. She said the man who bit her later apologized after he sobered up. A male Marine Corps officer who is a friend of the woman reported that he and the VMFAT-101 CO were standing and talking with the woman when she was bitten. The CO stated he had no recollection of witnessing the incident.

At least seven people reported that a Marine Corps officer assigned to the VMFAT-101 was involved in some fight or altercation during which he was pushed into a concrete planter on the pool patio and injured his back. The details of the various accounts of the incident were not consistent. According to the injured officer, at about 10:00 p.m. on Friday he was standing on the pool patio in the rain talking to an acquaintance who is a Naval Reserve officer. The Marine Corps officer said he had been drinking since 2:00 p.m. and was "feeling no pain." He started to splash water from rain puddles on the other officer who pushed him. As he fell backwards, the Marine officer's lower right back hit the corner of a concrete planter. He said hitting the planter made him "instantly sober" and "clear headed." He was advised by the squadron CO and a Navy flight surgeon to seek medical attention. The X-ray examination showed he had chipped some bones.

A Navy lieutenant said he witnessed a ballwalking incident that might have occurred in the VMFAT-101 suite. Our investigation disclosed that at least three VMFAT-101 squadron members ballwalked at Tailhook '91. One of the officers denied doing so until confronted with a photograph of him ballwalking.

MARINE AVIATION WEAPONS AND TACTICS SQUADRON 1 (MAWTS-1)
MARINE CORPS AIR STATION, YUMA, AZ

Hilton Suite Number: 356

Commanding Officer: COL Michael P. Delong, USMC (did not attend Tailhook '91)

Executive Officer: None at the time of Tailhook '91

Contributing Squadrons: VMFT-401 and VMFA-134

Squadron Members Attending: 17 from MAWTS-1, 4–6 from VMFT-401, and 5 from VMFA-134

Suite Financing: For MAWTS-1 members, initial voluntary payment of $75, with second voluntary assessment of $59; for VMFT-401 and VMFA-134, voluntary payments ranging from $25 to $50 for each attendee

Hours of Operation: Friday, 4:00 p.m. to 12:00 midnight; Saturday, 4:00 p.m. to Sunday, 3:00 a.m.

Type of Alcohol Served: Keg beer

Total Cost of Alcohol: $411.13

Total Cost of Suite Damage: $114.50 for carpet and sofa cleaning and damage to the telephone

The MAWTS-1 was organized and administered as a "staging place" for the squadron members to gather and socialize. There was no entertainment provided other than the display of various aircraft photographs, slide shows, and videos.

The suite coordinator told us that prior to the symposium, the CO decided to provide transportation for the squadron members to and from Las Vegas. Two enlisted personnel drove a Marine Corps Morale, Welfare, and Recreation (MWR) vehicle carrying the MAWTS-1 squadron members to the symposium. During the convention, the enlisted personnel stayed on temporary travel status at Nellis Air Force Base, Las Vegas, NV. Also prior to the symposium, two memoranda were sent to all potential squadron attendees discussing the logistical efforts and conduct in the suite. A copy of CAPT Ludwig's letter of August 15, 1991, regarding various problems at previous Tailhook conventions was made available for each attendee to read before attending the symposium. The CO, suite coordinator, and squadron attendees decided prior to the symposium that the suite would be managed in a professional manner. The squadron's intent was to advertise its operational capabilities of providing instructor-level training and certification and to recruit the "best of the best" to become future Marine Corps instructor pilots. To appear more professional, attendees were told to wear their MAWTS-1 black polo shirts on Friday night and their white polo shirts on Saturday night.

The activities in the MAWTS-1 suite were described by Tailhook attendees as "boring" as there was no alcohol available in the suite until 11:30 p.m. on Saturday night. Information provided by a squadron member indicated that "soft porno" pictures, specifically of naked women, were presented during one of the slide shows.

FIXED WING FLEET LOGISTICS SUPPORT SQUADRON 57 (VR-57) NAVAL AIR STATION, NORTH ISLAND, CA

Hilton Suite Number: 357

Commanding Officer: CDR Philip J. Swartz, USNR
                       (attended Tailhook '91)

Executive Officer: (attended Tailhook '91)

Contributing Squadrons: Ten C-9 (VR) squadrons

Squadron Members Attending: Seven VR-57 officers and an
                               undetermined number of
                               officers from the other 10 VR
                               squadrons

Suite Financing: Voluntary contributions (of no
                       pre-set amount) from members
                       of the various VR squadrons

Hours of Operation: Thursday, 6:00 p.m. to Friday,
                       2:00 a.m.; Friday, 12:00 noon
                       to Saturday, 2:00 a.m.;
                       Saturday, 12:00 noon to
                       Sunday, 2:00 a.m.

Type of Alcohol Served: Keg beer and mixed drinks

Total Cost of Alcohol: $1,115

Total Cost of Suite Damage: None

The VR-57 hospitality suite was administered by VR-57 and was
funded by squadron members throughout the VR community. The
squadrons are Naval Reserve units. The CO told us the primary purpose of the suite was to afford those Naval Reserve officers assigned
to the squadrons, as well as former officers, a place to meet and relax
while at Tailhook '91.

One squadron member said that before Tailhook '91, the CO held
an all-officers meeting to determine which squadron members would
be attending the convention. It was decided that duty officers would
be present in the hospitality suite whenever the suite was open and
further agreed that the squadron would hire a woman from the San
Diego area to tend bar in the suite during the evening hours. The
squadron paid the woman's transportation and lodging expenses

while she was in Las Vegas. The CO informed us that his directions for conduct at Tailhook '91 were that there was to be no activity in the suite that would be embarrassing for the squadron or the Navy.

By most accounts, the suite was one of the more subdued hospitality suites at the convention. The suite offered a full-service bar that was operated during the evening and early morning hours. The bartender told us that while in the suite she did not observe any improper conduct. She did note that on Friday evening two women entered the suite from the third-floor hallway after having had numerous drinks thrown on them by unknown aviators. The women were provided with dry clothing. The XO informed us that on Saturday evening, the duty officer identified an underage female in the room and escorted her out of the suite. The CO told us there was one reported incident of "leg shaving" in the suite. He learned of the incident after the convention and described it as an isolated matter and not a planned activity as in other suites. Although there were other reported incidents of "leg shaving" at Tailhook '91, no reliable information was developed regarding any other such incidents in the VR-57 suite.

Air Test and Evaluation Squadron Four (VX-4)
Naval Air Station, Point Mugu, CA

Hilton Suite Number:	360
Commanding Officer:	CAPT Thomas A. Perkins, USN (attended Tailhook '91)
Executive Officer:	(attended Tailhook '91)
Contributing Squadrons:	VX-4
Squadron Members Attending:	32
Suite Financing:	VX-4 Officer Fund, individual assessments, and the sale of T-shirts at air shows

Hours of Operation: Thursday, 5:00 p.m. to Friday,
                                       4:00 a.m.; Friday, 5:00 p.m.
                                       to Saturday, 4:30 a.m.;
                                       Saturday, 5:00 p.m. to
                                       Sunday, 5:00 a.m.

Type of Alcohol Served: Beer and "bushwhackers"

Total Cost of Alcohol: $8,500

Total Cost of Suite Damage:* $1,800

The CO and XO of the VX-4 advised that prior to Tailhook '91 they decided they wanted their suite to be a class act. The XO explained that, because the VX-4 is the operational and test evaluation unit for all of the Navy F-18 and F-14 air-to-air missile and related software products, he anticipated there would be a number of contractor executives and high-ranking naval officers visiting the suite. He also expected there would be a number of junior officers visiting the suite who might be interested in assignments with the VX-4. The XO said it was important, therefore, that the VX-4 suite be operated professionally and with decorum. He noted that, prior to Tailhook '91, he recieved a letter and a telephone call from CAPT Ludwig, the Tailhook Association President and former VX-4 CO, regarding appropriate behavior at the convention. The XO said CAPT Ludwig told him he wanted the VX-4 squadron to maintain its good image, and that CAPT Ludwig indicated he did not want strippers performing in the suites at Tailhook '91.

The CO and XO said they set ground rules for the operation of the suite. The suite was not open before 5:00 p.m. each day. The CO also said he denied a request from the squadron members to have strippers perform in the suite. The XO told us he and the CO decided not to have strippers in the suite because they did not know how the strippers might conduct themselves. Several squadron members

---

*The VX-4 CO advised that the Hilton Hotel billed the squadron $1,800 to replace carpet damaged by cigarette burns and spilled drinks. The squadron disputed those damages and asked the Tailhook Association to intervene with the hotel. The CO said he has been advised by Mr. Ron Thomas, the Executive Director of the Tailhook Association, that the Hilton Hotel decided not to pursue the matter.

stated that prior to Tailhook '91 they did receive instructions from the XO about such things as the administration of the suite, the dress code, and that the VX-4 suite was to be conducted with higher standards than some of the other squadron suites.

According to the primary suite coordinator, the suite was funded by collecting $10 per month over a one-year period from each of the squadron members who were planning to attend Tailhook '91. He said there was no command influence or coercion in collecting the money and if anyone refused to contribute, it meant they were not going to attend. The goal was to collect $4,000 to pay for the suite operation and any damages that might result. Another suite coordinator told us the funding also came from the sale of squadron T-shirts at air shows. He said after the initial $4,000 was spent in Las Vegas on the suite rental and the purchase of alcohol, approximately $4,500 more was raised by asking all VX-4 squadron officers to each contribute an additional $40 and by using a number of personal credit cards.

The VX-4 suite served beer and a specialty drink called "bush-whackers" made from rum and Kahlúa. The bushwhackers proved to be a popular drink, which apparently was the reason why the suite overspent on its alcohol budget. Early on Friday evening, the suite stopped serving bushwhackers for a time so as not to run out later. The suite had a drink machine and bar and showed videos of some VX-4 flight operations. According to information submitted by the VX-4 CO to the Naval Inspector General in November 1991, the suite hours of operation were from 5:00 p.m. to 3:00 a.m. each day. Several suite coordinators and bartenders stated, however, that the suite remained open until 4:30 a.m. or 5:00 a.m. all three days of the symposium.

The VX-4 squadron logo/mascot is the Playboy Bunny symbol. The VX-4 hired two cocktail waitresses, described as college-age girls dressed in rented Playboy Bunny costumes, consisting of short, black tuxedo jackets, leotards, and bunny ears and tails, to serve drinks in the suite. On Saturday night around 11:00 p.m. to 12:00 midnight, a drunken male reportedly grabbed one of the waitresses on the buttocks and tore off her bunny tail. The man was escorted out of the suite. The squadron also hired a female bartender who was reportedly dressed in shorts and a polo shirt. A male Air Force officer assigned to VX-4 stated he was given a squadron T-shirt that he wore while helping to distribute drinks. Several persons who visited the suite, including one female naval officer, described the bartender and cocktail waitresses as being conservatively and tastefully dressed.

A number of those who visited the suite described it as "mellow" and "dignified." One junior officer, who stated that he spent a good deal of time talking to people in the VX-4 suite because he was interested in getting assigned to that squadron, described the VX-4 members as a prestigious, clean, neat group. Another officer stated he was in and out of the VX-4 suite several times over the weekend and he remembered several fully clothed females, dressed in black, dancing in the suite.

The VX-4 squadron members who were interviewed consistently reported there were no strippers, pornographic movies, or other inappropriate entertainment in the suite. However, other persons gave descriptions of the VX-4 suite that contradicted those of the squadron members. Most notable were the several reports of strippers performing in the VX-4 suite. At least eight male Navy or Marine Corps officers, none of whom were VX-4 members, stated they either heard of or saw strippers performing in the VX-4 suite. It is important to note that only one of those officers said with certainty that he saw the stripper in the VX-4 suite. The recollections of the others were not as specific, but they all mentioned the VX-4 suite as possibly or probably where they saw or heard about strippers performing.

Two other specific accounts of strippers performing in the VX-4 suite came from two civilian women. The two women were interviewed independently and gave similar accounts of going into the VX-4 suite sometime just after 11:00 p.m. on Saturday night, immediately after being assaulted in the gauntlet. One of the victims said that while in the VX-4 suite she saw a woman dancing on a table who took off her top, baring her breasts. The other victim said that she observed two strippers dancing in the VX-4 suite. She said because of the crowd in the room she could only see the upper bodies of the women, both of whom had their breasts exposed. She commented that she thought the strippers were either standing on some elevated platform or were on someone's shoulders because their hands were touching the ceiling. She also recalled the rap song "Me So Horny" was playing on the stereo. Both witnesses said that at the same time they saw the strippers performing there was a pornographic movie playing on the television screen. Both women said, with some degree of certainty, that it was in the VX-4 suite where they witnessed those events. One of the women specifically mentioned relating the events to the Playboy Bunny symbol represented in the suite. The CO of the VX-4 was recontacted after his initial interview in an effort to reconcile the contradictory accounts of whether there were strippers in the suite. He reiterated his initial statements that he had denied the squadron's request for permission to have strippers perform, and he had no knowledge of strippers or pornographic entertainment in the VX-4 suite at Tailhook '91. The VX-4 CO also said he was in the immediate vicinity or actually in the VX-4 suite on Saturday night during the times when the two women gauntlet victims said they saw strippers in the suite.

Investigation disclosed that the VX-4 suite was located in the area where the gauntlet ended. Numerous people described being in the hallway near the VX-4 suite when they saw women exit the gauntlet who appeared to have been grabbed, groped, or more seriously assaulted. One female victim said she and another woman were assaulted in the gauntlet and that they sought refuge in the VX-4 suite. She stated they locked themselves in the suite bathroom and discussed their shock at being assaulted. There was one reported instance where a Navy lieutenant witnessed a visibly upset woman with a torn blouse, either in or near the VX-4 suite, who was being followed by three men who were laughing and urging the woman to come back to them. Investigation failed to identify either the woman or the three men. The lieutenant who witnessed the incident and who gave assistance to the woman was killed in an aircraft crash in February 1992. Other VX-4 squadron members reported hearing of the incident secondhand. The VX-4 CO reported that he heard the terms "gauntlet" and "admiral's aide" yelled from the hall while he was in the VX-4 suite. Aside from those reports, there were no VX-4 squadron members who admitted having witnessed gauntlet activity or seen women in distress.

CHIEF OF NAVAL AIR TRAINING (CNATRA)
NAVAL AIR STATION, CORPUS CHRISTI, TX
* * * * * * *
TRAINING SQUADRON 24 (VT-24)
TRAINING WING III
NAVAL AIR STATION, BEEVILLE, TX

Hilton Suite Number: 364

Commanding Officer:

RADM William P. McGowen, USN (attended Tailhook '91)

* * * * * * *

CDR Austin G. Abercrombie, USN (VT-24) (attended Tailhook '91)

Executive Officer:

(attended Tailhook '91)

Contributing Squadrons:

VT-24 and all other squadrons and miscellaneous commands within the CNATRA organizational structure

Squadron Members Attending: Approximately 400* CNATRA officers

Suite Financing:

$5,000 surplus from CNATRA hospitality suite at Tailhook '90 and individual assessments of $35 from participating officers

Hours of Operation:

Thursday, 2:00 p.m. to Friday, 2:00 a.m.; Friday, 2:00 p.m. to Saturday, 2:00 a.m.; Saturday, 2:00 p.m. to Sunday, 2:00 a.m.

Type of Alcohol Served:

Margaritas, beer, open bar

Total Cost of Alcohol:

Estimated at $5,000 to $7,000 (exact amount unavailable)

Total Cost of Suite Damage:

Some carpet damage reported (exact amount unavailable)

*The CNATRA records indicate that approximately 400 officers contributed funds for operation of the CNATRA suite. However, one naval officer in charge of transportation estimated that as many as 800 CNATRA officers attended.

The Chief of Naval Air Training (CNATRA) is a major Navy command responsible for the training of Navy and Marine Corps aviators and aviation support personnel such as landing signal officers (LSOs). The CNATRA is headquartered at NAS Corpus Christi, Texas. The CNATRA encompasses a large number of training squadrons and other subordinate commands located at various locations primarily in Texas, Florida,* and Mississippi.

By many accounts, the CNATRA has hosted one of the most popular hospitality suites at the Tailhook conventions. In recent years, many aviators told us they made it a point to visit the CNATRA suite in the hope of meeting persons they knew from flight school either as instructors or fellow students. Many of those who went to Tailhook '91 from the training commands were among the youngest officers at the convention and told us that was their first visit to Tailhook. No fewer than 400 people told us they visited the CNATRA suite at some point during Tailhook '91.

Historically, the CNATRA suite has been hosted by one of the training squadrons within the command, with responsibility to host the suite passing from one squadron to another each year. Reportedly, the suite was funded by contributions from officers assigned to the various CNATRA squadrons, with any surplus funds turned over to the squadron responsible for the next year's suite. A Navy commander responsible for the suite in 1985 and 1986 told us that in

*At the time of Tailhook '91, the CNATRA was organized into six training wings, each of which had subordinate training squadrons and/or other subordinate commands. Training Wing I, located at NAS Meridian, Mississippi, consists of training squadrons VT-7 and VT-19. Training Wing II, located at NAS Kingsville, Texas, consists of squadrons VT-21, VT-22, and VT-23. Training Wing III was located at NAS Beeville, Texas, and consisted of squadrons VT-24, VT-25, and VT-26. (Training Wing III and all three squadrons were decommissioned in 1992. The NAS Beeville, Texas was closed on February 1, 1993.) Training Wing IV, located at NAS Corpus Christi, Texas, includes squadrons VT-27, VT-28, and VT-31. Training Wing V, located at NAS Whiting Field, Florida, consists of squadrons VT-2, VT-3, and VT-6, a Marine Training Support Group (MATSG), and squadrons HT-8 and HT-18. Training Wing VI, located at NAS Pensacola, Florida, consists of squadrons VT-4, VT-10, and VT-86. Other CNATRA subordinate commands located at NAS Pensacola include the Navy Flight Demonstration Squadron (Blue Angels), the Navy Aviation School Command, and a Marine Training Support Group. The CNATRA also includes a Naval Air Training United located at Mather Air Force Base, California.

years prior to and including 1985 any CNATRA officers attending Tailhook would each donate $1. He said that additional funding in those years came from squadron-sponsored fund raisers such as pool parties and golf tournaments. He went on to say that at Tailhook '86, the CNATRA rented a larger suite at the Hilton Hotel. In order to raise the additional money needed to fund the larger suite, each person who attended was required to pay a $25 fee to "step" into the room and enjoy the bar and activities.

Several witnesses connected the CNATRA suite to incidents they recalled from past Tailhooks. For example, a Navy lieutenant commander, a member of the Tailhook Association since 1977 who had only missed one Tailhook convention in the last 15 years, told us about an incident he observed in the CNATRA suite during Tailhook '85. He said that a woman attempted to perform an amateur strip show in another suite but was escorted out. She then went to the adjacent CNATRA suite where she was encouraged by clapping and shouting. He observed the woman in a state of undress, bouncing on the bed. The officer recalled that one of the males in the suite removed his own clothing, got behind the woman while she was on all fours, and attempted to have sexual intercourse with her. He went on to say that he recalled the man was having some difficulty, he presumed because of the crowd of people watching.

Witnesses related instances of stripper performances, ballwalkers, other acts of indecent exposure, and public sex acts that took place in the CNATRA suite during the years 1985 through 1990. A Marine Corps officer told us that, in one particular incident during Tailhook '90, he witnessed four or five men throw a couch out of an open window in the CNATRA suite. Three other Navy lieutenants independently reported the same incident. The three lieutenants stated that although they had not personally witnessed the incident, they were certain it had occurred. Another five naval officers each reported they had heard of the event, but had no first-hand knowledge. Of the nine persons who mentioned the couch incident to us, not one could (or would) identify the persons who had done it. One of the three lieutenants who did not personally witness the incident, but who said he knew that it had actually happened, wrote an article about his squadron's experiences at Tailhook '90. In the September 21, 1990, edition of "The Flying K," a publication of the NAS Kingsville, Texas, the officer wrote:

> The 1990 Tailhook Symposium is over. The good news is that all Redhawks returned home relatively

unharmed and none were convicted of any crimes (felonies, that is). This is not to say that there was any lack of excitement at the 34th annual convention held in the Las Vegas Hilton.

The days were filled with interesting lectures, forums, and demonstrations, while the nights were characterized by celebration, joviality, and debauchery. Once again the CNATRA Suite proved to be the most hospitable and popular. . . .

In three fun filled nights, CNATRA visitors drained the suite of 40 kegs of beer, 450 gallons of margaritas containing 315 liters of tequila and 15 cases of liquor.

Conveniently located on the third floor overlooking the parking lot, the suite provided a base for the flight testing of various household objects. LT [name deleted] commented on this activity. "The couch failed its initial spin evaluation and suffered complete strike damage. The garbage cans proved, to the dismay of the 'engineers,' to be more aerodynamic than the couch."

Airborne furniture turned out to be just a portion of the fun, thanks to the entertainment committee of LT[s] [names deleted] . . . While [names deleted] called upon their management skills as "performer liaison officers," [name deleted] chose to entertain the crowd with his own rendition of the Vegas Shuffle. There was no encore.

The naval officer who wrote the article told us the amount of alcohol consumption reported in the article was factual. He also added that on the first night (Thursday) of Tailhook '90 there were trash cans thrown out of the CNATRA suite window. He said that, out of concern someone on the parking lot three floors below might be injured, it was decided to have the Hilton Hotel bolt the windows shut and that was accomplished by the second night. He said the couch was thrown out the window on Saturday night after someone apparently managed to unbolt the windows. He recalled the Hilton Hotel was paid $800 for the couch that had been destroyed.

The CNATRA suite at Tailhook '91 was hosted by training squadron VT-24 (now decommissioned) from the NAS Beeville, Texas.

According to the CNATRA command and the VT-24 CO, the squadron received $5,000, which represented surplus funds from Tailhook '90 when the CNATRA suite had been hosted by VT-22. According to the VT-24 CO and XO, an additional $10,000 to $15,000 was raised from individual $35 assessments levied on each of the participating CNATRA officers. According to the VT-24 CO, there was a surplus of approximately $5,000 after Tailhook '91. That money was divided equally and deposited to the Navy Recreation Funds at Pensacola, Florida, and Corpus Christi, Texas.

According to the CNATRA Chief of Staff, tickets were initially distributed to officers who paid their $35, but it was later ordered there not be any further tickets distributed for fear it might be misconstrued that the $35 payment was for travel to Tailhook on the Navy C-9 flights. Nonetheless, at least five officers told us they were under the impression their contribution went toward operation of the CNATRA suite and transportation to Las Vegas on the Navy C-9 flights.

The CNATRA command and the VT-24 CO told us instructions were given to the officers who served as duty officers in the suite and that the instructions included a prohibition on "dancing girls" (strippers), as well as the need for crowd control, suite clean-up details, authorized hours of operation, and the authority of duty officers to eject anyone who was "out of control." The VT-24 CO also stated that he instructed the four lieutenants who were primarily responsible for the operation of the suite that he did not want the men in the suite to act like animals, and he explicitly told them he did not want any strippers in the suite. The VT-24 XO told us he recalled that the CO instructed the primary suite coordinator that he wanted everything to be "by the book" and he expected appropriate behavior. The VT-24 CO said the four suite coordinators lodged in a suite on the third floor adjacent to the CNATRA suite.

The COs of some other training squadrons told us they also gave instructions to officers under their command. A Navy commander, who was the CO of VT-19 at the time of Tailhook '91, said that before the C-9 flight left for Las Vegas he advised his squadron not to embarrass the command, to be careful, and to take care of themselves. He added that he did not allow any students to attend Tailhook if they had never landed on a carrier. The CO of VT-22, who was the XO of the same squadron at the time of Tailhook '91, said that he encouraged all of his subordinate officers to attend. He also recalled giving the VT-22 squadron members his "sex, drugs, and rock and roll'' speech prior to the symposium. He said he cautioned his squadron about AIDS, one-night stands, and drinking to excess. He told them not to do anything about which they might be ashamed and that they would be held accountable for their actions at Tailhook. He said he told them to have a good time, but that they were expected to attend and participate in the official symposium professional presentations. He said he told them not to take their clothes off in public.

Junior officers assigned to the training squadrons at the time of Tailhook '91 said they went to Tailhook for various reasons. Some said they believed they were expected to attend and that it would reflect poorly on them if they did not go. Some said they were encouraged to attend Tailhook '91 in order to participate in the symposiums and mingle in the CNATRA suite where they could meet fellow aviators and build a foundation for their careers. Others said they attended Tailhook '91 primarily for the social aspects. According to the CNATRA command in its written submission to the Navy IG, "No mandatory attendance was required (of CNATRA officers) at any official event or social activity."

The VT-24 CO and XO said they periodically stopped at the CNATRA suite every day/evening of the symposium. The CO said he would check with the four lieutenants assigned as suite coordinators to get a verbal report on the evening's activities. He recalled he was told that on Friday night there were a few people thrown out of the suite because they had too much to drink. The VT-24 CO also recalled that at about 9:00 p.m. on Friday, a lieutenant from VT-26 told him that money had been collected from men in the CNATRA suite for a stripper performance. The CO said he was initially opposed to the idea, but he then gave permission for the stripper to perform for two songs. The CO said he was present when the stripper performed and he ensured that she left the suite after two songs. That was corroborated by the XO and by a lieutenant. The lieutenant told us that on Friday night the VT-24 CO approached him and instructed him to get the stripper out of the suite. The lieutenant recalled the CO gave him the keys to a suite adjoining the CNATRA suite where he escorted her after her performance. The lieutenant added that the stripper dressed and immediately left to do her act at another suite. He also recalled that the VT-24 CO was pretty upset the stripper was performing in the CNATRA suite.

Despite the CO's statements he had permitted a stripper in the CNATRA suite only for one brief performance on Friday evening, our investigation identified witnesses who stated there were strippers in the suite on other nights as well. At least 52 people told us there were strippers in the CNATRA suite at Tailhook '91. Eighteen of those said a stripper performed on Friday night. Eleven people said a stripper performed on Saturday, and two people recalled seeing a stripper in the CNATRA suite on Thursday. The other 21 witnesses recalled seeing a stripper in the CNATRA suite but could not specify the night. Most of the descriptions of the strippers' performances were consistent in that the acts were unremarkable and there was minimal contact between the strippers and the audience except for an occasional tip placed in the strippers' G-strings.

There was a ballwalking incident in the CNATRA suite on Saturday evening. A lieutenant junior grade admitted that he and four other officers ballwalked in the suite on a dare. A female Navy ensign stated she was assaulted on Saturday night in the suite when a drunken man placed his hands on her breasts.

There were two female cocktail waitresses serving drinks each night in the CNATRA suite. Both women wore black shorts and Tailhook '91 T-shirts provided by the suite coordinators and worked strictly for tips.

The waitresses described their experiences over the three days as unpleasant, reporting that they were continually pinched, grabbed, and groped by the men in the suite and that the men placed squadron stickers on their breasts and buttocks even though the women repeatedly told the men to stop. They also said the men looked down their T-shirts and suggested that they could make better tips if they cut their T-shirts to be more revealing. One waitress said the men grabbed her T-shirt, pulled it open, and looked at her breasts. Both waitresses said they were subjected to vulgar and lewd comments from the men in the suite. One waitress said she was bitten on the buttocks in the suite on Saturday night. The other woman said she saw men ballwalking in the suite on Saturday night. Both waitresses agreed that the behavior of the men in the suite got progressively more vulgar from Thursday to Saturday. One said the men in the suite went "crazy" during the Saturday night stripper performance and they subsequently refused to serve drinks while the stripper was performing. Only two of the male aviators we interviewed who stated they were in the CNATRA suite mentioned the treatment of the waitresses. Both men commented that they saw the waitresses get zapped on the buttocks with squadron stickers while one recalled that the waitresses seemed agreeable to the zapping and that they wore revealing clothing.

The admiral who commands CNATRA, RADM McGowen, told us he was in the CNATRA suite on Thursday and Friday evenings. That was consistent with other reports by junior officers. The admiral said he did not observe any unacceptable behavior while he was in the CNATRA suite but he later "learned that they had a stripper in there one night." He further said it was his understanding that the CO of VT-24 acted properly in having the stripper leave after just a short performance in which nothing improper occurred. He also told us he was not certain if he was on the third floor on Saturday night but was definitely not in the suite on Saturday.

STRIKE FIGHTER WING PACIFIC (STRKFIGHTWINGPAC) NAVAL AIR STATION, LEMOORE, CA

Hilton Suite Number:	371
Commanding Officer:	CAPT D. C. Kendall, USN (attended Tailhook '91)
Executive Officer:	(attended Tailhook '91)
Contributing Squadrons:	VFA-125, 27, 97, 113, 125, 127, 146, 151; VAQ-34; Strike Fighter Weapons School; and Association of Naval Aviation
Squadron Members Attending:	21 from VFA-125 and approximately 53 from the other contributing squadrons
Suite Financing:	$4,000 from the above-referenced contributing squadrons
Hours of Operation:	Thursday, 2:00 p.m. to Friday, 4:00 a.m.; Friday, 8:00 a.m. to Saturday, 3:00 a.m.; Saturday, 8:00 a.m. to Sunday, 3:00 a.m.

Type of Alcohol Served: Keg beer and premixed drinks

Total Cost of Alcohol: $1,030

Total Cost of Suite Damage: No damage; additional $100
                              cleaning fee

Strike Fighter Squadron One Two Five (VFA-125), Naval Air Station Lemoore, CA, was the host squadron for the hospitality suite in room 370. Although the suite was administered by the VFA-125, it was funded by the various squadrons that make up the STRKFIGHT-WINGPAC. Squadron members told us the purpose of the suite was to afford those officers from the VFA-125 and the other contributing squadrons a place to meet while at the convention. The suite was set up to display the activities and highlight the accomplishments of the Strike Fighter Wings. The focal point of the suite was a 5-hour video featuring the F/A-18 Hornet. According to Tailhook attendees, the suite also sponsored entertainment in the form of music and dancing, and served two specialty drinks, "cubi specials" and "hornet stingers." The suite coordinators informed us they used the services of two bartenders and three waitresses in the suite on Friday and Saturday evenings to assist in the serving of alcoholic beverages.

The VFA-125 XO told us that, prior to Tailhook '91, squadron members were lectured by the CO as to their conduct and behavior at the convention. Specific instructions were given prohibiting pornographic movies or the hiring of strippers as entertainment for the suite. Squadron members confirmed that such instructions were given by the CO and included information from CAPT Ludwig's letter of August 15, 1991, regarding problems at previous Tailhooks.

Information provided by VFA-125 members during the course of the investigation reflected that at previous Tailhooks (and recommended for use at future Tailhooks) the squadron used invitations or "invites" as a means to encourage female civilians to attend the convention. Documents obtained from the squadron reflected remarks regarding the use of such "invites." In part, the instructions read, "Invites are a nice thing to have and guys love to give them out. If you are really aggressive you could mail them out to the UNLV* sororities."

---

*Our investigation determined that eight UNLV female students were assaulted

FIGHTER SQUADRON 124 (VF-124)
NAVAL AIR STATION, MIRAMAR, CA

Hilton Suite Number: 373

Commanding Officer: CAPT George Moe, USN
(attended Tailhook '91)

Executive Officer: (attended Tailhook '91)

Contributing Squadrons: Fighter Squadrons VF-1, 2,
24, 51, 111, and 211

Squadron Members Attending: 78

Suite Financing: No individual assessment:
profits from the sale of
squadron memorabilia and
contributions of approximately
$4,500 from supporting
squadrons

Hours of Operation: Thursday, 3:00 p.m. to Friday,
2:00 a.m.; Friday, 3:00 p.m.
to Saturday, 2:00 a.m.;
Saturday, 3:00 p.m. to
Sunday, 2:00 a.m.; alcohol
served 3:00 p.m. to 2:00 a.m.

Type of Alcohol Served: Keg beer and margaritas

Total Cost of Alcohol: $1,954

Total Cost of Suite Damage: $412 for damage (stains) to the
furniture

The VF-124 suite was called the "Fightertown" suite as it represented other fighter squadrons based at Naval Air Station, Miramar,

---

at Tailhook '91; two other local female college students who attended Tailhook
'91 at the suggestion of UNLV students were also assaulted. Seven of the ten
college students were under the legal drinking age of 21.

CA, and derived some of its funding to support the suite from those squadrons. By most accounts, the "Fightertown" suite was organized and administered as an entertainment-type suite.

The squadron commander told us he received CAPT Ludwig's letter of August 15, 1991, regarding various problems at previous Tailhook conventions. The commander furnished documents pertaining to specific guidance and instructions given by him on the administration of the suite and conduct at the convention, to specifically include the treatment of female guests. During our interviews of squadron members, a number of them confirmed receiving such instructions at an all-officers meeting prior to Tailhook '91. The commander informed us he attended the convention out of an obligation to his squadron and he visited the suite to ensure everything was running smoothly. In addition to the commander, the squadron's executive officer attended Tailhook '91.

The entertainment in the suite, as described during the course of our investigation, consisted of a disk jockey being hired each evening to play music; one stripper hired for Friday evening and two strippers hired for Saturday evening. In addition, pornographic movies were shown at various times throughout the weekend and there were reported incidents of group ballwalking (involving as many as 10 men) and public sexual acts in the suite. Also, underage females reportedly had to be removed from the suite.

Witnesses stated that the stripper who performed on Friday evening received tips, in some instances by taking the money from the aviator (dollar bills) with her vagina. The performance of Saturday was further described as being lewd. On that night, the strippers performed as sadomasochists and lesbians. Sexual contact between a number of the aviators and the strippers was reported, to include the strippers fondling the exposed genitals or sitting on the faces of participating aviators. One of the strippers reportedly used a whip as part of her act, using it to draw onlookers to the "stage" where they then had physical contact with the strippers.

A number of aviators also said that, during the strippers' performance on Saturday evening, a male and female couple engaged in sexual intercourse in the rear of the suite directly behind aviators who stood watching the strippers perform.

The commander denied any previous knowledge of, or providing authorization for, the hiring of strippers. The executive officer told us that he had heard plans were being made for the hiring of strippers. During the course of our investigation, the President of the

Tailhook Association was questioned regarding the hiring of strippers to perform at the convention. He stated that he personally telephoned the commander of VF-124 prior to Tailhook '91 and asked him not to have strippers at Tailhook '91. Regarding the strippers' performances, which occurred late in the evenings, squadron members informed us that the suite was very crowded at the time; that an announcement as to the performance was made; that women were present; and that the door to the suite was closed during the show.

A number of photographs were provided during our investigation that depicted men (who were later identified as naval aviators) wearing T-shirts imprinted with "HE-MAN WOMAN HATER CLUB" and "WOMEN ARE PROPERTY." Our investigation determined that the T-shirts originated sometime prior to Tailhook '91 and were not specifically made for the convention. The T-shirts were originally sold by individuals associated with the VF-124.

Squadron members were not entirely candid during the interview process. The graphic descriptions of the strippers' performances in the hospitality suite and the information on the public sex acts taking place were told to us by Tailhook attendees who, for the most part, were not associated with the VF-124.

NAVY FIGHTER WEAPONS SCHOOL (TOP GUN)
NAVAL AIR STATION, MIRAMAR, SAN DIEGO, CA

Hilton Suite Number: 379 and 380

Commanding Officer: CAPT J. A. Robb, USN
(attended Tailhook '91)

Executive Officer: (attended Tailhook '91)

Contributing Squadrons: None

Squadron Members Attending: 24

Suite Financing: Squadron dues from the TOP GUN Officers' Fund

Hours of Operation: Thursday, 4:00 p.m. to Friday,
4:00 a.m.; Friday, 4:00 p.m.
to Saturday, 4:00 a.m.;
Saturday, 4:00 p.m. to
Sunday, 4:00 a.m.

Type of Alcohol Served: Open bar drinks and keg beer

Total Cost of Alcohol: $1,020

Total Cost of Suite Damage: $75 for carpet cleaning and
wallpaper damage

The Navy Fighter Weapons School hospitality suite was commonly referred to as the TOP GUN suite. By most accounts, the TOP GUN suite was organized and administered as an entertainment-type suite.

The XO told us he received CAPT Ludwig's letter of August 15, 1991. During a squadron briefing, the CO instructed his staff that he was happy to have them attend Tailhook '91 but they were to conduct themselves professionally. The XO and suite coordinators were told to ensure that the suite was a "class act." The CO further instructed the staff that, since TOP GUN routinely hosted high-level corporate, Navy, Marine Corps, and Air Force management during the symposium, a positive atmosphere was imperative. The suite coordinators were directed to screen for underage guests and not to allow any inebriated individuals into the suite. Although there was one report of University of Nevada Las Vegas students in the suite, the XO told us that, while he bartended, he did not "card" anyone.

The entertainment in the suite, as described during the course of our investigation, consisted of a display of aircraft weaponry and tactical videos from the Persian Gulf War. The suite was described by squadron members as "quiet" and "docile" in comparison to other suites. One female Navy attendee related that she "felt comfortable in that suite because the guys were really nice." An open bar serving beer, sodas, and mixed drinks featured "cubi specials" as the suite's specialty drink. One squadron member told us that 12 full kegs of beer and 14 to 21 bottles of liquor were consumed in the suite. Hot dogs were also served. The TOP GUN administrative officer provided $3,000 to the suite coordinators to finance the purchase of liquor and hot dogs. The money had been obtained from the sale of TOP GUN T-shirts and other collectibles from the TOP GUN

Memorabilia Shop at the Naval Air Station Miramar. Two female civilian attendees stated they purchased Tailhook T-shirts in the suite for $10.

One squadron member related that, before the symposium, everyone attending had to sign up for jobs in the suite such as bartending, serving hot dogs, changing videotapes, or selling T-shirts. The "working list" was posted on the wall in the suite. Most squadron members stated the bartending duties were fulfilled by members of the squadron; however, one witness identified a civilian working as a bartender in the suite.

Despite the information received from squadron members as described above, it became evident during the course of our investigation that TOP GUN members had not been candid in providing any information concerning suite activities such as pornographic videos, stripper performances, indecent exposure, and discussions in the suite about assaults that had occurred in the hallway. Specifically, there were two reports of pornographic videos shown in the suite, six reports of stripper performances, two reports of indecent exposure, and three discussions about assaults that occurred in the hallway. Each of the instances was reported by members of either other military units or civilian Tailhook attendees. There were no reports of those incidents by current or prior TOP GUN squadron members.

Regarding the pornographic videos, a Navy officer could not recall which night he saw the videos, saying it could have been Thursday, Friday, or Saturday night. A female civilian distinctly recalled looking for one of the TOP GUN instructors and entering the suite between 9:00 p.m. to 10:00 p.m. on Saturday night when the lights were dimmed, the curtains were drawn, and a pornographic video was playing.

Some of the witnesses to the stripper performances were able to recall which nights the strippers performed while other witnesses were not. Two of the most vivid recollections were from one Navy officer and one Marine Corps officer. The Navy officer reported that at approximately 11:00 p.m. on Saturday night two strippers were in the suite. While the audience cheered and clapped, one stripper performed while the other handled the music. The Marine Corps officer reported that he entered the suite, finding it "really packed" while "several" professional strippers were performing on a "makeshift" stage of coffee tables pulled together.

Other information not provided by TOP GUN members related to discussions of assaults. Every TOP GUN member interviewed said they did not have any information concerning the assaults that took place in the hallway; however, information developed through interviews of other military personnel, at best, appeared contrary. On three separate occasions, conversations held in the suite indicated that TOP GUN members were aware of assaults taking place in the hallway. Specifically, one female attendee stated she told suite attendees that she did not want to go down the hallway because men had grabbed her buttocks when she went down it before. Another individual recalled being told by suite occupants to go around rather than through the hallway because women were getting grabbed there. A third conversation took place when a Navy officer came into the suite and said to the effect, "Hey, some guys down at the end of the hallway just picked up a naked girl and dropped her [on the floor]."

Several witnesses related that the Secretary of the Navy, numerous admirals, and various civilians and contractors visited the suite at different times throughout the symposium. In particular, one squadron member recalled having "to throw an admiral" and four other men out of the suite at 5:00 a.m. Friday morning.

Appendix F
Individual Victim/Assault
Summaries

Victim Number 1

Status/Service/Rank: Lieutenant (O-3)
United States Navy/Female

Date/Time of Incident: Thursday, September 5, 1992 —
7:00 p.m.

Place of Incident: Hallway, Third Floor, Las Vegas
Hilton

Victim 1 is a 29-year-old Navy lieutenant.

According to the victim, she entered the third-floor hallway at approximately 7:00 p.m. As she walked up the hallway, she was bitten on the buttocks. The victim turned, kicked her assailant in the shins, and threw her drink on him. She was able to identify her attacker as a foreign exchange pilot.

The victim felt that she handled the incident and objected to being labeled as a "victim" despite the fact that the bite caused a bruise on her buttocks.

Victim Number 2

Status/Service/Rank: Lieutenant (O-3)
United States Navy/Female

Date/Time of Incident: Thursday, September 5, 1991 —
8:00 p.m.

Place of Incident: Hallway (just outside CNATRA
suite), Third Floor, Las Vegas
Hilton

Victim 2 is a 31-year-old Navy lieutenant. She attended Tailhook '87
but did not participate in the related social activities in that year.

According to the victim, she was talking to friends in the hallway
outside of the CNATRA suite when she was approached from behind
and bitten on the buttocks by an unidentified white male. She felt
something touch her buttocks, looked down and noticed a man bent
over with his face next to her buttocks. Before she realized she had
been bitten, the male fled the vicinity.

The victim witnessed the individual return to the area within 5
minutes of her attack and bite her female friend on the buttocks. The
man again quickly left the area. The victim and her friend subsequently referred to the individual as "Shark," as they had heard
other witnesses to the incidents use the name in describing the individual.

VICTIM NUMBER 3

Status/Service/Rank: Civilian/Female

Date/Time of Incident: Thursday, September 5, 1991 —
9:00 p.m.
Friday, September 6, 1991–2:00
a.m.

Place of Incident: VMFAT-101 Administrative
Suite, Room 355
Hallway, Third Floor, Las Vegas
Hilton

Victim 3 is a 32-year-old civilian who resides in the San Diego,
California area. She attended Tailhook '91 with her friend, a male
Marine captain.

According to the victim, she and her friend were sitting in the
VMFAT-101 administrative suite, room 355, when she was bitten.
She described the assault as follows:

"A British pilot came up to me and bit me on the left hip. He bit me hard enough that his one tooth went through my cloths [*sic*] and broke the skin. The bite hurt me but I did not know I was bleeding until I lifted up my clothes to look. I could smell alcohol and I think he was very drunk." Her friend admonished the man, who apologized and walked away. At around 2:00 a.m. on Friday, the victim was in the hallway on the third floor in the area of room 307. "The same British guy came up behind me and bit me on the buttocks. The British man had bitten me so hard that he left a welt on my buttocks. It left a red mark and a large bruise."

According to the victim's friend, he and the victim were standing in the VMFAT-101 administrative suite when a man he recognized as a foreign military exchange officer approached the victim from behind and bit her on the buttocks. The victim shouted "Ouch!" and the witness told the man to "Knock it off. What are you doing?" The witness opined that the foreign officer had had too much to drink.

We note that this victim objected to being classified as a "victim" despite the fact that she was the subject of a physical assault.

VICTIM NUMBER 4

Status/Service/Rank: Civilian/Female

Date/Time of Incident: Thursday, September 5, 1991 —
                              10:00–11:00 p.m.

Place of Incident: Pool Patio, Third Floor, Las
                              Vegas Hilton

Victim 4 is a Federal Government employee.

According to the victim, she was standing on the pool patio talking with some friends when an unidentified man came up behind her and bit her on the buttocks. She turned and told the man, "Don't ever do that again." Approximately 30 minutes later, while the victim was still on the pool patio, the same man again approached her and bit her on the buttocks. She turned and admonished the man. She described him as being a white male who spoke with an Australian or English accent. About 30 minutes after the incident, the victim remained on the pool patio. She was talking with two unidentified men whom she described as senior Navy officers. While talking to the two officers, a different man came up behind her, put his arms around her, and grabbed both her breasts. She turned and yelled at the man. One of two men she had been talking to said to the man, "There are some people you don't do that to." The man then apologized but held up a "flight tag" and said, "See this ID, this gives me the right."

VICTIM NUMBER 5

Status/Service/Rank: Lieutenant (O-3)
                          United States Navy/Female

Date/Time of Incident: Thursday, September 5, 1991
                          Evening, Time Unknown

Place of Incident: Administrative Suite, Third Floor
                          Las Vegas Hilton

Victim 5 is a 25-year-old Navy lieutenant. She attended Tailhook '91 with one male and two female friends both of whom are Navy officers.

According to the victim, she went to the third floor of the Hilton Hotel on Thursday evening and entered one of the administrative suites in the vicinity of room 307. She was engaged in conversation with two male military officers, when an unknown male approached her and attempted to place his hand up her dress. The victim grabbed the man by the collar and slammed him into a wall. She told him that she was a Navy officer and an aviator, and she did not want him to touch her. A few moments later the same man bit her on the right side of her buttocks. The victim smashed her elbow into the man's body; he fell to the ground, and crawled out the suite door into the hallway. She described her assailant as having an accent that she believed to be Australian. He was "around 6', sort of dumpy, weighing between 175 and 200 pounds, with light brown hair."

VICTIM NUMBER 6

Status/Service/Rank: Civilian/Female

Date/Time of Incident: Thursday, September 5, 1991—
                           9:00–11:30 p.m.

Place of Incident: Unknown Hospitality Suite
                           Hallway, Third Floor, Las Vegas
                           Hilton

Victim 6 is a 24-year-old civilian from the Las Vegas, Nevada, area, who attended the Tailhook Association convention on Thursday, September 5, 1991, with her spouse who is an Air Force captain.

According to the victim, she and her husband visited several hospitality suites on the third floor of the Hilton. While standing in one of the suites, an unknown male walked by her and grabbed her buttocks with one hand. She turned around and told the man not to touch her again. She stated that the individual appeared to be "extremely intoxicated" and he continued to the bar to get a drink. The same individual returned to her, walked by, and grabbed her again. She told her husband what had occurred, and her husband told the individual not to do it again.

At approximately 11:30 p.m., she and her husband walked down the third-floor hallway to exit the area. The hallway was crowded with intoxicated males who were grabbing and pinching women as they walked down the hallway. She was grabbed on the buttocks with "full hand grabs" three or four times and men intentionally tried to rub up against her chest as she pushed through the crowded hallway. She was unable to determine who grabbed her because "hands would just come out from the sides and grab me."

VICTIM NUMBER 7

Status/Service/Rank: Lieutenant (O-3)
                           United States Navy/Female

Date/Time of Incident: Thursday, September 5, 1991
                           10:30–11:00 p.m.

                           Saturday, September 7, 1991
                           7:30–9:30 p.m.

Place of Incident: Hallway, Third Floor, Las Vegas
                           Hilton

Victim 7 is a 30-year-old female United States Navy lieutenant. She attended Tailhook '91 with two female friends, one civilian and one Naval Reserve officer. This was the second convention she attended, the first in 1990.

The victim told us that at Tailhook '90, she went down the hallway and was grabbed. She believed that the "brass" knew about the harassment and lewd behavior toward women in the hallway at Tailhook '90 and assumed they would address the behavior. Thus, she did not report her assault nor anything she saw to any higher authority.

According to the victim, while outside on the pool patio area at approximately 10:30 to 11:00 p.m. on Thursday, September 5, 1991, several males placed squadron stickers on her buttocks. Also on that evening, two to three males touched and patted her on the buttocks. Later, while in a suite, possibly the TOP GUN suite, she attempted to enter the rest room. A male blocked the doorway and would not let her enter. She told the male that her friend was in the rest room, but he still would not let her in. When she tried to go around him, he grabbed her shoulder with one hand to stop her. She told the male to take his hands off her and pushed his hand away. The male then grabbed her again, and she pushed him away from her. The male called her a "cunt," whereupon she threw her drink on him and ran out the door. The male began to follow, until she stopped to talk to three older men. She told the male that the older men were her protection, and he left her alone.

The victim told us that as a result of her being assaulted in the hallway at Tailhook '90, she knew to avoid the hallway in 1991 and was able for the most part to do so. The only exception was one incident on Saturday, when she was escorted by three other naval officers, one female and two males. According to the victim, while walking down the main hallway of the third floor, she was grabbed on the crotch by a male. She turned around, grabbed the male's arm, and punched him with her free hand. The victim felt very capable of dealing with the crowd because she had other "guys" with her; she indicated that she is not the "type to let some guy get away with pawing me if I can help it."

The victim explained that the gauntlet, as experienced and witnessed by her, "was not a formal organized thing; it was a bunch of drunken men in the hallway abusing women as they walked by." The victim stated that the gauntlet started at the elevator bays and continued along the hallway through room 360.

VICTIM NUMBER 8

Status/Service/Rank: Civilian/ Female

Date/Time of Incident: Thursday, Friday, Saturday,
                            September 5–7, 1991

Place of Incident: CNATRA Suite (Room 364),
                            Third Floor, Las Vegas Hilton

Victim 8 is a 24-year-old woman. At the time of Tailhook '91, she had just graduated from bartenders' school and, on graduation, the victim and a second female bartender were asked to serve drinks in the CNATRA suite on a tips-only basis. They worked from 5:00 p.m. until 3:00 a.m. on each of the three nights.

According to the victim, on Thursday, while she served drinks in the suite, males pinched and grabbed her on the buttocks. She told them to stop and they would for a time. Later, they resumed pinching and grabbing her. She stated that that happened five or six times during the evening. Also, some males "zapped" her on the buttocks with various squadron emblems. She told them to stop, but they continued to place the stickers on her throughout the evening.

On Friday she was grabbed and pinched on her buttocks and breasts throughout the evening with more frequency than on Thursday. The behavior in the suite was more "rowdy" than on the previous evening. She and her friend left the suite twice and they were both grabbed and pinched walking down the hallway.

The victim stated that the behavior was the worst on Saturday. She was constantly grabbed and pinched. The aviators would grab her T-shirt, pull it open from the neck, and try to look down her shirt to see her breasts. In addition, they would verbally abuse her by saying things like "Are those your tits, are they real," "You got big tits," and "I'd like to f— you."

The victim witnessed two males exposing themselves in the CNATRA suite on Friday evening. She also saw a blond stripper in the suite. After her performance, the stripper left the suite and returned later, wrapped in a towel, crying and upset. The victim thought the stripper had had sex with some of the males from the suite.

The victim said she returned each night because she is a single parent and needed the money.

VICTIM NUMBER 9

Status/Service/Rank: Civilian/Female

Date/Time of Incident: Thursday, Friday, Saturday, September 5–7, 1991

Place of Incident: CNATRA Suite (Room 364), Third Floor, Las Vegas Hilton

Victim 9 is a 23-year-old woman. At the time of Tailhook '91, she had just graduated from bartenders' school. The victim and a second female bartender were hired to serve drinks in the CNATRA suite. She worked from 5:00 p.m. until 3:00 a.m. on each of the three nights.

According to the victim, on Thursday while she served drinks in the suite, males "zapped" her on her breasts and buttocks with various squadron emblems. She told them to stop but they continued to place the stickers on her throughout the evening.

On Friday, she was grabbed and pinched on her buttocks and breasts throughout the evening. The men were more vulgar and their behavior was more aggressive than on the previous evening. The men continually tried to "look down her shirt" and were lewd and abusive in their comments. Remarks such as, "I want to get down your pants," "Cute ass," "Nice tits," were directed at her throughout the night.

The victim also witnessed two males exposing themselves in the CNATRA suite. On Friday evening, the men in the suite told her to look over at two men across the room who were ballwalking. She did not know what the term meant until she saw the men exposing their testicles. The men in the suite acted as though it was extremely funny. The victim stated that the behavior was the worst on Saturday, when most of the aviators were drunk. She noted that when strippers entered the suite and performed, the men went "crazy." After the show, the victim was pinched and grabbed all night long. The more the victim would tell the men not to touch her, the worse the grabbing got.

At one point, the victim was bitten on the buttocks while she was serving drinks. A white male came up behind her and very forcefully bit her buttocks. The bite was hard enough to cause a bruise. The man who bit her was in the suite all three nights. The aviators who saw the incident merely laughed about it. The victim also stated that the hallway was extremely crowded and grew progressively worse each night. She needed to go through the hallway to get to the elevators on her way to dinner. She and several other women entered the hallway and were pinched and grabbed. On subsequent trips to dinner, she took a male bartender with her to help protect her from the crowd.

VICTIM NUMBER 10

Status/Service/Rank: Lieutenant Junior Grade (0–2)
United States Navy/Female

Date/Time of Incidents: Friday and Saturday, September 1990
Saturday, September 7, 1991
Times Unknown

Place of Incidents: Guest Room and Hallway, Third Floor, Las Vegas Hilton—1990
VMFP-3 Administrative Suite, Room 308, Las Vegas Hilton—1991

Victim 10 is a 24-year-old female Navy lieutenant junior grade. She attended Tailhooks '90 and '91.

On Saturday night during Tailhook '91, the victim went into the "Rhino" administrative suite with a male Navy aviator acquaintance. She saw a rhino mural with "a very large rhino penis on it—they wanted women to come in there and please the rhino." The aviator accompanying the victim pushed her head up toward the attached dildo on the rhino mural, "close enough to it that they wanted me to put this in my mouth." She believed that she would not be allowed to leave the suite until she "pleased" the rhino. As the victim was shoved up to the rhino, she resisted, and a liquid substance from the dildo was squirted on her face and clothing. She was finally able to back away from the rhino when the attention in the suite shifted from her to another female who willingly stepped up to the rhino and "sucked the dildo." At that point the victim quickly exited the "Rhino" suite.

This woman was the alleged victim of an attempted rape while at Tailhook '90.

VICTIM NUMBER 11

Status/Service/Rank: Civilian/Female

Date/Time of Incident: Friday, September 6, 1991 —
                              10:00 p.m.

Place of Incident: VMFP-3 Administrative Suite
                              Third Floor, Las Vegas Hilton

Victim 11 is an 18-year-old student at the UNLV. She attended Tailhook '91 with another female student.

According to the victim, she and four or five female friends from UNLV went to the third floor of the Hilton Hotel to attend the party. The hallway was crowded with men and "there was puke everywhere," so they decided to cut through one of the administrative suites and go out to the pool patio. The victim and her friends entered a suite single file with the victim at the end of the line. She was holding her friend's hand so she would not be separated from the group. There were between 10 and 20 men in the room. The victim and her friends were the only females in the suite. Suddenly four men "jerked me away" from her friends and circled her. They began chanting and pushing her toward a painting of a rhinoceros with a penis attached. The victim did not know why they were pushing her toward the rhino, but she "knew it had something to do with that [penis]." She struggled and screamed for her friends to help her. One of her friends grabbed her arm and pulled her out of the suite. The victim later met a Navy officer and told him what had happened to her in the suite. The officer told the victim that the men in the suite were Marines.

VICTIM NUMBER 12

Status/Service/Rank: Civilian/Female

Date/Time of Incident: Friday, September 6 or Saturday,
September 7, 1991 — Time
Unknown

Place of Incident: Patio Area, Third Floor, Las
Vegas Hilton

Victim 12 is a 21-year-old female student at the UNLV. She attended Tailhook '91 with six other UNLV students.

According to the victim, sometime during the evening, an unidentified male came up behind her, bit her on the buttocks, and ran away.

A second incident also occurred on the same evening that involved another individual. She was asked by a male what she would do if he grabbed her breasts. He then proceeded to grab her breasts. Another male in the vicinity then gave the victim a drink, which she threw on the male who grabbed her.

VICTIM NUMBER 13

Status/Service/Rank: Civilian/Female/Tailhook
Association Employee

Date/Time of Incident: Friday, September 6, 1991 —
Evening, Time Unknown

Place of Incident: Pool Patio, Las Vegas Hilton

Victim 13, a 23-year-old San Diego resident, is employed by the Tailhook Association.

According to the victim, on Friday evening, September 6, 1991, she and her sister were standing on the third-floor pool patio of the Hilton Hotel. They were in front of the MAWTS-1 administrative suite, which was located in room 356. An unidentified male grabbed her around the waist from behind, squatted down behind her and bit her on the buttocks. The bite was not hard enough to hurt her or break the skin, but she was shocked. She spun around and faced her attacker, whom she described as an obviously intoxicated white male, 190 pounds, 5'10" tall with a "Marine" haircut.

As she turned around, the individual saw her Tailhook Association name tag; he got down on his knees and exclaimed, "I'm sorry. I'm sorry, I didn't know who you were." She told him that he was going to hurt someone or get in trouble, and he could be ejected from the convention for such behavior. Several aviators standing in the area asked her if she wanted them to do anything, and she replied that she was "just going to let this one go."

VICTIM NUMBER 14

Status/Service/Rank:	Ensign (O-1) United States Navy/Female
Date/Time of Incident:	Friday, September 6, 1991 — 8:00–9:00 p.m.
Place of Incident:	Hallway, Third Floor, Las Vegas Hilton

Victim 14 is a 22-year-old Navy ensign. She attended Tailhook '91 with a friend who is a male Navy officer.

According to the victim, she was walking in the crowded hallway on the third floor with three male Navy officers when an unidentified young male pinched her on the buttocks. She turned around and pushed him up against the wall.

She felt that she resolved the situation and does not consider herself to be a victim of an assault, even though the pinch was nonconsensual.

VICTIM NUMBER 15

(See page 246)

VICTIM NUMBER 16

Status/Service/Rank:	Civilian/Female

Date/Time of Incident: Thursday or Friday, September 5
                         or 6, 1991—10:30–11:30 p.m.

Place of Incident: Hallway, Third Floor, Las Vegas
                         Hilton

Victim 16 is a 20-year-old student at the UNLV. She attended Tailhook '90 and '91 with a female friend from the UNLV.

According to the victim, Tailhook '91 "really got out of hand." The hallway was full of crowds of drunken men. When she attempted to walk through the crowd, she was grabbed on the buttocks. The victim also saw a man with his testicles hanging outside his pants. She tried to ignore the incident but was embarrassed. She was not able to identify the men who grabbed her or the man who exposed himself.

VICTIM NUMBER 17

Status/Service/Rank: Civilian/Female

Date/Time of Incident: Friday, September 6, 1991—9:00
                         p.m. to Saturday, September 7,
                         1991—1:00 a.m.

Place of Incident: Hallway, Third Floor, Las Vegas
                         Hilton

Victim 17 is a 24-year-old Federal Government employee. She attended Tailhook '91 with two female civilian friends.

According to the victim, she arrived on the third floor of the Hilton Hotel and "tons of people" were in the hallway. She ventured into one of the administrative suites and saw an unidentified man exposing his penis/testicles. He said, "What do you think of this?" She and her friends left the suite and walked out into the hallway. A man picked up her friend and began twirling her around. (See Victim 44.) She yelled at him to put her friend down, which he eventually did. No matter where she walked, men stood by doorways waiting for women to pass by so they could grab them. The victim recalled being grabbed several times but could not recognize any of the men who grabbed her.

VICTIM NUMBER 18

Status/Service/Rank: Lieutenant Junior Grade (O-2)
United States Navy/Female

Date/Time of Incident: Friday, September 6, 1991—
10:00 p.m.

Place of Incident: Hallway, Third Floor, Las Vegas
Hilton

Victim 18 is a 26-year-old Navy lieutenant junior grade.

According to the victim, she and a male friend, who is a Navy officer, were walking down the hallway of the third floor of the Hilton Hotel when an unidentified man grabbed her on the buttocks. She quickly turned around and gave the man an angry look. He walked away. The victim did not tell her friend about the incident because she was afraid he would retaliate, and she did not want him to get into trouble. She told her friend she wanted to leave, and they departed the third floor.

VICTIM NUMBER 19

Status/Service/Rank: Lieutenant (O-3)
United States Navy Reserve/
Female

Date/Time of Incident: Friday, September 6, 1991—3:30
p.m.

Place of Incident: Hallway, Third Floor, Las Vegas
Hilton

Victim 19 is a 31-year-old Navy Reserve lieutenant.

According to the victim, she went to the third floor of the Hilton Hotel to locate a friend. She exited the main passenger elevator and walked 20 or 30 feet down the hallway when two unidentified males approached her. One of the men, who had a short "military cut" hairstyle, pushed her up against the wall.

Both men put their hands between her legs and grabbed her crotch. They then fondled her breasts. She broke free of the men and immediately left the third floor.

VICTIM NUMBER 20

Status/Service/Rank: Lieutenant (O-3)
                            United States Navy/Female

Date/Time of Incident: Friday, September 6, 1991 —
                            11:00 p.m.

Place of Incident: Hallway, Third Floor, Las Vegas
                            Hilton

Victim 20 is a 25-year-old Navy lieutenant.

According to the victim, she was walking down the hallway on the third floor of the Hilton Hotel when she was slapped or brushed on the buttocks. She turned around but no one was looking at her, and she was unable to determine who may have touched her.

As she walked back down the hallway toward the main passenger elevators, in the area of the HS-1 administrative suite in room 315, she was grabbed on the buttocks. She turned and saw two men, whom she believed to be Marines because of their short haircuts, in the doorway of the suite. She said, "You guys better watch what you're doing." She then told them that she was a Navy lieutenant and they had better be careful. The men did not believe her and responded, "Yeah, right." She did not report the incident to anyone, felt that she had taken care of the situation herself, and opined to us that she did not feel she had been "assaulted."

VICTIM NUMBER 21

Status/Service/Rank: Civilian/Female

Date/Time of Incident: Friday, September 6, 1991 —
                            12:00 midnight

Place of Incident: "Rhino" Suite

[*193*]

Victim 21 is a 23-year-old female who resides in California. She attended Tailhook '91 with two female civilian friends. At the time of Tailhook '91, the victim had a cast on her leg and was on crutches, as a result of an accident which occurred prior to the convention.

According to the victim, when she and one of her friends arrived on the third-floor hallway of the Hilton, they saw a large group of males toward the end of the hall and decided they did not want to go any further into the hallway. They then entered the "Rhino" suite and immediately saw the rhino mural. Suddenly a male grabbed one of the victim's crutches and pulled her toward the mural. The victim recalled that she looked specifically at the area of the dildo and noticed that an unidentified male standing behind the mural had removed the dildo and placed his penis in the hole where the dildo had been. The male stood there exposing his penis to the victim and others in the suite. At that point, the victim's friend pried the other male's hands off the victim's crutch, and they (the victim and her friend) immediately left the suite. The victim stated that she did not get upset at the incident and did not feel that she was assaulted.

VICTIM NUMBER 22

Status/Service/Rank	Lieutenant Junior Grade (O-2) United States Navy/Female
Date/Time of Incident:	Friday, September 6, 1991 — 6:00 p.m.
Place of Incident:	Hallway, Third Floor, Las Vegas Hilton

Victim 22 is a 23-year-old lieutenant junior grade in the United States Navy.

According to the victim, she and her boyfriend, a Navy lieutenant junior grade, went to the third floor of the Hilton Hotel on Friday, September 6, 1991, at approximately 6:00 p.m. They exited the passenger elevators and turned to walk up the hallway. A group of four or five men were walking toward her and, as they passed by, one of them reached out and grabbed her buttocks. She immediately turned around and saw one of the men looking at her.

Neither she nor her boyfriend recognized any of the men, but she described them as "definitely military" because of their short haircuts.

VICTIM NUMBER 23

Status/Service/Rank: Civilian/Female

Date/Time of Incident: Friday, September 7, 1991—
Time Unknown

Place of Incident: Hallway, Third Floor, Las Vegas
Hilton

Victim 23 is a 41-year-old civilian who resides in Arizona. She attended Tailhook '91 with a group of female civilian friends.

According to the victim, she and two female friends were walking down the third-floor hallway of the Hilton Hotel when they were suddenly "swarmed" by men. The victim was grabbed in the breasts and crotch. She and her friends tried to continue down the hallway, but they were thrown to the floor and grabbed repeatedly. The men threw their drinks on the women while the victims screamed and yelled at the men to stop. One of the victim's friends was crying, and the victim told her not all of the men at the convention acted like this and she should not allow this incident to ruin her entire weekend.

During Tailhook '91, the victim learned that the hallway was called the gauntlet. She did not recognize any of the men who assaulted her, but she believed them to be lower-ranking young military men.

VICTIM NUMBER 24

Status/Service/Rank: First Lieutenant (O-2)
United States Air Force/Female

Date/Time of Incident: Saturday, September 7, 1991—
12:30 a.m.

Place of Incident: Hallway, Third Floor, Las Vegas
Hilton

Victim 24 is a 23-year-old Air Force first lieutenant. She attended Tailhook '91 with two male friends both of whom are military officers.

According to the victim, she arrived on the third floor at about 10:30 p.m. on Friday evening. On entering the hallway area, she noted it was extremely crowded and that people were pouring out the doorways of the administrative suites. Her initial impression was, "I can't believe the Navy is paying for this." As she walked alone through the hallway, men made suggestive comments and obstructed her passage by standing in front of her. She again attempted to walk through the hallway at 12:30 a.m., at which time she was grabbed on the buttocks. Men cornered her and pressed close to her, intentionally brushing their chests against her breasts. Leers and provocative comments were directed at her. The victim also noticed that as other women walked through the hallway, they too were grabbed on the buttocks by men in the crowd.

The victim told us that she did not file a complaint because of repercussions she experienced in filing a previous complaint against fellow Air Force officers.

VICTIM NUMBER 25

Status/Service/Rank: Civilian/Female

Date/Time of Incident: Friday or Saturday, September 6–7, 1991—9:00 p.m. or 10:00 p.m.

Place of Incident: Hallway, Third Floor, Las Vegas Hilton

Victim 25 is a 19-year-old student at the UNLV.

According to the victim, she went to the Tailhook Association convention with two female friends on either Friday or Saturday evening and arrived on the third floor at approximately 9:00 or 10:00 p.m.

She became separated from her friends and began looking for them in the administrative suites. As she left one of the suites to go into the hallway, a man stopped her and said, "I don't think you want to go through there.'' She did not think anything was wrong except that there was a ''tremendous crowd and lots of noise.''

She entered the crowded hallway and felt numerous hands grabbing at her breasts, crotch, and buttocks. Men were making ''sexual comments'' to her as they grabbed at her body. She swung out with her arms and continued down the hallway. She tripped and fell down on her hands, falling out of the crowd. She looked back at the hallway through which she had just come and saw men ''lined up alongside the walls.'' She was not able to identify anyone in the hallway.

VICTIM NUMBER 26

Status/Service/Rank: Civilian/Female

Date/Time of Incident: Friday or Saturday, September 6
                            or 7, 1991—10:00 p.m.

Place of Incident: Hallway, Third Floor, Las Vegas
                            Hilton

Victim 26 is a 19-year-old student at the UNLV. She attended Tailhook '91 with several friends from the UNLV.

According to the victim, she walked through the third-floor hallway of the Hilton Hotel with two friends. The hallway was crowded with men who appeared to be drunk. The victim believed the men to be in the military because of their short haircuts. Her female friend walked ahead of the victim and a male friend walked behind her. Suddenly, men reached out, grabbing and groping the victim on the breasts, buttocks, and crotch. She screamed and covered herself with her arms. She could see that her female friend was also being assaulted. They finally got to the end of the crowd and left the hallway. After the incident, the victim spent the rest of the evening on the pool patio and avoided the third-floor hallway.

VICTIM NUMBER 27

Status/Service/Rank: Civilian/Female

Date/Time of Incident: Friday or Saturday, September 6 or 7, 1991—10:00 p.m.

Place of Incident: Unknown Suite(s), Third Floor, Hilton Hotel

Victim 27 is a 19-year-old female student at the UNLV. She attended Tailhook '91 with two girlfriends who are also students at the UNLV.

According to the victim, she and her friends went to the third floor of the Hilton Hotel at 10:00 p.m. on either Friday or Saturday. The victim went from suite to suite and stated that what she saw was "hard to believe." In one suite, the victim saw a green statue with an exposed "dildo" protruding from it that dispensed a margarita drink. She observed a girl on her hands and knees drinking from it.

As the victim walked through the suite's doorway to get to the pool patio area, two males on each side of the doorway reached out and grabbed her breasts and buttocks. The victim could not identify her assailants.

The victim and her friends also witnessed an instance of indecent exposure in another suite. As they entered this suite, a male tapped one of the victim's friends on the shoulder to get her attention. He then exhibited his "private parts." The victim remembers that two other males were laughing about it. The victim and her friends quickly left the area.

VICTIM NUMBER 28

Status/Service/Rank: Civilian/Female

Date/Time of Incident: Friday or Saturday Evening, September 6 or 7, 1991—Time Unknown

Place of Incident: Unknown

Victim 28 is a 44-year-old spouse of a Navy officer and resides in California.

According to the victim, she was on the third floor of the Hilton Hotel on Friday and Saturday evening, when a military junior officer "goosed" her on the buttocks. Another individual put his hand up her long dress to her knees. She told her husband about the incidents and they both laughed about it. She advised us that she did not consider herself a victim of assault.

VICTIM NUMBER 29

Status/Service/Rank: Civilian/Female

Date/Time of Incident: Friday and Saturday, September 6–7, 1991 — 11:30 p.m.

Place of Incident: Hallway, Third Floor, Las Vegas Hilton

Victim 29 is a 29-year-old woman who resides in Arizona.

According to the victim, on Friday night she was in the hallway when a man put his hands inside her top and grabbed her breasts. She chased him as he ran and was able to catch him because he fell. While he was on the ground, the victim proceeded to hit him. There were other persons present who saw the incident and laughed.

On Saturday she visited several suites on the third floor. At 11:00 p.m., she came out of a suite into the hallway and noticed about 15 military men standing on each side of the hall making various noises. She was with several friends and they all joined hands in an attempt to get to the elevators. The victim said that she and her friends were grabbed on the breasts and buttocks. She stated there were hands everywhere and the men looked like they were "in heat." She and her friends were shaken up by the incident and left the hotel.

VICTIM NUMBER 30

Status/Service/Rank: Lieutenant Commander (O-4), United States Navy, Female

Date/Time of Incident: Saturday, September 7, 1991 — 6:30 p.m.

Place of Incident: Hallway, Third Floor, Las Vegas Hilton

Victim 30 is a 36-year-old female United States Navy lieutenant commander. She has attended Tailhook Association conventions in 1987, 1989, 1990, and 1991.

According to the victim, on Saturday, September 7, 1991, at 6:30 p.m., she entered the third-floor hallway of the Las Vegas Hilton Hotel by way of the main passenger elevators. When she reached the area of the hallway between rooms 303 and 306, she felt someone reach around and through her right arm from behind and fondle her right breast. She immediately turned around and observed a group of five men with their backs to her. She believed one of those men committed the assault, but she did not confront them, and she continued to walk through the hallway.

During one previous Tailhook convention, she was grabbed in the crotch by an unknown male while she walked through the third-floor hallway. She immediately confronted the individual responsible, grabbed the man by his genitals, and asked, "How do you like it?" The man was quite surprised by her reaction and did not respond. She left the area feeling that she had dealt with the situation.

VICTIM NUMBER 31

Status/Service/Rank: Spouse of Naval Reserve Officer

Date/Time of Incident: Saturday, September 7, 1991—
                            10:30 p.m.

Place of Incident: Hallway, Third Floor, Las Vegas
                            Hilton

Victim 31, a 48-year-old spouse of a Navy Reserve officer, attended the Tailhook Association convention in 1991 with her daughter, son-in-law, who is a naval officer, and two female civilian friends. She had attended Tailhook conventions in 1986 and 1990 with her husband. He did not attend the Tailhook convention in 1991.

According to the victim, on Saturday evening, September 7, 1991, she, her friends, her daughter, and son-in-law left the "Rhino" suite (room 308) to go to the VR-57 suite (room 357). The hallway was packed with men lining both sides of the hallway. They proceeded to walk down the hallway with her son-in-law leading them single file. As she walked through the hallway, she was pinched several times. She turned around to find her friend, and her friend said, "Let's get out of here." She and her friend quickly exited through a nearby suite and out onto the pool patio where they met with the rest of their party.

Even though she was pinched, she was not fearful that anything would happen to her because she has "been associated with the Navy and pilots most of my life." However, she was concerned for her friend, who is 60 years old and probably does not know how a group of aviators having fun might behave.

VICTIM NUMBER 32

(See page 245)

VICTIM NUMBER 33

Status/Service/Rank: Civilian/Female

Date/Time of Incident: Saturday, September 7, 1991 —
                          After 10:00 p.m.

Place of Incident: Hallway, Third Floor, Las Vegas
                          Hilton

Victim 33, a 23-year-old woman from California, attended the Tailhook Association Symposium in 1991 with several friends who were female active-duty naval officers. This was the first Tailhook convention she attended.

According to the victim, on Saturday evening, September 7, 1992, after 8:00 p.m., she entered the third-floor hallway to look for her friends. She asked a male, whom she did not know, to escort her through the hallway because she had heard rumors that at past Tailhook conventions men grabbed and pawed women as they walked through the third-floor hallway, and she did not want to be grabbed. She was unable to identify the man, but stated that she nicknamed him "Smiley," and he was a Navy pilot.

After entering the hallway with Smiley, she was almost instantly caught up in a "rush" of people. As she walked through the hallway, a "wall of people" closed in behind her, and she was catapulted forward. She was grabbed and pawed by numerous hands. She believed she was being grabbed at random and that men who walked through the hallway were also being grabbed.

She was pushed through the hallway so quickly she did not have time to see who was assaulting her. She was unable to identify her assailants or anyone else in the hallway.

VICTIM NUMBER 34

Status/Service/Rank: Civilian/Female

Date/Time of Incident: Sunday, September 8, 1991 —
                             2:00 a.m.

Place of Incident: Hallway, Third Floor, Las Vegas
                             Hilton

Victim 34, a 20-year-old woman from Nevada, attended the Tailhook Association convention in 1991 with a female civilian friend.

According to the victim, she, her friend, and two male Navy lieutenants went to the third floor of the Hilton Hotel at approximately 2:00 a.m. on Sunday, September 8, 1991.

As they exited the passenger elevators and began to walk down the hallway, an unidentified male reached out and grabbed her buttocks. She quickly whirled around and one of the male lieutenants she was with pushed the individual and said, "You're an embarrassment to the Navy." She did not know the individual who grabbed her.

A Navy lieutenant who witnessed the incident stated that as he and the victim exited the elevators on the third floor of the Hilton on Sunday morning, September 8, 1991, and began to walk up the hallway, he observed an unknown male grab the victim on the buttocks. He physically pushed the man away and made "some type of remark" to him.

VICTIM NUMBER 35

(See page 246)

VICTIM NUMBER 36

Status/Service/Rank: Lieutenant (O-3)
                              United States Navy/Female

Date/Time of Incident: Saturday, September 7, 1991—
                              After 9:00 p.m.

Place of Incident: Hallway, Third Floor, Las Vegas
                              Hilton

Victim 36 is a 29-year-old Navy lieutenant.

According to the victim, she was on the third floor of the Hilton Hotel on Saturday, September 7, 1991, when she was "involved in a gauntlet incident." She was walking through the crowded hallway with a male Navy lieutenant, and "had no idea that this was a gauntlet." Suddenly, hands began grabbing at her. She crossed her arms over her breasts and ran through the closest administrative-suite door to escape from the gauntlet. She heard the man she was with yell at her attackers, but does not recall what he said. She was not able to identify any of the men in the gauntlet.

VICTIM NUMBER 37

Status/Service/Rank: Civilian/Female

Date/Time of Incident: Saturday, September 7, 1991
                              Evening—Time Unknown

Place of Incident: Hallway, Third Floor, Las Vegas
                              Hilton

Victim 37 is a 31-year-old civilian woman who resides in California. She attended Tailhook '91 with two female civilian friends.

According to the victim, prior to attending Tailhook '91, she was warned by another female friend that it was not a good idea to go on the third floor after 11:00 p.m. On Saturday evening, the victim did go into the third-floor hallway to look for her friends. The hallway was crowded and as she proceeded through the hallway men began to grab at her. They grabbed her shirt and ripped her brassiere. She ran through the hallway to a less crowded area.

The victim stated that since she had been warned about the third floor and she went anyway, she should not be labeled a victim even though she was subjected to indecent assault.

VICTIM NUMBER 38

Status/Service/Rank: Civilian/Female

Date/Time of Incident: Saturday, September 7, 1991 —
                              7:30 p.m.

Place of Incident: Hallway, Third Floor, Las Vegas
                              Hilton

Victim 38 is a 36-year-old Federal Government employee.

According to the victim, she and a female friend were walking down the third-floor hallway of the Hilton on Saturday evening at approximately 7:30 p.m. She knew from attending previous Tailhook Association conventions that the hallway could get "crazy," but at the time, the hallway did not appear "packed with people," and she felt that everything was "calm."

As she walked down the hallway, she was "suddenly surrounded by men." They started grabbing her on the buttocks and "everywhere else." She started pushing to get to an exit, screaming, "Leave me alone."

She noted that she "knew the hallway was trouble," and she "should have known better."

VICTIM NUMBER 39

Status/Service/Rank: Civilian/Female

Date/Time of Incident: Saturday, September 7, 1991 —
                              11:00 p.m.

Place of Incident: Hallway, Third Floor, Las Vegas
                              Hilton

Victim 39 is a 35-year-old woman who resides in California. She is the ex-spouse of an enlisted Marine and attended previous Tailhook Association conventions with her spouse. She attended the convention in 1991 with her sister.

According to the victim, she and her sister went to the third floor of the Hilton at approximately 11:00 p.m. on Saturday evening. They went into several administrative suites and walked down the hallway. She was "grabbed on the buttocks two or three times while walking through the gauntlet." As she felt hands grabbing her buttocks, she turned to see who had done it but was unable to determine who had touched her.

The individuals standing in the area all had "short, military-style haircuts." She could not identify anyone standing in the hallway.

VICTIM NUMBER 40

Status/Service/Rank: Civilian/Female

Date/Time of Incident: Saturday, September 7, 1991 —
                            11:30 p.m.

Place of Incident: Hallway, Third Floor, Las Vegas
                            Hilton

Victim 40 is a 38-year-old civilian from Massachusetts.

According to the victim, she traveled to the Tailhook Association convention in 1991 by herself.

She went to the third floor of the Hilton Hotel on Saturday evening, and at approximately 11:30 p.m., she and an unidentified male naval officer from the VF-1 squadron walked out into the hallway. There were "males lining both sides of the hallway." As they approached the vicinity of room 312, two males, one on each side of the hall, grabbed her on the breasts and buttocks simultaneously. She turned around in shock, but the hall was so crowded she could not determine who grabbed her. The man she was with did not observe her assault.

VICTIM NUMBER 41

Status/Service/Rank: Civilian/Female

Date/Time of Incident: Saturday, September 7, 1991—
                            10:30 p.m.

Place of Incident: Hallway, Third Floor, Las Vegas
                            Hilton

Victim 41, a 29-year-old Las Vegas resident, attended the Tailhook Association conventions in 1990 and 1991. On Saturday, September 7, 1991, she and two friends arrived on the third floor of the Hilton at approximately 10:30 p.m.

According to the victim, the hallway was extremely crowded as they walked through to go to the pool patio exit. As she walked through the crowd, several men attempted to place unit stickers on her breasts and buttocks. Two men slapped her on the buttocks, affixing unit stickers. When she objected, the men began to throw the stickers at her.

She then retreated into one of the hospitality suites to use the bathroom. She discovered the bathroom door in that suite was locked, so she went back out into the hallway to look for another bathroom. As she stepped back out into the hallway, someone removed the baseball cap she was wearing and threw it down the hallway into the crowd. She began to walk down the hallway to retrieve her hat.

As she walked into the crowd, men began hooting and hollering at her. A group of men surrounded her and began "groping" her body. Several men ran their hands down her top and grabbed her breasts inside her bra. Several other men ran their hands up her legs inside her loose-fitting shorts and grabbed and fondled her buttocks. She attempted to defend herself by striking out at the men, but as she twisted and turned, another group of men fondled her breasts and buttocks from behind.

She was finally ejected from the crowd with such force that she was thrown against a man standing in the doorway of one of the administrative suites, and she fell down on top of him. Someone picked her up, stood her against the wall, and told her not to go back down the hallway. She was extremely frightened and crying. She told the man who picked her up that she was just trying to get her hat. She saw someone in the crowd wearing her hat, and the man who picked her up retrieved the hat for her and, at her request, escorted her back to her friends.

After finding her friends, she was approached by several men who apologized for what had occurred, one of them stating, "One person can't control this crowd." She subsequently walked out on the pool patio where she saw a line of six men walking around the pool deck completely naked.

VICTIM NUMBER 42

Status/Service/Rank: Civilian/Female

Date/Time of Incident: Saturday, September 7, 1991 —
           11:00 p.m.–12:00 midnight

Place of Incident: Hallway, Third Floor, Las Vegas
           Hilton

Victim 42 is a 40-year-old victim who resides in Florida. She attended the Tailhook Association convention with two female friends.

According to the victim, she entered the hallway on the third floor of the Hilton Hotel at approximately 11:00 or 12:00 midnight on Saturday evening. The hallway was "body to body," and men in the hallway were standing there "like they were waiting and wanting people to walk by." She heard men saying things like "Oh, baby, baby," and "Look at the tits on that." She was pinched on the buttocks about six times.

She did not like being pinched on the buttocks by strangers even though there was a "party atmosphere" on the third floor. She felt that, when she was walking through the hallway, "the guys had a definite plan in mind, they were all in on it, and it was not a random activity. They were planning to pinch and touch women walking through the hall."

VICTIM NUMBER 43

Status/Service/Rank: Civilian/Female

Date/Time of Incident: Saturday, September 7, 1991 —
           9:30 p.m.

Place of Incident: Hallway, Third Floor, Las Vegas Hilton

Victim 43 is a 19-year-old student and resides in Las Vegas. She attended Tailhook '91 with two female civilian friends.

According to the victim, she and her friends arrived on the third floor of the Hilton Hotel at approximately 9:30 p.m. and exited the passenger elevators. As they walked down the hallway to the administrative suite located in room 315, she found she had to push her way through the crowd that lined both sides of the hallway. She was pinched on her buttocks while she walked through the hallway. She could not identify anyone who was in the hallway at that time.

VICTIM NUMBER 44

Status/Service/Rank: Civilian/Female

Date/Time of Incident: Saturday, September 7, 1991 — 9:30 p.m.

Place of Incident: Hallway, Third Floor, Las Vegas Hilton

Victim 44 is a 24-year-old student at the UNLV. She attended Tailhook '91 with two female friends who were also students at the UNLV.

According to the victim, she attended the party on the third floor of the Hilton Hotel from approximately 9:00 p.m. until 11:00 p.m. on Saturday, September, 7, 1991. At some time during the evening, she and her friends walked down the hallway on the third floor. As they pushed through the crowd, a tall blond male, approximately 6'2" in height, picked her up and began to spin her around in circles. She became very dizzy and screamed for him to put her down. Her friends were also screaming at him. He ignored their screams until another unidentified man stopped the individual from spinning.

One of the victim's friends witnessed the incident. The witness stated that while walking down the hallway, a tall man picked the victim up in the air and twirled her around and around. They both screamed at the man to put her down, which he finally did.

The victim related another incident that shocked and upset her.

Shortly after she arrived at the party, she and her friends walked into one of the administrative suites located in room 302, 303, 304, or 305 of the Hilton Hotel. While in the suite, a dark-complexioned male exposed his penis/testicles to her. He appeared to be of Hispanic or Italian ethnic background, 5'6" to 5'8" in height, with short black hair. He was standing next to two other males. One of the other males reached down, grabbed the man's exposed penis/testicles, and shook them at her and her friends, saying, "Hey ladies, have you ever seen anything like this before?" She was shocked and could not believe what she had just seen. She and her friends quickly exited the suite. (See Victim 17.)

VICTIM NUMBER 45

Status/Service/Rank: Civilian/Female

Date/Time of Incident: Saturday, September 7, 1991—
                           9:30–11:00 p.m.

Place of Incident: Hallway, Third Floor, Las Vegas
                           Hilton

Victim 45 is a 34-year-old civilian who resides in Nevada. She attended Tailhook '91 with a female civilian friend.

According to the victim, she and her friend went up to the third floor of the Hilton Hotel via the guest elevator near room 364. She began walking down the hallway, which she described as filled with drunken, rowdy men. As she proceeded, she was pushed and shoved as men grabbed at her breasts and buttocks. When she got to the area of the hallway between rooms 304 and 305, she realized that she had lost the pager she wore at her waist. One of the men in the crowd immediately yelled out to the other men in the hallway that she had lost her beeper. The victim stated, "The whole crowd stopped and looked for the pager." The victim saw other women in the hallway who were also being grabbed on the breasts and buttocks.

The victim's friend was a witness to the incident. According to the witness, she and the victim began to walk down the third-floor hallway and were "touched all over the place." The victim was wearing a dress and the witness saw men reach up her dress and grab at her. The witness also corroborated the victim's statement relative to her lost pager, noting that the pager and other personal articles were found and returned to the victim without further incident.

VICTIM NUMBER 46

Status/Service/Rank: Civilian/Female

Date/Time of Incident: Saturday, September 7, 1991 —
                                10:30 p.m.

Place of Incident: Hallway, Third Floor, Las Vegas
                                Hilton

Victim 46 is a 31-year-old civilian from California.

According to the victim, she and a female friend went to Las Vegas on vacation. Her friend's cousin, a male Navy lieutenant junior grade, invited them to attend Tailhook '91.

She, her friend, her friend's cousin, and two other male Navy officers arrived on the third floor of the Hilton Hotel at approximately 10:30 p.m. on Saturday. They exited the passenger elevators and started walking up the long hallway that had ''guys standing on both sides, like a gauntlet at a high school football game.'' She walked closely behind her friend's cousin and felt men from both sides of the hallway intentionally grab her buttocks and attempt to grab her breasts. She pressed her front to the back of her friend's cousin to protect her breasts. She was firmly grabbed on the buttocks by at least six different men. One man grabbed her T-shirt and would not let go. That frightened her, as she did not know what he was going to do next, but he finally released his grip.

As she was walking through the hallway, she thought, ''Why did I do this?'' A part of her felt guilty for even being there. She did not report the incident or tell anyone about it because she did not want anyone to know she had gone to the Tailhook party.

VICTIM NUMBER 47

Status/Service/Rank: Civilian/Female

Date/Time of Incident:　　　Saturday, September 7, 1991—
　　　　　　　　　　　　　　7:00–8:00 p.m.

Place of Incident:　　　　　Hallway, Third Floor, Las Vegas
　　　　　　　　　　　　　　Hilton

Victim 47 is a 34-year-old Federal Government employee who is married to a Navy officer. She attended the Tailhook Association convention with her husband and has attended three or four conventions in the past.

According to the victim, she, her husband, and several friends were visiting one of the administrative suites on the third floor of the Hilton Hotel on Saturday evening. She and one of the other females decided to leave the suite to look for a friend. She was aware, from attending previous Tailhook conventions, that the third-floor hallway could be dangerous, but she thought that it was early in the evening, and people were moving freely through the crowded hallway. As she and her friend entered the crowd, men began to encircle them. She felt hands grabbing at her breasts, genitalia, and buttocks. The attack was so forceful that she was surprised she was not bruised. She pushed herself up against her friend, who was also being attacked. They were finally able to extract themselves from the crowd. The attack took place between rooms 302 and 308. She did not recognize any of the men in the hallway at the time of the assault.

The victim stated she felt humiliated and was upset with herself for not recognizing a known problem and avoiding the hallway. She was aware that there was gauntlet-type activity at previous Tailhook conventions. In the past, she had seen women emerge from the crowded hallway who were upset and had articles of clothing removed. The activity always seemed to take place between rooms 302 and 308. She had not been able to recognize anyone in the hallway at that time, except that some of the men participating in the gauntlet during the 1988 and 1989 Tailhook conventions wore "elephant hats."*

---

*Investigation disclosed that a Prowler squadron (VA-128) wore hats decorated with a mock fuel probe. The probe was described by at least one witness as resembling an elephant's trunk. Similarly, some VMFP-3 "Rhino" squadron members wore rhinoceros-horn headpieces that could also appear to be an elephant's trunk.

VICTIM NUMBER 48

Status/Service/Rank: Lieutenant (O-3)
United States Navy/Female

Date/Time of Incident: Saturday, September 7, 1991 —
Evening, Time Unknown

Place of Incident: Hallway, Third Floor, Las Vegas
Hilton

Victim 48 is a 30-year-old Navy lieutenant.

According to the victim, she was walking alone down the hallway on the third floor of the Hilton Hotel on Saturday evening when she suddenly felt men intentionally touching her body. She described the touching as a "group grope" with hands everywhere. She was touched and grabbed on her buttocks, breasts, and crotch. As she continued down the hall, the men began chanting and whistling at her. She was wearing a strapless evening dress, and someone grabbed the top of her dress under her arm. She brought her arm down with enough force to dislodge the hand from her dress. She then screamed out, "OK, guys, that's enough," after which the men stopped their grabbing and she was able to exit the hallway.

VICTIM NUMBER 49

Status/Service/Rank: Civilian/Female

Date/Time of Incident: Saturday, September 7, 1991 —
Evening, Time Unknown

Place of Incident: Hallway, Third Floor, Las Vegas
Hilton

Victim 49 is a 42-year-old civilian from Las Vegas, Nevada. She attended Tailhook '91 with a female civilian friend.

According to the victim, she and her friend arrived on the third floor of the Hilton Hotel on Saturday evening. As they started to walk down the hallway, she was "touched all over the place" by the men in the hallway. She was in a state of shock and embarrassed that she had been grabbed all over her body. She pushed through the hallway and at the end of the crowd, a man who said he was a Navy lieutenant advised her to hold his hand and nothing else would happen to her. She took his hand and was escorted from the hallway without further incident. She and her friend then noticed that several items had fallen from their handbags when they were in the hallway. She told the officer who had offered his help about the missing items, and he immediately turned to the crowd and yelled for the men to look for the items. The men in the hallway searched for the items, found them, and returned them to the victim and her friend.

VICTIM NUMBER 50

Status/Service/Rank: Lieutenant (O-3)
United States Navy/Female

Date/Time of Incident: Saturday, September 7, 1991—
11:30 p.m.

Place of Incident: Hallway, Third Floor, Las Vegas
Hilton

Victim 50 is LT Paula Coughlin. At the time of Tailhook '91, she was aide to RADM John W. Snyder, United States Navy, Commander, Naval Air Test Center.

According to LT Coughlin, she arrived at the third-floor hallway of the Hilton Hotel alone at approximately 11:30 p.m. Saturday evening. She entered the hotel from the pool patio through the doors at the main passenger elevators, turned right and proceeded up the hallway.

As she approached the hallway, she found it to be loud and rowdy. Both sides of the hallway were lined with men leaning on the walls. As she began to walk up the hallway, there were approximately six to eight of the young men on each side of the hallway and two in the center of the hallway. Each had their backs to her at the head of the group. As she attempted to pass the man on the right side, the man intentionally bumped into her with his right hip. LT Coughlin excused herself, and one of the men lining the hallway yelled loudly, "Admiral's aide!"

LT Coughlin turned to look at the man who yelled. She described the man who had first bumped into her as having dark skin with short dark hair, perhaps Hispanic or a light-skinned black. She was grabbed by the buttocks with such force that it lifted her off the ground and ahead a step. LT Coughlin turned around and yelled at the man, "What the f— do you think you are doing?" As she said that, she was grabbed on the buttocks by someone from behind. She turned and asked that individual the same question. The men in the group began grabbing her breasts as well as her buttocks. LT Coughlin described the assault as follows:

"The man with the dark complexion moved in immediately behind me with his body pressed against mine. He was bumping me, pushing me forward down the passageway where the group on either side was pinching and then pulling at my clothing. The man then put both his hands down the front of my tanktop and inside my bra where he grabbed my breasts. I dropped to a forward crouch position and placed my hands on the wrists of my attacker in an attempt to remove his hands . . . I sank my teeth into the fleshy part of the man's left forearm, biting hard. I thought I drew blood . . . I then turned and bit the man on the right hand at the area between the base of the thumb and base of the index finger." The man removed his hands, and another individual "reached up under my skirt and grabbed the crotch of my panties. I kicked one of my attackers . . . I felt as though the group was trying to rape me. I was terrified and had no idea what was going to happen next."

LT Coughlin attempted to escape into one of the administrative suites, but her route was blocked by men who stood in the doorway and would not allow her through. The men in the crowd continued to grab at her buttocks and breasts, and she noticed that one of the men in the crowd turned and began to walk away. "I reached out and tapped him on the right hip, pleading with the man to just let me get in front of him. The man stopped, turned . . . and pivoted to a position directly in front of me. With this action, the man raised both his hands and put one on each of my breasts."

LT Coughlin broke free and ran past him into an open door that led to one of the administrative suites. She sat in the room in the dark, "attempting to understand what had happened to me . . . I was appalled not only by the brutality of the incident, but the fact that the group did that to me knowing I was both a fellow officer and an admiral's aide."

According to one witness, a male Federal Government civilian employee, "I remember Coughlin entered the hallway. Coughlin stood in the hallway for a couple of minutes and then proceeded down the hall. As she advanced through the area, the gauntlet collapsed around her blocking her from my view. I recall Coughlin wrenching around as she disappeared from sight. I never saw her exit the gauntlet." There were approximately 100 men in the hallway at the time, none of whom the witness recognized.

A male Navy lieutenant stated that he saw a woman walk into the crowded hallway. He saw her get pinched on the buttocks by an unknown male. As the woman turned to confront the man, another male from the other side of the hallway pinched her on the buttocks. During the confrontation, he heard someone yell, "Admiral's aide!" Later, when the witness saw LT Coughlin on television, he realized that she was probably the woman he witnessed being assaulted in the hallway.

Another male Federal Government employee witnessed part of the assault on LT Coughlin. The witness saw a man standing in the hallway whom he described as the "master of ceremonies." The man appeared to be moving about in an animated fashion, trying to get women to walk through the gauntlet where the men in the hallway would then surround them. If a woman did not want to walk down the hallway, the man would physically pick her up and carry her down the hallway. The witness saw LT Coughlin conversing with the "master of ceremonies," and it appeared that she was telling him she was a lieutenant and an admiral's aide. The witness saw a man come up behind LT Coughlin and grab her from behind, wrapping his arms all the way around her. LT Coughlin started to struggle, bending over forward. At the same time LT Coughlin was being assaulted, another woman standing behind the witness was being grabbed by men in the hallway. The witness left the area before LT Coughlin emerged from the hallway.

During the course of our investigation, we received several allegations indicating that LT Coughlin engaged in improper activity while at Tailhook '91. We investigated all such allegations but found that the allegations were based on hearsay testimony or were otherwise without merit. None of the people who told us about the alleged incidents or improper conduct involving LT Coughlin actually witnessed the incidents themselves, nor could they provide the identity of any eyewitnesses.

When interviewed, LT Coughlin denied all allegations of impropriety. No credible information was found to support the allegations of misconduct on the part of LT Coughlin. As noted by one male officer, it appeared the allegations were fabricated to discredit LT Coughlin for her public disclosure of facts concerning assaults at Tailhook '91.

VICTIM NUMBER 51

Status/Service/Rank: Civilian/Female

Date/Time of Incident: Saturday, September 7, 1991 — 11:00 p.m.

Place of Incident: Hallway, Third Floor, Las Vegas Hilton

Victim 51 is a female from California.

According to the victim, she was exiting the hallway of the third floor when she was grabbed on the buttocks by an unidentified white male. She turned and asked, "What the hell are you doing?" The man then apologized to the victim. Even though she was a victim of an assault, she did not want to be "listed" as a victim and requested confidentiality.

VICTIM NUMBER 52

Status/Service/Rank: Civilian/Female

Date/Time of Incident: Saturday, September 7, 1991 — 10:00 p.m.

Place of Incident: Hallway, Third Floor, Las Vegas Hilton

Victim 52 is a 23-year-old Federal Government employee. She attended Tailhook '91 with two female civilian friends.

According to the victim, she and her friends exited the main passenger elevators on the third floor of the Hilton Hotel at approximately 10:00 p.m. on Saturday evening. As they began to walk up the hallway, an unidentified male grabbed the victim and pushed her toward the crowd. She recalled men yelling "Women" or "Girls" and yelling something like "Woo woo." As she was pushed through the crowd, men grabbed her on the arms, legs, and buttocks. She exited the crowd and did not return to the hallway.

VICTIM NUMBER 53

Status/Service/Rank: Civilian/Female

Date/Time of Incident: Saturday, September 7, 1991—
10:30 p.m.

Place of Incident: Hallway, Third Floor, Las Vegas
Hilton

Victim 53 is a 28-year-old civilian who resides in Las Vegas, Nevada. She attended Tailhook '91 with a female civilian friend.

According to the victim, she and her friend took the stairs to the third floor of the Hilton Hotel. They stepped out of the stairwell into the hallway that was crowded with people, mostly men. A man asked the victim if she ever "gone through the line before." She did not know what he was talking about and told him she had not. He replied "Be careful." Suddenly a man came up behind her, put his head between her legs, and lifted her up on his shoulders. The man started walking her through the crowd in the hallway. Men reached out and grabbed her on the breasts, buttocks, and crotch, and she was hit in the mouth. They put their hands up under her shirt to grab at her, while she feverishly attempted to protect herself with her arms. She described the crowd in the hallway as a "riot" and she was extremely frightened. As she was being carried down the hallway, she squeezed her eyes shut and was "totally in shock." At the end of the crowd, the man "dumped" her off his shoulders onto the floor and asked if she was all right. He then disappeared into the crowd. She could not identify any of her assailants because the military men all looked alike to her with their short haircuts.

VICTIM NUMBER 54

Status/Service/Rank: Civilian/Female

Date/Time of Incident: Saturday, September 7, 1991 —
9:00–10:00 p.m.

Place of Incident: Hallway, Third Floor, Las Vegas
Hilton

Victim 54 is a 23-year-old civilian who resides in Las Vegas, Nevada. She attended Tailhook '91 with six friends: four female civilians, one male Navy officer, and one male Marine officer.

According to the victim, she entered the hallway through the door of one of the administrative suites on the third floor of the Hilton Hotel. As she entered the hallway, "there was no turning back. There were millions of guys and they had total control." She was pushed along the hallway, and men reached up under her skirt to grab at her buttocks. She twisted and swung out at them, but as she turned, more hands would grab her from behind. She heard cheering and chanting as she was propelled down the hallway. Men were blocking the doorways to the suites so she could not escape. She finally made her way into one of the suites and went through to the pool patio to find her friends. She could not recognize anyone in the hallway, because there were so many who looked alike with short haircuts.

VICTIM NUMBER 55

Status/Service/Rank: Civilian/Female

Date/Time of Incident: Saturday, September 7, 1991 —
9:30 p.m.

Place of Incident: Hallway, Third Floor, Las Vegas
Hilton

Victim 55 is a 25-year-old civilian from Las Vegas, Nevada. She attended Tailhook '91 with three civilian female friends and their dates who were male Navy or Marine officers.

According to the victim, she and her friends arrived on the third floor of the Hilton Hotel at approximately 9:30 p.m. on Saturday. As they began to walk down the crowded hallway, she heard someone yell, "Deck clear." As she walked through the crowd, men began grabbing her breasts and buttocks and attempted to get their hands inside her shorts. She saw one of her friends get picked up by one man and carried screaming down the hallway. The victim tried to go to her friend's aid, but men blocked her way, still grabbing at her breasts and crotch. She knocked one man's hands away and told him she would hit him if he touched her again. He laughed at her.

After the incident in the hallway, the victim and her friends visited three of the administrative suites to get drinks. In all three suites, she was confronted by men who grabbed at her breasts or crotch. She was asked several times by men in the suites if she wanted to "f—." She was unable to identify any of the men who assaulted her.

VICTIM NUMBER 56

Status/Service/Rank: Lieutenant (O-3)
                        United States Navy/Female

Date/Time of Incident: Saturday, September 7, 1991—
                        10:00–11:00 p.m.

Place of Incident: Hallway, Third Floor, Las Vegas
                        Hilton

Victim 56 is a 29-year-old Navy lieutenant who resides in Virginia. She attended Tailhook '91 with a female friend who is a Navy officer and two civilian female friends.

According to the victim, she entered the third-floor hallway, walking behind three male Navy friends. She described the assault as follows:

"I was immediately pounced on. I had several hands on every part of my body, my breasts, my buttocks, and my crotch. There were approximately 30 guys in the hallway. I wasn't punching, but I was throwing my arms to move through the crowd." The victim considered striking one man who had grasped her breast, but instead she stared at him and he released her. The victim provided a description of the man to the San Diego Police Department, and a composite drawing was prepared. She lost sight of her companions in the crowd, but thought one of them may have witnessed her emergence from the crowd. The victim later viewed photographs of possible suspects, but was unable to make a positive identification.

A Navy officer who accompanied the victim through the hallway told us that he did, in fact, witness her exit the crowd. She passed by a group of five men, and one of them reached out and grabbed her. A second man pushed the victim, and she punched one of the men. The witness walked up to the victim and offered her some assistance. He then escorted her from the area. The witness could not identify any of the men in the hallway at the time and could only describe them as having a general military appearance.

VICTIM NUMBER 57

Status/Service/Rank: Civilian/Female

Date/Time of Incident: Saturday, September 7, 1991 — 9:00–10:00 p.m.

Place of Incident: Hallway, Third Floor, Las Vegas Hilton

Victim 57 is a 30-year-old civilian who resides in California. She attended Tailhooks '85, '87, '89, '90, and '91.

According to the victim, she was walking down the hallway when an unidentified male placed his hand on her buttocks. She removed his hand and told him to stop touching her. She recalled that at Tailhook '85, she was walking down the hallway when several aviators tried to grab her breasts and buttocks. She covered herself with her arms and ran from the hallway.

VICTIM NUMBER 58

Status/Service/Rank: Lieutenant (O-3)

Date/Time of Incident: Saturday Night, September 7, 1991 — Time Unknown

Place of Incident: Hallway, Outside VF-124 Suite, Third Floor, Las Vegas Hilton

Victim 58 is a 31-year-old Navy lieutenant. She went to Tailhook '91 accompanied by her husband who is also a lieutenant in the Navy. She has not attended any other Tailhook conventions.

As the victim and her husband were leaving the VF-124 suite, a male naval officer sitting on the floor just outside the suite reached up her shorts and tried to grab her. The victim slapped the man and continued down the hall. The victim stated that the man looked surprised. She described the attitude as, "It was OK to cop a free feel." The male appeared to be very drunk.

The victim stated that, prior to going to the convention, she was warned not to go on the third floor after 11:00 p.m. because of the gauntlet. She stated that, in a matter of 30 minutes, the hallway underwent a major transformation. At 10:00 p.m., it was a quiet place with perhaps 20 people in the hallway. By 10:30 p.m., however, it was apparent to the victim that the gauntlet was starting. People were coming out of the suites into the hallway as though prearranged. The victim stated that the gauntlet started at the VS-41 suite (room 304) and continued to the VMFP-3 suite (room 308).

The victim and her husband left the third-floor area because they did not want to be in the area when things got out of control.

VICTIM NUMBER 59

Status/Service/Rank: Civilian/Female

Date/Time of Incident: Saturday, September 7, 1991 —
                            9:00 p.m.

Place of Incident: Hallway, Third Floor, Las Vegas
                            Hilton

Victim 59 is a 27-year-old woman who resides in the Las Vegas, Nevada, area. This was the first Tailhook that the victim attended.

According to the victim, as she was wandering down the hall, a white male picked her up and threw her over his shoulder. He then ran the length of the hallway with her. As she was yelling for help, she remembered hearing other men in the hallway cheering and laughing. At the end of the hallway, as the man let her down, he spilled a drink on her. The victim although angry, did not show it because she was afraid of what he might do. The victim was not surprised to learn that other women were also assaulted.

During the hour and a half the victim was at Tailhook, she also saw a man mooning as she turned the corner to go into a suite.

VICTIM NUMBER 60

Status/Service/Rank: Lieutenant Junior Grade (O-2)
                                United States Navy/Female

Date/Time of Incident: Saturday, September 7, 1991 —
                                10:00 p.m.

Place of Incident: Hallway, Third Floor, Las Vegas
                                Hilton

Victim 60 is a 24-year-old Navy lieutenant junior grade who resides in California.

According to the victim, she arrived on the third floor on Saturday evening to look for a friend to go out to dinner. She started to walk down the hallway when it occurred to her that there were "lots of men lined up along the sides of the hallway, leaving a cleared path down the middle." She estimated there were 200 or 300 men lining the hallway at that time, which looked "very strange" to her. She looked around at the men in the hallway, but did not see anyone she knew other than one Navy lieutenant who was "just standing around," but "close enough to the gauntlet that he would have to have seen what happened to me." She also saw two hotel security guards in the area. She stood at the beginning of the hallway for about five minutes looking around for someone she might know. While she stood there, several men walked through the clear passage in the hallway and "nothing happened to them, so I figured it was OK and went too."

The victim stated that as she entered the hallway, she was immediately converged on by five or six men. She describes her attack as follows:

"My arms were either held down at my sides or behind my back. I remember one guy was behind me and had both his hands grabbing my breasts. I think maybe they were trying to pick me up off the ground so I was struggling downwards. I don't recall specifically how or when it stopped.''

The victim recalled that she grabbed the wrist of a man who was grabbing her buttocks, swung around with her right hand, and "hit him in the face as hard as I could." The men in the crowd began booing her. She recalled seeing the same lieutenant she recognized from before her attack, still standing there, a little closer to the hallway. During the attack, she saw a Navy captain she knew standing in the area of the hallway. She stated, "I was shocked to realize that he knew what was going on and hadn't done anything to stop it . . . In my opinion, it would have been impossible for anyone to have been there and not know that something strange was going on."

The victim stated that she ". . . wandered around in shock for a while, looking for someone I knew." She saw someone from her squadron and she asked him to escort her to the VF-126 administrative suite in room 306 where she began crying profusely. She then asked a male Navy officer friend to walk her back to her hotel.

The Navy lieutenant identified by the victim as having been a possible witness to the assault was interviewed. He denied seeing or hearing anything unusual in the hallway at the time of the victim's assault, except to say that he witnessed a female he recognized as being a Navy officer punch a man in the face. He did not see what precipitated the punch, and the female left the area.

The victim related that two months after Tailhook '91, she again encountered the lieutenant. She stated, "He laid into me and chewed me out for about an hour. He said that men have been treating women like that since 'caveman days.' . . . All the guys think like he does . . . He continually told me it was my fault for being there in the first place. He said since I'm . . . not a Naval aviator, I had no business being there in the first place. He also implied that I was stupid or dumb for not recognizing the gauntlet and knowing what would/could happen to me if I walked down it.''

VICTIM NUMBER 61

Status/Service/Rank: Civilian/Female

Date/Time of Incident: Saturday, September 7, 1991 —
                                   11:00 p.m.

Place of Incident: Hallway, Third Floor, Las Vegas
Hilton

Victim 61 is a 34-year-old civilian woman who resides in California. She and a civilian female friend (victim number 69) were staying at the Hilton on vacation during Tailhook '91.

According to the victim, at approximately 11:00 p.m. on Saturday, she and her friend, accompanied by at least one male aviator, went to the third floor. As they exited the elevator and turned right, she noticed numerous men on each side of the hallway, laughing and drinking. As the victim walked 10 or 20 feet down the hall, the crowd got denser. A chant started which, to her, had no distinguishable words. At the same time, the victim felt a bump behind her, which pushed her forward into the crowd. The hooting and hollering became louder and men began grabbing her buttocks, breasts, and crotch. The victim was wearing a white blouse and black skirt both of which the men were trying to lift. While she held her skirt, many pairs of hands continued to grab her breasts, legs, buttocks, and crotch. The victim looked back at her friend who was also being assaulted and saw her friend throw a drink at one of the men. After that, drinks were flung in all directions. As she was forced through the gauntlet, the victim's blouse was soaked with alcohol, beer, and some kind of pink-colored drink.

Immediately after the assault, the victim was approached by a Marine aviator whom both she and her friend knew. He was covered with alcohol and apologized to the victim for what had happened. The Marine stated that the victim's friend had punched him in the stomach. The victim now thinks that individual may have been in the crowd and participated in the assault.

The victim and her friend left the area, returned to their room, and discussed the incident. Early Sunday morning, they decided to call the police. The victims had difficulty contacting the Las Vegas Metropolitan Police through the Hilton switchboard. Once contacted, the police referred the matter to the Hilton Hotel security. The victims filed reports with Hilton security and the Las Vegas Metropolitan Police. The incident was the only assault found to have been reported to the police.

VICTIM NUMBER 62

Status/Service/Rank: Commander (O-5)
United States Navy/Female

Date/Time of Incident: Saturday, September 7, 1991 —
                           10:00 p.m.

Place of Incident: Hallway, Third Floor, Las Vegas
                           Hilton

Victim 62 is a 37-year-old Navy commander whose husband is also a Navy officer. The victim attended Tailhook conventions in the past.

According to the victim, on Thursday, when she first arrived at the Hilton, she went to the third floor at 3:00 p.m. While she was walking through the hallway, she was lifted off her feet by a young, tall, broad white male wearing a military haircut. His breath indicated he had been drinking. She told him to put her down several times, but he refused and continued his attempts to engage her in conversation. After a minute, a second male identified her as a commander and the young male quickly put her down and apologized.

On Saturday at approximately 10:00 p.m., she entered the third-floor hallway via the main elevators. As she was trying to push her way through the crowd in the hall, two stickers were "zapped" on either side of her buttocks by unknown person(s). When moving through the hallway, she heard comments such as "You're ugly" and "Flag wife." The men in the hallway straightened up immediately when the last comment was heard. The victim told us that, in her opinion, she was not a "victim" of an assault merely because she was "zapped" without her consent.

VICTIM NUMBER 63

Status/Service/Rank: Civilian/Female

Date/Time of Incident: Saturday, September 7, 1991 —
                           12:00 midnight

Place of Incident: Hallway, Third Floor, Las Vegas
                           Hilton

Victim 63 is a 30-year-old civilian from California, who went to Las Vegas with a girlfriend to attend a concert. They were invited by an unidentified person to a party on the third floor of the Hilton after the concert.

According to the victim, on arriving on the third floor, she met a male Navy lieutenant who asked her to go with him to look for some of his friends. As they began to walk up the hallway, she saw that it was lined with men. As she entered the crowd, the men immediately converged upon her. She felt hands reach out and grab, pinch, and touch her on her breasts, buttocks, and crotch. The men cheered and yelled as they grabbed at her. She lowered her head and began to swing her arms in an attempt to break free. The Navy lieutenant, who was behind her, grabbed her waist and pushed her through the crowd into one of the administrative suites.

The victim was surprised and shocked over the incident but could not identify anyone in the hallway other than the Navy lieutenant she was with.

According to the Navy lieutenant, he and the victim were in the hallway near the "Rhino room" (room 308) when he noticed the victim start "jumping around." She subsequently opened the door to one of the hospitality suites and pulled him inside. The victim told him that the men in the hallway were groping her breasts and buttocks and had reached up under her skirt. The officer told us that he wanted to go back out to the hallway to identify those responsible but the victim was adamant about not wanting to go back there. They went out to the pool patio through the administrative suite and did not return to the hallway area.

VICTIM NUMBER 64

Status/Service/Rank: Civilian/Female

Date/Time of Incident: Saturday, September 7, 1991—
                           10:00 p.m.

Place of Incident: Hallway, Third Floor, Las Vegas
                           Hilton

Victim 64 is an 18-year-old student who resides in Las Vegas. She attended Tailhook '91 with two female civilian friends at the suggestion of a female friend who is a student at the UNLV.

According to the victim, she and her friends spent the majority of the evening in the "Helicopter Suite," which was located in room 315. The victim drank beer and margaritas that were prepared and served in the suite. She and her friends danced and talked and were given alcoholic drinks by the men in the suite. The victim became intoxicated. As evidenced by a poster signed by some of the men in the suite and given to the victim, the men were aware that she was under the legal age for consuming alcohol.

The victim next remembered being out in the hallway and being thrown in the air by a crowd of men. The crowd stripped the victim of her slacks and panties and dropped her on the floor. Security guards helped her dress behind a sheet and then took her to the Security Office to contact her parents.

The assault was witnessed by dozens of the people interviewed. One witness stated he saw several males standing in the hallway near the door of the helicopter squadron administrative suite (room 315). He observed the victim in the hallway and saw her surrounded by the men in the hallway. The witness observed an article of clothing thrown into the air above the crowd. Suddenly, the crowd dispersed and within a matter of seconds, the hallway was cleared of people. The witness saw the victim sitting on the floor against a wall near room 315. Security guards picked up the victim and led her down the hallway.

A male Navy officer stated that he observed the victim in the helicopter squadron administrative suite. She was drinking alcohol and was very intoxicated. He and one of the squadron members picked the victim up from where she had fallen on the floor and carried her out to the hallway. They sat her in the hallway, went back inside the suite, and closed the door. Moments later, the witness heard a loud commotion in the hallway. He looked out into the hallway and saw that it was completely cleared of people. The victim was sprawled in the middle of the hallway and, he believed, she was wearing only a pair of underpants. He watched as security guards came and removed the girl from the hallway. The witness stated that he was "embarrassed and ashamed" about taking the victim into the hallway.

Another witness, a male Navy officer, was standing in the hallway when he saw a fully clothed female being passed along hand-over-hand above the crowd in the hallway. He thought about participating, but decided against it. He watched as men began stripping off the victim's clothing. Someone yelled, "Broken arrow," and the victim was dropped to the floor. The witness started moving toward the victim because he thought she might have been hurt, but he suddenly realized that he was the only person in the hallway going toward the victim, while everyone else was running away from the incident. He too then turned and went through one of the other administrative suites and out to the pool patio.

Several Navy aviators we interviewed witnessed the assault; however, all stated they were merely observers and none were able to identify any individual who removed the victim's clothing. We obtained a photograph from a naval aviator that depicted the minor, nude from the waist down, being escorted from the hallway by security officers.

VICTIM NUMBER 65

Status/Service/Rank: Civilian/Female

Date/Time of Incident: Saturday, September 7, 1991 —
                          9:00 p.m.

Place of Incident: Hallway, Third Floor, Las Vegas
                          Hilton

Victim 65 is a 20-year-old civilian who attended Tailhook '91 with three civilian female friends and her fiancé, a Navy officer.

According to the victim, as the group walked through the crowded hallway on the third floor, she was pinched on the buttocks. She quickly turned around but could not determine who had pinched her. She was upset over the incident and told her fiancé what had happened. The victim and her friends then went out to the pool patio, where they stayed for the remainder of the evening.

VICTIM NUMBER 66

Status/Service/Rank: Civilian/Female

Date/Time of Incident: Saturday, September 7, 1991 —
                          8:30 p.m.

Place of Incident: Hallway, Third Floor, Las Vegas
                          Hilton

Victim 66 is a 32-year-old spouse of a Navy lieutenant commander. She attended the Tailhook Association convention with her husband, her mother, and her mother's two female friends.

According to the victim, she, her husband, and one of her mother's friends walked out of the VMFP-3 administrative suite in room 308 of the Hilton Hotel to go to the VR-57 administrative suite in room 357. As they proceeded down the hallway, they walked single file because the hallway was so crowded. Her husband led the way, followed by the victim and the friend. As she walked down the hallway, she was suddenly grabbed around the waist by two men and lifted into the air. She was wearing a formal black cocktail dress and the men lifted the skirt of the dress above her waist. She was not wearing nylons or pantyhose, and the men placed their hands between her legs and attempted to get their fingers inside her panties. The men appeared to be drunk and were laughing while they held her in the air. She did not say anything to them, but thought to herself, "If looks could kill, you would be a goner." She was placed back on the ground, and she hurried down the hall to find her husband. She did not recognize the men, but remembered thinking that they were military, "young west coast aviators," because of their haircuts. She felt helpless and feared the men were going to rip her dress off. Immediately after the assault, she went to her room and changed into shorts because she "did not want to be mistaken for a prostitute." She felt "helpless, angry, violated, and humiliated."

The victim told her husband what had happened, and, together, they decided to keep the assault private, even after other assaults that took place at the Tailhook convention became public. The reason for the reluctance to come forward was the fear that, if they acknowledged or reported the assault, her husband's naval career would be jeopardized. Despite that fact, both the victim and her spouse cooperated fully in the investigation.

VICTIM NUMBER 67

Status/Service/Rank: Civilian/Female

Date/Time of Incident: Saturday, September 7, 1991 —
                            10:00 p.m.

Place of Incident: Hallway, Third Floor, Las Vegas
                      Hilton

Victim 67 is a 33-year-old civilian.

According to the victim, she went to the Tailhook '91 convention accompanied by her sister. They went to the third floor at 10:00 p.m. on Saturday. As they entered and attempted to proceed through the hallway, a group of men attacked them. The victim's buttocks was grabbed at least twice. When she turned, she saw a crowd of men with short hair, most wearing polo shirts and jeans, laughing at her. The victim described the men in the hallway as "rowdy, drunk, throwing up. . . ." She stated that, since the men all looked alike, she could not identify her assailants. She added that after the attack, she felt awful and just wanted to get away. The victim's sister was also assaulted.

VICTIM NUMBER 68

Status/Service/Rank: Civilian/Female

Date/Time of Incident: Saturday, September 7 or
                        Sunday, September 8, 1991 —
                        1:00 a.m.

Place of Incident: Hallway, Third Floor, Las Vegas
                        Hilton

Victim 68 is a 20-year-old female student at the UNLV. She attended Tailhook '91 with four friends.

According to the victim, at 1:00 a.m. on Saturday or Sunday, the victim was walking down the hallway alone when she was forcibly grabbed in her private areas. She was frightened and did not make eye contact with anyone as she tried to move through the crowd. When she got through, she looked back and saw another girl being thrown around. The victim said it appeared the crowd was stripping this girl's clothes off. The incident seemed so unbelievable and violent that she immediately went to the pool area. She was followed by a dark-complexioned male, either Italian or Hispanic, who commented about the girl being stripped naked. He acted as if it was fun, like a "great event" had just occurred.

The victim witnessed three or four incidents of ballwalking throughout the evening. The victim also saw naked people in the hot tub. She noted that, although she was not then of legal age, she had no trouble getting alcoholic drinks since no one asked her for identification.

VICTIM NUMBER 69

Status/Service/Rank:	Civilian/Female
Date/Time of Incident:	Saturday, September 7, 1991 — 11:00 p.m.
Place of Incident:	Hallway, Third Floor, Las Vegas Hilton

Victim 69 is a 33-year-old civilian woman who resides in California. She and her civilian female friend (victim number 61) were staying at the Hilton on vacation during Tailhook '91.

According to the victim, at approximately 11:00 p.m. on Saturday, she and her female friend, accompanied by at least one male aviator, went to the third floor. As they exited the elevator and turned right, she noticed numerous men whom she believed to be young, apparently military officers in the hall. The victim followed her friend down the hall. A few feet into the crowd she began to hear a chant. There were no words to the chant, just sounds such as "ooh" and "ah." At the same time, the crowd closed in around her and she felt hands all over her. Hands reached up her dress and grabbed her crotch; other hands grabbed her breasts and buttocks. She tried to fight them off, but was unable to because of the number. She threw her drink at someone, then drinks were thrown on her. She also punched someone in the stomach, but did not see whom she hit. Eventually, the crowd thinned out and she was able to extricate herself. At that time, she rejoined victim number 61 and the aviator who was with them when they first entered the gauntlet. They were also joined by a second aviator who was holding his stomach. The second aviator, who was known to both victims, told the victim she had punched him in the stomach.

The victim added that she was so concerned with fighting off the men who were grabbing her, and keeping her dress down, that she never realized whom she had punched until the aviator approached her. She now believes that he was either an active participant in the gauntlet or encouraged it.

The victim said that both she and her friend had tried to report the incident that night to the Las Vegas Police through the hotel switchboard, but instead, the hotel security came to their room. The security officer was more concerned about the damage to the victims' clothing than what happened to them. The victims filled out reports for the hotel and also filed reports with the Las Vegas Police on Sunday morning prior to leaving.

Both victims have provided several statements to authorities that differ slightly in some details, but are consistent with the account of their assault.

VICTIM NUMBER 70

Status/Service/Rank: Civilian/Female

Date/Time of Incident: Saturday night, September 7, 1991 — 12:00 midnight

Place of Incident: Hallway, Third Floor, Las Vegas Hilton

Victim 70 is a 24-year-old who resides in the Los Angeles area. She attended the Tailhook Association convention with the female spouse of a Navy officer.

According to the victim, at approximately 12:00 midnight on Saturday night, September 7, 1991, she left the VAW-110 administrative suite located in room 303 of the Hilton Hotel to look for a friend. As she stepped out into the hallway, she noticed there were many men lined up along the hallway, seemingly minding their own business. As she walked up the hallway, about 10 feet, she was suddenly attacked by at least seven men. She was wearing a "tube top" that was pulled down to expose her breasts. The men grabbed her breasts and buttocks while she attempted to cover herself with her arms. She fell to the ground, where the assault continued. During the attack, she bit several of the men on their arms and other places in an attempt to make them stop grabbing her. She did not recognize any of the men in the hallway at that time, but believed they were Marines because of their haircuts and demeanor. Finally, they stopped their assault and allowed her to get up. Immediately after the attack, she was approached in the hallway by a Marine aviator she had met the night before. She was crying profusely, and he told her it is an annual tradition at Tailhook conventions to harass women physically and verbally in the hallway and she should not worry about it. After escaping from her attackers, she looked back down the hallway and observed a white female screaming and fighting her way through the hallway as she was being assaulted. She related her experience to her boyfriend, a Navy lieutenant. Her boyfriend advised her not to tell anyone she was there because they would think she was a "slut."

VICTIM NUMBER 71

Status/Service/Rank: Civilian/Female

Date/Time of Incident: Saturday, September 7, 1991 —
                              Exact Time Unknown

Place of Incident: Hallway, Third and Fourteenth
                              Floors, Las Vegas Hilton

Victim 71 is a 24-year-old civilian currently residing in Arizona.

According to the victim, after she had consumed several drinks, she met an individual who asked her to follow him down the hallway. As they proceeded down the hallway, he disappeared. She heard males yelling and screaming. She was grabbed and eventually knocked down onto the floor. She got up, then continued down the hallway. Thinking the fire exit was a dead end, the victim turned around and came back through the crowd as she tried to escape the area completely. Again she was grabbed everywhere on her body, including her groin and breasts. She related that hands were all over her and that, although the incident lasted only about 5 minutes, it seemed to last forever. When the victim reached the wall near the service area, she stopped and cried. At that time, the man who had asked her to proceed down the hallway reappeared and said the males were "a bunch of jerks" and suggested that the victim come with him and that everything would be okay.

He took the victim to a guest room on the 14th floor. The amount of alcohol the victim had consumed impaired her ability to recall exactly what happened next. The victim remembered being naked in the shower when the man grabbed her by the arm and threw her out in the hallway. The victim screamed and cried out to him for her clothes, but he pushed her out of the room and shut the door. The victim recalled that, as he propelled her out the door, she scratched him hard enough to leave marks. In an effort to avoid being seen, she attempted to reenter the room she thought she had been in. When she knocked on the door, no one responded. Hotel security appeared shortly thereafter with a sheet to cover her.

A month or two after Tailhook '91, the victim recalled being in the shower with the man, prior to being thrown out of the room. Although she cannot remember anything that happened from the time she entered the room until she woke up naked in the shower, she believes she engaged in consensual sex with the man.

The victim expressed she now believes that the man knew she would be assaulted when he led her down the hallway.

VICTIM NUMBER 72

Status/Service/Rank: Civilian/Female

Date/Time of Incident: Saturday, September 7, 1991 —
         12:00 midnight

Place of Incident: Hallway and Pool Patio, Third
         Floor, Las Vegas Hilton

Victim 72 is a 21-year-old State employee.

According to the victim, she and three female friends traveled to Las Vegas from New York on vacation. While in Las Vegas, they met several Navy aviators who invited them to a "Navy party" at the Las Vegas Hilton.

While on the pool patio, she was assaulted by "military party attendees." She was approached by a man who grabbed her arms and shook her "in order to watch my breasts shake." He then grabbed her left breast with his right hand. She reacted by stepping back, swearing at him, and throwing her drink in his face. The man became "very angry" and attempted to hit her. At that point one of the men she was with stepped in and told the man to leave her alone. She was very upset and crying.

She and her friends decided to leave the party after the incident. They walked through the hallway on the third floor to go to the passenger elevators. While walking through the hallway, she noticed there were "several inebriated men lined up against both sides of the hallway." As she and her friends passed through, the men made "crude remarks" and then "pawed and grabbed" at the women.

After they left the Hilton, the Navy aviators they were with apologized to the women for taking them to the party.

VICTIM NUMBER 73

Status/Service/Rank: Civilian/Female

Date/Time of Incident: Saturday, September 7, 1991 —
                            5:00 p.m.

Place of Incident: Pool Patio, Las Vegas Hilton

Victim 73 is a 35-year-old civilian from California. She attended the Tailhook Association convention in 1991 with her spouse, a civilian, and her brother, an officer in the United States Navy.

According to the victim, at 5:00 p.m., while standing on the pool patio with her brother and her husband, she felt someone brushing up against her. At first she thought the individual was just trying to push through the crowd. She turned around and observed a "white male aviator" walking away. Her brother immediately asked her if she realized that the unidentified man "had his [penis] in her hair." She denied observing the individual's penis, but requested to leave the third floor. She does not believe she could identify the individual who assaulted her.

The victim's brother was a witness to the incident. He stated that he saw an individual standing "unusually close" behind his sister. As he looked at the man, he observed the man's penis was exposed, and he either wrapped his penis in the victim's waist-length hair, or was brushing his penis against her hair. When the victim turned to look, the man immediately turned, walked away, and got lost in the crowd. He stated that "Even if I could, I don't think I would identify the guy." He said that what happened to his sister was not "wrong in the context of the Tailhook party," and "nobody was hurt."

Another witness, a Navy lieutenant (O-3) stated he was standing on the pool patio when he heard someone in the group yell that someone he knew had just made a bet, and he was about to "wrap a girl's hair around his penis." He looked over in the direction of the activity and saw the suspect standing behind a girl with long hair. His view was obstructed, so he did not actually see the subject expose his penis. He saw the girl turn around and the suspect disappeared into the crowd. The witness identified the suspect.

VICTIM NUMBER 74

(See page 246)

VICTIM NUMBER 75

(See page 246)

VICTIM NUMBER 76

Status/Service/Rank:	Civilian/Female
Date/Time of Incident:	Saturday, September 7, 1991 — Time Unknown
Place of Incident:	Hallway, Third Floor, Las Vegas Hilton

Victim 76 is a 23-year-old civilian who resides in California.

According to the victim, she attended the Tailhook Association convention in 1991 with three female friends. They went to the third floor of the Hilton on Saturday, September 7, 1991, sometime after 7:00 p.m. and remained there until 3:00 a.m. Sunday morning, visiting all the administrative suites.

It was very crowded in the hallway and as she walked through the part of the hallway known as the "gauntlet" area, she was pinched on the buttocks by several unknown males. She did not let it bother her and "blew it off," thinking of the men, "What jerks."

VICTIM NUMBER 77

Status/Service/Rank: Ensign (O-1) United States Navy/
Female

Date/Time of Incident: Sunday, September 8, 1991—
3:00 a.m.

Place of Incident: CNATRA Suite, Room 364

Victim 77 is a 23-year-old Navy ensign. Tailhook '91 was the first convention she had attended.

According to the victim, she and several unidentified males were discussing women in combat in the CNATRA suite when an unidentified drunk male approached her and placed his hands on her breasts. He said in essence, "Can I touch your boobs?" She was shocked and angry. She pushed the male away with both of her fists in his chest and said, "I'm a naval officer, and I don't appreciate that at all." The male responded "Oh, shit," which the victim interpreted to mean he had really "screwed up" because she was not some girl who just happened to be there, and she could find him later. Friends of the male took him away and apologized for his behavior. The victim described the male as a "drunken ass" and stated that she doubted the man was even aware of what he was doing.

The victim told us that she did not consider herself a victim of any criminal activity. She felt she took care of the situation when it occurred and that it was over.

VICTIM NUMBER 78

Status/Service/Rank: Civilian/Female

Date/Time of Incident: Saturday, September 7, 1991—
12:00 midnight

Place of Incident: VMFP-3 ("Rhino" Suite) and
Patio, Third Floor, Las Vegas
Hilton

Victim 78 is a 26-year-old woman who resides in New York. She and two of her female friends were invited to Tailhook '91 by two aviators.

According to the victim, she entered the "Rhino" suite at approximately 12:00 midnight and was asked if she wanted a drink. An aviator then took her hand, introducing her to people in the suite. The victim stated that as everyone started chanting her name, a crowd of people stepped away from a wall on which hung a mural of a rhinoceros. The mural had a hose-like contraption attached to the rhinoceros' genital area which dispensed drinks. The victim was expected to kneel on the floor and drink from the "penis." The crowd surrounding her laughed and the man who escorted her into the room grabbed her arms and stood in front of her to restrain her from leaving. One of the aviators who had invited her assisted her in leaving the suite.

Later, while the victim was talking to people in the patio area, a man lifted her culottes shorts with a plastic drink straw. She demanded that he stop three times; the fourth time, she turned and slapped the man, as well as the male friend who encouraged him.

VICTIM NUMBER 79

Status/Service/Rank: Civilian/Female

Date/Time of Incident: Saturday, September 7, 1991—
Time Unknown
Sunday, September 8, 1991—
Early Morning

Place of Incident: Pool Patio, Third Floor, Las
Vegas Hilton
VMFP-3 Administrative Suite,
Third Floor, Las Vegas Hilton

Victim 79 is the wife of a Navy lieutenant. She attended Tailhook '91 with her husband.

According to the victim, she and a female friend were standing on the pool patio sometime on Saturday evening when they were approached by an unidentified white male. He cupped her buttocks in one of his hands and asked, "Do you mind if I do this?" She told him he was "pathetic." He told her he had been watching her and "they dared me," indicating a group of men standing nearby.

Later Saturday evening or Sunday morning, the victim and her friend were walking through the third-floor hallway. They were in front of the VMFP-3 administrative suite, known as the "Rhino" suite, when a man wearing a "Rhino" horn hat on his head stepped out of the suite and grabbed her arm. He began pulling her into the suite by the arm, at which point her friend grabbed her other arm and tried to pull her back out into the hallway. She was screaming for them to stop because they were "yanking my arms out." Her friend released her arm, and she was pulled into the "Rhino" suite. The man who pulled her in asked her name. He told her that no one in the room could have a drink until she stroked and sucked the "penis" on the rhino mural. About 50 people in the room began cheering and taunting, chanting her name over and over. As she was pulled toward the rhino mural, she kept refusing, saying no, and she crossed her arms in front of her. The man finally let her go and her friend grabbed her and pulled her from the room. As they left, the crowd began chanting "We hate [her name]. We hate [her name]." The incident left her shaken and unnerved.

She described the man who pulled her into the suite as a white male, 5'10" tall, weighing 160 pounds, slight build, dark hair, wearing an open print shirt and a "Rhino" horn hat. According to a witness, she and the victim were on the pool patio on Saturday evening when a man approached them and placed his hands on the victim's buttocks. Both women were surprised and upset by the incident, but did not do anything about it at the time. The witness stated that she and the victim were in the "Rhino" suite when one of the men in the room tried to coerce the victim into drinking from the rhinoceros "penis" attached to a mural of a rhinoceros. The people in the suite began chanting the victim's name, but she resisted the man and refused to touch the rhino. The witness then grabbed the victim by the arm and pulled her out of the suite.

VICTIM NUMBER 80

Status/Service/Rank:	Lieutenant (O-3) United States Navy/Female
Date/Time of Incident:	Saturday, September 7, 1991— 10:00 p.m.

Place of Incident: Hallway, Third Floor, Las Vegas
                            Hilton

Victim 80 is a 23-year-old Navy lieutenant. She attended Tailhooks '89 and '91.

According to the victim, she and a male Navy officer friend decided to go down the hallway even though it was very crowded. Her friend walked in front of her, pushing a path through so she could follow. She soon lost sight of him and began to yell his name. Suddenly men began grabbing her breasts and body "all over." Her friend looked back and saw that she had been stopped by the crowd and he started pushing his way back toward her. A man behind her whom she did not know said, "Let's get you out of here." He put his arms around her and pulled her out of the crowd.

VICTIM NUMBER 81

Status/Service/Rank: Lieutenant (O-3)
                            United States Navy/Female

Date/Time of Incident: Saturday, September 7, 1991—
                            Evening, Time Unknown

Place of Incident: CNATRA Suite (Room 364) and
                            Hallway, Third Floor, Las Vegas
                            Hilton

Victim 81 is a 27-year-old Navy lieutenant from California.

According to the victim, she was in the CNATRA administrative suite conversing with two male Navy officers when a third male Navy officer approached her and began to rub her leg from her knee to her ankle. She told him to stop, but he continued to rub her leg. She told him again to stop and asked his name and unit. The man stopped rubbing her leg and told her he was a surface warfare officer. The victim was very offended by the act.

On Friday or Saturday night at approximately 6:00–7:00 p.m. the victim was grabbed on the buttocks while she walked in the hallway on the third floor. She immediately turned to see who had grabbed her, but was unable to identify anyone in the hallway.

The victim related that on Saturday evening she was conversing in the hallway with a male acquaintance who is a Navy lieutenant commander. He asked her if she was breast-feeding her infant and she replied that she was. He in turn told her he would like to try breast-feeding from her. Judging from the drink in his hand, the victim concluded that he must have been intoxicated to have made such a remark.

VICTIM NUMBER 82

Status/Service/Rank: Civilian/Female

Date/Time of Incident: Sunday, September 8, 1991—
                           1:00 a.m.

Place of Incident: Hallway, Third Floor, Las Vegas
                           Hilton

Victim 82 is a 24-year-old woman who attended Tailhook '91 with two female civilian friends.

According to the victim, she was walking alone through the crowded hallway on the third floor of the Hilton Hotel when a man she described as "sloppy looking" head-butted her in the stomach. The blow caused her to fall back and someone standing behind her grabbed her buttocks. In response to being grabbed, the victim kicked backwards, making contact. She heard someone say, "Nice kick, babe." The victim was surprised and irritated by what had happened and did not go into the third-floor hallway again.

VICTIM NUMBER 83

Status/Service/Rank: Civilian/Female

Date/Time of Incident: Saturday, September 7, 1991—
                           11:45 p.m.

Place of Incident: Hallway, Third Floor, Las Vegas
                           Hilton

Victim 83, a 26-year-old civilian from the San Juan Capistrano, California, area, attended the Tailhook Association convention in 1991 with several friends. She stated that the majority of her friends are either Marine or Navy aviators.

According to the victim, on Saturday evening, September 7, 1991, at 11:45 p.m., she and a friend began to walk through the crowd in the third-floor hallway. They had walked only a few steps, when she felt someone grab her crotch. She described the grab as being "very intense," and she looked up to see a man grinning at her. She asked if he had grabbed her and he replied that he had. She immediately punched the man in the face, which caused him to fall to the ground. The men in the hallway began booing her and grabbing at her buttocks as she continued through the hallway. The incident took place near room 307.

She stated she did not know any of the men in the hallway at the time of the incident; however, she identified the man she punched as "apparently a naval aviator" because he was wearing an "Annapolis" ring and a necklace with an anchor pendant.

VICTIM NUMBER 84
(See page 246)

VICTIM NUMBER 85
(See page 246)

VICTIM NUMBER 86

Status/Service/Rank: Civilian/Female

Date/Time of Incident: September 1991—Date and Time Unknown

Place of Incident: Hallway, Third Floor, Las Vegas Hilton

Victim 86 is a 33-year-old Federal Government employee.

When the victim was interviewed by NIS investigators in December 1991 regarding her attendance at Tailhook '91, she indicated she was grabbed and pinched while walking through the third-floor hallway.

She was contacted for an interview by an investigator from the OIG, DoD, in August 1992, at which time she refused to provide any information regarding her assault.

VICTIM NUMBER 87

Status/Service/Rank: Civilian/Female

Date/Time of Incident: Saturday, September 7, 1991 —
                              8:00 p.m.

Place of Incident: Hallway, Third Floor, Las Vegas
                              Hilton

Victim 87 is a 25-year-old woman from California.

According to the victim, on Saturday, September 7, 1991, she exited the elevators on the third floor of the Las Vegas Hilton and turned toward the hallway where she saw a line of men on both sides of the hallway. She had no idea what was about to happen. As she walked through the hallway, men began intentionally and deliberately grabbing her breasts, buttocks, and crotch. She attempted to hit the men's hands away from her body, but that only seemed to intensify their groping and grabbing and she was firmly grabbed six or seven times while she walked through the hallway.

Although she was not physically injured, she was stunned and shocked and experienced a loss of breath. She remembered thinking while the men were grabbing at her body, "I can't believe this is really happening."

She indicated she was unable to identify any of the men in the hallway at the time of the assault.

The victim's cousin, a male Navy lieutenant, was in the area when the victim got out of the crowd. He told us that the victim had advised him that she had been touched and grabbed. He also recalled that the victim remarked that passing through the hall had been a lot like going to a gynecologist.

VICTIM NUMBER 88

Status/Service/Rank: Civilian/Female

Date/Time of Incident:	Saturday, September 7, 1991 — 11:30 p.m.
Place of Incident:	Hallway, Third Floor, Las Vegas Hilton

Victim 88 is a 46-year-old civilian who resides in California. She attended Tailhooks '90 and '91.

According to the victim, she was grabbed on the buttocks in the hallway of the Hilton Hotel during Tailhook '90, so she avoided the hallway at Tailhook '91.

On Saturday evening, the victim entered the third-floor hallway through one of the hospitality suites. As she walked up the hallway and neared room 308, she was grabbed on the buttocks. She pressed her back against the wall and stood there until she felt she could safely leave the hallway.

VICTIM NUMBER 89

Status/Service/Rank:	Civilian/Female
Date/Time of Incident:	Saturday, September 7, 1991 — 10:00 p.m.
Place of Incident:	Pool Patio, Third Floor, Las Vegas Hilton

Victim 89 is a 23-year-old civilian who resides in California. She attended Tailhook '91 with a female friend.

According to the victim, she entered a hospitality suite on the third floor of the Hilton Hotel to obtain a beer. A man, whom she described as a large Marine, pinned her arms against her sides, picked her up, and twirled her around several times. She screamed for him to put her down, but her screams could not be heard over the loud music in the suite. Some of the people in the suite looked at her as if they thought the incident was funny, but no one came to her aid. The victim said she was "dragged" out of the suite and onto the pool patio where her assailant sat down in a plastic chair, pulling her down into his lap so that she faced him. He raised her shirt to completely expose her breasts, and he roughly applied his mouth to her breasts, neck, and face. The man continued his assault for several minutes and then directed that the victim wait while he went to the bathroom. As soon as the man turned to leave, the victim ran from the area. The victim told us she was shaking, crying, and walking around in a daze, as well as shocked and frightened at the violence of the assault. She told several Marine Corps officers what had happened shortly after the assault.

VICTIM NUMBER 90

Status/Service/Rank: Civilian/Female

Date/Time of Incident: Thursday, Friday, or Saturday, September 5, 6, or 7, 1991 — Evening, Time Unknown

Place of Incident: Casino, Las Vegas Hilton

Victim 90 is a civilian who resides in California. She attended Tailhook '91 with a civilian female friend.

According to the friend, the victim told her she was in the Hilton Hotel casino playing blackjack with a male Navy officer, when another Navy officer at the table leaned across and grabbed her breast.

The victim acknowledged the assault to us, but stated that she would not provide further details.

MALE VICTIMS

Summary:

The following summaries concern seven male naval officers who reported they were assaulted on the third floor of the Las Vegas Hilton at Tailhook '91:

Victim Number 32 is a 27-year-old Navy lieutenant who was pinched on the buttocks in the hallway by an unknown person. The hallway was so crowded he "could not tell who was doing what."

Victim Number 75 is a 33-year-old Navy lieutenant commander. While in the VS-41 administrative suite located in room 304, he was approached by a "tall woman in a knit dress" who walked up to him, grabbed his genitals through his clothing, and yelled "package check." She then offered to perform a sex act for money.

Victim Number 35 is a 26-year-old Navy lieutenant. While walking through the hallway, he was pinched on the buttocks by an unknown woman. A short time later he was grabbed in the crotch by a different woman. He retaliated by pinching the woman on the buttocks.

Victim Number 74 is a 41-year-old Marine lieutenant colonel. He was standing on the pool patio when he was pinched on the left buttock by an unknown woman. Our investigation disclosed that the "victim" provided false statements to investigators regarding other acts of impropriety at Tailhook '91. When confronted with those discrepancies, he retracted his previous statements. Although he continued to maintain that his statements regarding his assault are truthful as reported, he requested that the matter not be further pursued.

Victim Number 15 is a 32-year-old Navy lieutenant. He was pinched on the buttocks by an unknown person in the hallway.

Victim Number 85 is a 29-year-old Marine captain. While in the VMFP-3 administrative suite (room 308), two women pulled his shorts down to his knees.

Victim Number 84 is a 22-year-old Navy ensign. He was pinched on the buttocks by military men in the hallway.

VICTIMS ASSAULTED DURING PRIOR TAILHOOK CONVENTIONS

Summary:

The following 10 indecent assaults occurred in the hallway of the third floor at the Las Vegas Hilton during Tailhook conventions in years *prior to* Tailhook '91:

Victim Number 91 is a 29-year-old female Government contractor employee. At Tailhook '90, she was grabbed in the crotch and breasts. She could not identify the man, so she did not report the incident.

Victim Number 92 is a 29-year-old female Navy lieutenant. At Tailhook '89 she was pinched and grabbed on the buttocks. She did not report the assault because she could not identify her assailant.

Victim Number 93 is a 33-year-old female civilian who resides in Nevada. At Tailhook '90, she was "grabbed" in the hallway on the third floor of the Las Vegas Hilton.

Victim Number 94 is a 31-year-old female Navy lieutenant. She attended Tailhooks '86, '87, '90, and '91. At one convention prior to Tailhook '91, she was pinched, and at another Tailhook, she was picked up by a man and carried down the hallway.

Victim Number 95 is a 27-year-old female civilian who resides in California. She attended Tailhook '90 at the invitation of a friend who is a male Navy lieutenant commander. As she approached a crowd of men in the hallway, they closed in on her and began to push her through the passageway. They grabbed her breasts, crotch, and buttocks. Men lifted up her skirt and placed squadron stickers on her crotch and buttocks. They unbuttoned her blouse and ripped her sleeve. She escaped the crowd through one of the administrative suites. When she described what happened to her to the male Navy officer who invited her to Tailhook, he responded, "Boys will be boys."

Victim Number 96 is a 24-year-old female Navy lieutenant. She attended Tailhooks '89, '90, and '91. At Tailhook '89, she was standing on the pool patio when she saw a man, who appeared to be extremely intoxicated, walking around with his penis/testicles exposed. The man came up behind the victim, grabbed her hips, and pressed his body against her buttocks. She threw her drink in his face.

Victim Number 97 is a 31-year-old female Navy lieutenant. She attended Tailhooks '89 and '91. As she walked through the hallway on the third floor of the Hilton Hotel, she was pinched on the buttocks and grabbed on the breasts by unknown males.

Victim Number 98 is a 41-year-old female former employee of the Hilton Hotel. During Tailhook '89, she was a blackjack dealer in the casino on the first floor of the hotel. Four or five men from the ''Tail Gunners'' convention sat at her table, yelling comments such as ''Show us your tits.'' While on her break, one of those men came up behind her and ran his hand up her skirt.

Victim Number 99 is a 28-year-old female Navy lieutenant who attended Tailhooks '86, '87, '88, '89, and '91. At Tailhook '87, she was grabbed on the breasts by men in the ''gauntlet.'' She still went on the third floor in subsequent years, but avoided the hallway when it was crowded.

Victim Number 100 is a 25-year-old female military spouse who attended Tailhook '90 with a female friend. She entered the third floor of the Hilton Hotel by way of the passenger elevators. As she walked down what appeared to be a path in the crowded hallway, the men on either side of the hallway suddenly collapsed around her. Approximately 20 men began to grab, pinch, and touch her breasts, buttocks, and crotch. One man got his hand inside her clothing and grabbed her bare buttocks. The men verbally abused the victim, calling her ''bitch'' and saying ''I'd like to f--- you.'' She fought the crowd, screaming, ''Leave me alone.''

Appendix G
List of Flag Officers

Thirty-two active duty flag/general officers attended Tailhook '91:

ADM Robert J. Kelly
ADM Frank B. Kelso
VADM William C. Bowes
VADM Richard M. Dunleavy
VADM John H. Fetterman, Jr.
VADM Edwin R. Kohn, Jr.
VADM Anthony A. Less
VADM Jerry L. Unruh
LT GEN Duane A. Wills, USMC
RADM Riley D. Mixson
MG GEN Clyde L. Vermilyea, USMC
RADM (SEL) Philip S. Anselmo
RADM (SEL) Paul W. Parcells
RADM (SEL) Luther F. Schriefer
RADM (L) Don W. Baird
RADM (L) Joseph J. Dantone, Jr.
RADM (L) James H. Finney
RADM (L) Robert P. Hickey
RADM (L) Jay L. Johnson
RADM (L) John A. Lockard
RADM (L) William P. McGowen
RADM (L) John A. Moriarty
RADM (L) William E. Newman
RADM (L) Bernard J. Smith
RADM (L) Robert J. Spane
RADM (L) Frank L. Tillotson
RADM (L) Joseph S. Walker
RADM (L) (SEL) Charles S. Abbot
RADM (L) (SEL) John M. Luecke
RADM (L) (SEL) John W. Snyder, Jr.
RADM (L) (SEL) Jay W. Sprague
RADM (L) (SEL) Jay B. Yakeley, III

Three Reserve flag officers attended Tailhook '91:

RADM Wilson F. Flagg
RADM (L) Ronald R. Morgan
RADM (SEL) Kenneth W. Pettigrew

Acronyms/Designators:

ADM   = Admiral
VADM   = Vice Admiral
LT GEN = Lieutenant General
MG GEN = Major General
RADM   = Rear Admiral

(L)   = Lower Half
(SEL) = Select
USMC   = U.S. Marine Corps